Mr. Whittier in 1885

THE POETICAL WORKS

OF

JOHN GREENLEAF WHITTIER

IN FOUR VOLUMES

VOLUME IV.

PERSONAL POEMS
THE TENT ON THE BEACH, ETC.

BOSTON AND NEW YORK
HOUGHTON, MIFFLIN AND COMPANY
The Riverside Press, Cambridge

The Riverside Press, Cambridge, Mass., U. S. A.
Electrotyped and Printed by H. O. Houghton & Co.

CONTENTS

CONTENTS

CONTENTS

POEMS BY ELIZABETH H. WHITTIER.

APPENDIX.

I. EARLY AND UNCOLLECTED VERSES.

Note. The portrait prefacing this volume is from an engrav-
ing on steel by J. A. J. Wilcox in 1888, after a photograph taken
by Miss Isa E. Gray in July, 1885.

PERSONAL POEMS

A LAMENT.

> "The parted spirit,
> Knoweth it not our sorrow ?   Answereth not
> Its blessing to our tears ? "

THE circle is broken, one seat is forsaken,
One bud from the tree of our friendship is shaken;
One heart from among us no longer shall thrill
With joy in our gladness, or grief in our ill.

Weep! lonely and lowly are slumbering now
The light of her glances, the pride of her brow;
Weep! sadly and long shall we listen in vain
To hear the soft tones of her welcome again.

Give our tears to the dead!   For humanity's claim
From its silence and darkness is ever the same;
The hope of that world whose existence is bliss
May not stifle the tears of the mourners of this.

For, oh! if one glance the freed spirit can throw
On the scene of its troubled probation below,
Than the pride of the marble, the pomp of the dead,
To that glance will be dearer the tears which we
    shed.

Oh, who can forget the mild light of her smile,
Over lips moved with music and feeling the while,
The eye's deep enchantment, dark, dream-like, and
          clear,
In the glow of its gladness, the shade of its tear.

And the charm of her features, while over the
          whole
Played the hues of the heart and the sunshine of
          soul ;
And the tones of her voice, like the music which
          seems
Murmured low in our ears by the Angel of dreams !

But holier and dearer our memories hold
Those treasures of feeling, more precious than gold,
The love and the kindness and pity which gave
Fresh flowers for the bridal, green wreaths for the
          grave!

The heart ever open to Charity's claim,
Unmoved from its purpose by censure and blame,
While vainly alike on her eye and her ear
Fell the scorn of the heartless, the jesting and jeer.

How true to our hearts was that beautiful sleeper !
With smiles for the joyful, with tears for the
          weeper !
Yet, evermore prompt, whether mournful or gay,
With warnings in love to the passing astray.

For, though spotless herself, she could sorrow for
          them
Who sullied with evil the spirit's pure gem ;

And a sigh or a tear could the erring reprove,
And the sting of reproof was still tempered by
    love.

As a cloud of the sunset, slow melting in heaven,
As a star that is lost when the daylight is given,
As a glad dream of slumber, which wakens in bliss,
She hath passed to the world of the holy from this.
    1834.

TO THE MEMORY OF CHARLES B. STORRS,

Late President of Western Reserve College, who died at his
post of duty, overworn by his strenuous labors with tongue and
pen in the cause of Human Freedom.

THOU hast fallen in thine armor,
    Thou martyr of the Lord!
With thy last breath crying " Onward! "
    And thy hand upon the sword.
The haughty heart derideth,
    And the sinful lip reviles,
But the blessing of the perishing
    Around thy pillow smiles!

When to our cup of trembling
    The added drop is given,
And the long-suspended thunder
    Falls terribly from Heaven, —
When a new and fearful freedom
    Is proffered of the Lord
To the slow-consuming Famine,
    The Pestilence and Sword!

When the refuges of Falsehood
    Shall be swept away in wrath,
And the temple shall be shaken,
    With its idol, to the earth,
Shall not thy words of warning
    Be all remembered then?
And thy now unheeded message
    Burn in the hearts of men?

Oppression's hand may scatter
    Its nettles on thy tomb,
And even Christian bosoms
    Deny thy memory room;
For lying lips shall torture
    Thy mercy into crime,
And the slanderer shall flourish
    As the bay-tree for a time.

But where the south-wind lingers
    On Carolina's pines,
Or falls the careless sunbeam
    Down Georgia's golden mines;
Where now beneath his burthen
    The toiling slave is driven;
Where now a tyrant's mockery
    Is offered unto Heaven;

Where Mammon hath its altars
    Wet o'er with human blood,
And pride and lust debases
    The workmanship of God, —
There shall thy praise be spoken,
    Redeemed from Falsehood's ban,

When the fetters shall be broken,
  And the slave shall be a man !

Joy to thy spirit, brother !
  A thousand hearts are warm,
A thousand kindred bosoms
  Are baring to the storm.
What though red-handed Violence
  With secret Fraud combine ?
The wall of fire is round us,
  Our Present Help was thine.

Lo, the waking up of nations,
  From Slavery's fatal sleep ;
The murmur of a Universe,
  Deep calling unto Deep !
Joy to thy spirit, brother !
  On every wind of heaven
The onward cheer and summons
  Of Freedom's voice is given !

Glory to God forever !
  Beyond the despot's will
The soul of Freedom liveth
  Imperishable still.
The words which thou hast uttered
  Are of that soul a part,
And the good seed thou hast scattered
  Is springing from the heart.

In the evil days before us,
  And the trials yet to come,

In the shadow of the prison,
　　Or the cruel martyrdom, —
We will think of thee, O brother!
　　And thy sainted name shall be
In the blessing of the captive,
　　And the anthem of the free.

1834.

LINES

ON THE DEATH OF S. OLIVER TORREY, SECRETARY OF
THE BOSTON YOUNG MEN'S ANTI-SLAVERY SOCIETY.

GONE before us, O our brother,
　　To the spirit-land!
Vainly look we for another
　　In thy place to stand.
Who shall offer youth and beauty
　　On the wasting shrine
Of a stern and lofty duty,
　　With a faith like thine?

Oh, thy gentle smile of greeting
　　Who again shall see?
Who amidst the solemn meeting
　　Gaze again on thee?
Who when peril gathers o'er us,
　　Wear so calm a brow?
Who, with evil men before us,
　　So serene as thou?

Early hath the spoiler found thee,
　　Brother of our love!

Autumn's faded earth around thee,
  And its storms above !
Evermore that turf lie lightly,
  And, with future showers,
O'er thy slumbers fresh and brightly
  Blow the summer flowers !

In the locks thy forehead gracing,
  Not a silvery streak ;
Nor a line of sorrow's tracing
  On thy fair young cheek ;
Eyes of light and lips of roses,
  Such as Hylas wore, —
Over all that curtain closes,
  Which shall rise no more !

Will the vigil Love is keeping
  Round that grave of thine,
Mournfully, like Jazer weeping
  Over Sibmah's vine ; [1]
Will the pleasant memories, swelling
  Gentle hearts, of thee,
In the spirit's distant dwelling
  All unheeded be ?

If the spirit ever gazes,
  From its journeyings, back ;
If the immortal ever traces
  O'er its mortal track ;
Wilt thou not, O brother, meet us
  Sometimes on our way,
And, in hours of sadness, greet us
  As a spirit may ?

Peace be with thee, O our brother,
  In the spirit-land!
Vainly look we for another
  In thy place to stand.
Unto Truth and Freedom giving
  All thy early powers,
Be thy virtues with the living,
  And thy spirit ours!

1837.

TO ——,

WITH A COPY OF WOOLMAN'S JOURNAL.

"Get the writings of John Woolman by heart." — *Essays of Elia.*

MAIDEN! with the fair brown tresses
  Shading o'er thy dreamy eye,
Floating on thy thoughtful forehead
  Cloud wreaths of its sky.

Youthful years and maiden beauty,
  Joy with them should still abide, —
Instinct take the place of Duty,
  Love, not Reason, guide.

Ever in the New rejoicing,
  Kindly beckoning back the Old,
Turning, with the gift of Midas,
  All things into gold.

And the passing shades of sadness
  Wearing even a welcome guise,

As, when some bright lake lies open
 To the sunny skies,

Every wing of bird above it,
 Every light cloud floating on,
Glitters like that flashing mirror
 In the self-same sun.

But upon thy youthful forehead
 Something like a shadow lies;
And a serious soul is looking
 From thy earnest eyes.

With an early introversion,
 Through the forms of outward things,
Seeking for the subtle essence,
 And the hidden springs.

Deeper than the gilded surface
 Hath thy wakeful vision seen,
Farther than the narrow present
 Have thy journeyings been.

Thou hast midst Life's empty noises
 Heard the solemn steps of Time,
And the low mysterious voices
 Of another clime.

All the mystery of Being
 Hath upon thy spirit pressed, —
Thoughts which, like the Deluge wanderer,
 Find no place of rest:

That which mystic Plato pondered,
　　That which Zeno heard with awe,
And the star-rapt Zoroaster
　　In his night-watch saw.

From the doubt and darkness springing
　　Of the dim, uncertain Past,
Moving to the dark still shadows
　　O'er the Future cast,

Early hath Life's mighty question
　　Thrilled within thy heart of youth,
With a deep and strong beseeching:
　　What and where is Truth?

Hollow creed and ceremonial,
　　Whence the ancient life hath fled,
Idle faith unknown to action,
　　Dull and cold and dead.

Oracles, whose wire-worked meanings
　　Only wake a quiet scorn, —
Not from these thy seeking spirit
　　Hath its answer drawn.

But, like some tired child at even,
　　On thy mother Nature's breast,
Thou, methinks, art vainly seeking
　　Truth, and peace, and rest.

O'er that mother's rugged features
　　Thou art throwing Fancy's veil,
Light and soft as woven moonbeams,
　　Beautiful and frail!

O'er the rough chart of Existence,
   Rocks of sin and wastes of woe,
Soft airs breathe, and green leaves tremble,
   And cool fountains flow.

And to thee an answer cometh
   From the earth and from the sky,
And to thee the hills and waters
   And the stars reply.

But a soul-sufficing answer
   Hath no outward origin ;
More than Nature's many voices
   May be heard within.

Even as the great Augustine
   Questioned earth and sea and sky,[2]
And the dusty tomes of learning
   And old poesy.

But his earnest spirit needed
   More than outward Nature taught ;
More than blest the poet's vision
   Or the sage's thought.

Only in the gathered silence
   Of a calm and waiting frame,
Light and wisdom as from Heaven
   To the seeker came.

Not to ease and aimless quiet
   Doth that inward answer tend,
But to works of love and duty
   As our being's end ;

Not to idle dreams and trances,
    Length of face, and solemn tone,
But to Faith, in daily striving
    And performance shown.

Earnest toil and strong endeavor
    Of a spirit which within
Wrestles with familiar evil
    And besetting sin ;

And without, with tireless vigor,
    Steady heart, and weapon strong,
In the power of truth assailing
    Every form of wrong.

Guided thus, how passing lovely
    Is the track of Woolman's feet !
And his brief and simple record
    How serenely sweet !

O'er life's humblest duties throwing
    Light the earthling never knew,
Freshening all its dark waste places
    As with Hermon's dew.

All which glows in Pascal's pages,
    All which sainted Guion sought,
Or the blue-eyed German Rahel
    Half-unconscious taught :

Beauty, such as Goethe pictured,
    Such as Shelley dreamed of, shed
Living warmth and starry brightness
    Round that poor man's head.

Not a vain and cold ideal,
   Not a poet's dream alone,
But a presence warm and real,
   Seen and felt and known.

When the red right-hand of slaughter
   Moulders with the steel it swung,
When the name of seer and poet
   Dies on Memory's tongue,

All bright thoughts and pure shall gather
   Round that meek and suffering one, —
Glorious, like the seer-seen angel
   Standing in the sun!

Take the good man's book and ponder
   What its pages say to thee;
Blessed as the hand of healing
   May its lesson be.

If it only serves to strengthen
   Yearnings for a higher good,
For the fount of living waters
   And diviner food;

If the pride of human reason
   Feels its meek and still rebuke,
Quailing like the eye of Peter
   From the Just One's look!

If with readier ear thou heedest
   What the Inward Teacher saith,
Listening with a willing spirit
   And a childlike faith, —

Thou mayst live to bless the giver,
    Who, himself but frail and weak,
Would at least the highest welfare
    Of another seek;

And his gift, though poor and lowly
    It may seem to other eyes,
Yet may prove an angel holy
    In a pilgrim's guise.

1840.

LEGGETT'S MONUMENT.

William Leggett, who died in 1839 at the age of thirty-seven, was the intrepid editor of the *New York Evening Post* and afterward of *The Plain Dealer.* His vigorous assault upon the system of slavery brought down upon him the enmity of political defenders of the system.

"Ye build the tombs of the prophets." — *Holy Writ.*

YES, pile the marble o'er him! It is well
    That ye who mocked him in his long stern
            strife,
And planted in the pathway of his life
The ploughshares of your hatred hot from hell,
    Who clamored down the bold reformer when
    He pleaded for his captive fellow-men,
Who spurned him in the market-place, and sought
    Within thy walls, St. Tammany, to bind
In party chains the free and honest thought,
    The angel utterance of an upright mind,
Well is it now that o'er his grave ye raise
The stony tribute of your tardy praise,

For not alone that pile shall tell to Fame
Of the brave heart beneath, but of the builders'
    shame!
  1841.

TO A FRIEND,

ON HER RETURN FROM EUROPE.

How smiled the land of France
Under thy blue eye's glance,
    Light-hearted rover!
Old walls of chateaux gray,
Towers of an early day,
Which the Three Colors play
    Flauntingly over.

Now midst the brilliant train
Thronging the banks of Seine:
    Now midst the splendor
Of the wild Alpine range,
Waking with change on change
Thoughts in thy young heart strange,
    Lovely, and tender.

Vales, soft Elysian,
Like those in the vision
    Of Mirza, when, dreaming,
He saw the long hollow dell,
Touched by the prophet's spell,
Into an ocean swell
    With its isles teeming.

Cliffs wrapped in snows of years,
Splintering with icy spears
    Autumn's blue heaven :
Loose rock and frozen slide,
Hung on the mountain-side,
Waiting their hour to glide
    Downward, storm-driven !

Rhine-stream, by castle old,
Baron's and robber's hold,
    Peacefully flowing ;
Sweeping through vineyards green,
Or where the cliffs are seen
O'er the broad wave between
    Grim shadows throwing.

Or, where St. Peter's dome
Swells o'er eternal Rome,
    Vast, dim, and solemn ;
Hymns ever chanting low,
Censers swung to and fro,
Sable stoles sweeping slow
    Cornice and column !

Oh, as from each and all
Will there not voices call
    Evermore back again?
In the mind's gallery
Wilt thou not always see
Dim phantoms beckon thee
    O'er that old track again?

New forms thy presence haunt,
New voices softly chant,

New faces greet thee!
Pilgrims from many a shrine
Hallowed by poet's line,
At memory's magic sign,
    Rising to meet thee.

And when such visions come
Unto thy olden home,
    Will they not waken
Deep thoughts of Him whose hand
Led thee o'er sea and land
Back to the household band
    Whence thou wast taken?

While, at the sunset time,
Swells the cathedral's chime,
    Yet, in thy dreaming,
While to thy spirit's eye
Yet the vast mountains lie
Piled in the Switzer's sky,
    Icy and gleaming:

Prompter of silent prayer,
Be the wild picture there
    In the mind's chamber,
And, through each coming day
Him who, as staff and stay,
Watched o'er thy wandering way,
    Freshly remember.

So, when the call shall be
Soon or late unto thee,
    As to all given,

Still may that picture live,
All its fair forms survive,
And to thy spirit give
        Gladness in Heaven !

1841.

LUCY HOOPER.

Lucy Hooper died at Brooklyn, L. I., on the 1st of 8th mo.,
1841, aged twenty-four years.

THEY tell me, Lucy, thou art dead,
        That all of thee we loved and cherished
        Has with thy summer roses perished ;
And left, as its young beauty fled,
An ashen memory in its stead,
The twilight of a parted day
        Whose fading light is cold and vain,
        The heart's faint echo of a strain
Of low, sweet music passed away.
That true and loving heart, that gift
        Of a mind, earnest, clear, profound,
Bestowing, with a glad unthrift,
        Its sunny light on all around,
Affinities which only could
Cleave to the pure, the true, and good ;
        And sympathies which found no rest,
        Save with the loveliest and best.
Of them — of thee — remains there naught
        But sorrow in the mourner's breast ?
A shadow in the land of thought ?
No ! Even my weak and trembling faith
        Can lift for thee the veil which doubt

And human fear have drawn about
The all-awaiting scene of death.

Even as thou wast I see thee still;
And, save the absence of all ill
And pain and weariness, which here
Summoned the sigh or wrung the tear,
The same as when, two summers back,
Beside our childhood's Merrimac,
I saw thy dark eye wander o'er
Stream, sunny upland, rocky shore,
And heard thy low, soft voice alone
Midst lapse of waters, and the tone
Of pine-leaves by the west-wind blown,
There's not a charm of soul or brow,
   Of all we knew and loved in thee,
But lives in holier beauty now,
    Baptized in immortality!
Not mine the sad and freezing dream
   Of souls that, with their earthly mould,
   Cast off the loves and joys of old,
Unbodied, like a pale moonbeam,
   As pure, as passionless, and cold;
Nor mine the hope of Indra's son,
   Of slumbering in oblivion's rest,
Life's myriads blending into one,
   In blank annihilation blest;
Dust-atoms of the infinite,
Sparks scattered from the central light,
And winning back through mortal pain
Their old unconsciousness again.
No! I have friends in Spirit Land,
Not shadows in a shadowy band,

Not others, but themselves are they.
And still I think of them the same
As when the Master's summons came ;
Their change, — the holy morn-light breaking
Upon the dream-worn sleeper, waking, —
A change from twilight into day.

They 've laid thee midst the household graves,
    Where father, brother, sister lie ;
Below thee sweep the dark blue waves,
    Above thee bends the summer sky.
Thy own loved church in sadness read
Her solemn ritual o'er thy head,
And blessed and hallowed with her prayer
The turf laid lightly o'er thee there.
That church, whose rites and liturgy,
Sublime and old, were truth to thee,
Undoubted to thy bosom taken,
As symbols of a faith unshaken.
Even I, of simpler views, could feel
The beauty of thy trust and zeal ;
And, owning not thy creed, could see
How deep a truth it seemed to thee,
And how thy fervent heart had thrown
O'er all, a coloring of its own,
And kindled up, intense and warm,
A life in every rite and form,
As, when on Chebar's banks of old,
The Hebrew's gorgeous vision rolled,
A spirit filled the vast machine,
A life " within the wheels " was seen.

Farewell !   A little time, and we
    Who knew thee well, and loved thee here,

One after one shall follow thee
    As pilgrims through the gate of fear,
Which opens on eternity.
Yet shall we cherish not the less
    All that is left our hearts meanwhile;
The memory of thy loveliness
    Shall round our weary pathway smile,
Like moonlight when the sun has set,
A sweet and tender radiance yet.
Thoughts of thy clear-eyed sense of duty,
    Thy generous scorn of all things wrong,
The truth, the strength, the graceful beauty
    Which blended in thy song.
All lovely things, by thee beloved,
    Shall whisper to our hearts of thee;
These green hills, where thy childhood roved,
    Yon river winding to the sea,
The sunset light of autumn eves
    Reflecting on the deep, still floods,
Cloud, crimson sky, and trembling leaves
    Of rainbow-tinted woods,
These, in our view, shall henceforth take
A tenderer meaning for thy sake;
And all thou lovedst of earth and sky,
Seem sacred to thy memory.

1841.

FOLLEN.

ON READING HIS ESSAY ON THE "FUTURE STATE."

Charles Follen, one of the noblest contributions of Germany to American citizenship, was at an early age driven from his professorship in the University of Jena, and compelled to seek shelter from official prosecution in Switzerland, on account of his liberal political opinions. He became Professor of Civil Law in the Uni versity of Basle. The governments of Prussia, Austria, and Russia united in demanding his delivery as a political offender; and, in consequence, he left Switzerland, and came to the United States. At the time of the formation of the American Anti-Slavery Society he was a Professor in Harvard University, honored for his genius, learning, and estimable character. His love of liberty and hatred of oppression led him to seek an interview with Garrison and express his sympathy with him. Soon after, he attended a meeting of the New England Anti-Slavery Society. An able speech was made by Rev. A. A. Phelps, and a letter of mine addressed to the Secretary of the Society was read. Whereupon he rose and stated that his views were in unison with those of the Society, and that after hearing the speech and the letter, he was ready to join it, and abide the probable consequences of such an unpopular act. He lost by so doing his professorship. He was an able member of the Executive Committee of the American Anti-Slavery Society. He perished in the ill-fated steamer Lexington, which was burned on its passage from New York, January 13, 1840. The few writings left behind him show him to have been a profound thinker of rare spiritual insight.

FRIEND of my soul! as with moist eye
   I look up from this page of thine,
Is it a dream that thou art nigh,
   Thy mild face gazing into mine?

That presence seems before me now,
   A placid heaven of sweet moonrise,
When, dew-like, on the earth below
   Descends the quiet of the skies.

The calm brow through the parted hair,
   The gentle lips which knew no guile,
Softening the blue eye's thoughtful care
   With the bland beauty of their smile.

Ah me! at times that last dread scene
   Of Frost and Fire and moaning Sea

Will cast its shade of doubt between
　The failing eyes of Faith and thee.

Yet, lingering o'er thy charmëd page,
　Where through the twilight air of earth,
Alike enthusiast and sage,
　Prophet and bard, thou gazest forth,

Lifting the Future's solemn veil;
　The reaching of a mortal hand
To put aside the cold and pale
　Cloud-curtains of the Unseen Land;

In thoughts which answer to my own,
　In words which reach my inward ear,
Like whispers from the void Unknown,
　I feel thy living presence here.

The waves which lull thy body's rest,
　The dust thy pilgrim footsteps trod,
Unwasted, through each change, attest
　The fixed economy of God.

Shall these poor elements outlive
　The mind whose kingly will they wrought?
Their gross unconsciousness survive
　Thy godlike energy of thought?

Thou livest, Follen! not in vain
　Hath thy fine spirit meekly borne
The burthen of Life's cross of pain,
　And the thorned crown of suffering worn.

Oh, while Life's solemn mystery glooms
   Around us like a dungeon's wall,
Silent earth's pale and crowded tombs,
   Silent the heaven which bends o'er all !

While day by day our loved ones glide
   In spectral silence, hushed and lone,
To the cold shadows which divide
   The living from the dread Unknown ;

While even on the closing eye,
   And on the lip which moves in vain,
The seals of that stern mystery
   Their undiscovered trust retain ;

And only midst the gloom of death,
   Its mournful doubts and haunting fears,
Two pale, sweet angels, Hope and Faith,
   Smile dimly on us through their tears ;

'T is something to a heart like mine
   To think of thee as living yet ;
To feel that such a light as thine
   Could not in utter darkness set.

Less dreary seems the untried way
   Since thou hast left thy footprints there,
And beams of mournful beauty play
   Round the sad Angel's sable hair.

Oh ! at this hour when half the sky
   Is glorious with its evening light,
And fair broad fields of summer lie
   Hung o'er with greenness in my sight ;

While through these elm-boughs wet with rain
    The sunset's golden walls are seen,
With clover-bloom and yellow grain
    And wood-draped hill and stream between;

I long to know if scenes like this
    Are hidden from an angel's eyes;
If earth's familiar loveliness
    Haunts not thy heaven's serener skies.

For sweetly here upon thee grew
    The lesson which that beauty gave,
The ideal of the pure and true
    In earth and sky and gliding wave.

And it may be that all which lends
    The soul an upward impulse here,
With a diviner beauty blends,
    And greets us in a holier sphere.

Through groves where blighting never fell
    The humbler flowers of earth may twine;
And simple draughts from childhood's well
    Blend with the angel-tasted wine.

But be the prying vision veiled,
    And let the seeking lips be dumb,
Where even seraph eyes have failed
    Shall mortal blindness seek to come?

We only know that thou hast gone,
    And that the same returnless tide
Which bore thee from us still glides on,
    And we who mourn thee with it glide.

On all thou lookest we shall look,
    And to our gaze erelong shall turn
That page of God's mysterious book
    We so much wish yet dread to learn.

With Him, before whose awful power
    Thy spirit bent its trembling knee;
Who, in the silent greeting flower,
    And forest leaf, looked out on thee,

We leave thee, with a trust serene,
    Which Time, nor Change, nor Death can
        move,
While with thy childlike faith we lean
    On Him whose dearest name is Love!
1842.

TO J. P.

John Pierpont, the eloquent preacher and poet of Boston.

NOT as a poor requital of the joy
    With which my childhood heard that lay of
        thine,
    Which, like an echo of the song divine
At Bethlehem breathed above the Holy Boy,
    Bore to my ear the Airs of Palestine, —
Not to the poet, but the man I bring
In friendship's fearless trust my offering:
How much it lacks I feel, and thou wilt see,
Yet well I know that thou hast deemed with me
Life all too earnest, and its time too short
For dreamy ease and Fancy's graceful sport;

And girded for thy constant strife with wrong,
Like Nehemiah fighting while he wrought
    The broken walls of Zion, even thy song
Hath a rude martial tone, a blow in every thought!
    1843.

CHALKLEY HALL.

Chalkley Hall, near Frankford, Pa., was the residence of Thomas Chalkley, an eminent minister of the Friends' denomination. He was one of the early settlers of the Colony, and his *Journal*, which was published in 1749, presents a quaint but beautiful picture of a life of unostentatious and simple goodness. He was the master of a merchant vessel, and, in his visits to the West Indies and Great Britain, omitted no opportunity to labor for the highest interests of his fellow-men During a temporary residence in Philadelphia, in the summer of 1838, the quiet and beautiful scenery around the ancient village of Frankford frequently attracted me from the heat and bustle of the city. I have referred to my youthful acquaintance with his writings in *Snow-Bound*.

How bland and sweet the greeting of this breeze
    To him who flies
From crowded street and red wall's weary gleam,
Till far behind him like a hideous dream
    The close dark city lies!

Here, while the market murmurs, while men throng
    The marble floor
Of Mammon's altar, from the crush and din
Of the world's madness let me gather in
    My better thoughts once more.

Oh, once again revive, while on my ear
    The cry of Gain

And low hoarse hum of Traffic die away,
Ye blessed memories of my early day
    Like sere grass wet with rain !

Once more let God's green earth and sunset air
    Old feelings waken ;
Through weary years of toil and strife and ill,
Oh, let me feel that my good angel still
    Hath not his trust forsaken.

And well do time and place befit my mood :
    Beneath the arms
Of this embracing wood, a good man made
His home, like Abraham resting in the shade
    Of Mamre's lonely palms.

Here, rich with autumn gifts of countless years,
    The virgin soil
Turned from the share he guided, and in rain
And summer sunshine throve the fruits and grain
    Which blessed his honest toil.

Here, from his voyages on the stormy seas,
    Weary and worn,
He came to meet his children and to bless
The Giver of all good in thankfulness
    And praise for his return.

And here his neighbors gathered in to greet
    Their friend again,
Safe from the wave and the destroying gales,
Which reap untimely green Bermuda's vales,
    And vex the Carib main.

To hear the good man tell of simple truth,
    Sown in an hour
Of weakness in some far-off Indian isle,
From the parched bosom of a barren soil,
    Raised up in life and power :

How at those gatherings in Barbadian vales,
    A tendering love
Came o'er him, like the gentle rain from heaven,
And words of fitness to his lips were given,
    And strength as from above :

How the sad captive listened to the Word,
    Until his chain
Grew lighter, and his wounded spirit felt
The healing balm of consolation melt
    Upon its life-long pain :

How the armed warrior sat him down to hear
    Of Peace and Truth,
And the proud ruler and his Creole dame,
Jewelled and gorgeous in her beauty came,
    And fair and bright-eyed youth.

Oh, far away beneath New England's sky,
    Even when a boy,
Following my plough by Merrimac's green shore,
His simple record I have pondered o'er
    With deep and quiet joy.

And hence this scene, in sunset glory warm, —
    Its woods around,
Its still stream winding on in light and shade,

Its soft, green meadows and its upland glade, —
    To me is holy ground.

And dearer far than haunts where Genius keeps
    His vigils still ;
Than that where Avon's son of song is laid,
Or Vaucluse hallowed by its Petrarch's shade,
    Or Virgil's laurelled hill.

To the gray walls of fallen Paraclete,
    To Juliet's urn,
Fair Arno and Sorrento's orange-grove,
Where Tasso sang, let young Romance and Love
    Like brother pilgrims turn.

But here a deeper and serener charm
    To all is given ;
And blessed memories of the faithful dead
O'er wood and vale and meadow-stream have shed
    The holy hues of Heaven !

    1843.

GONE.

ANOTHER hand is beckoning us,
    Another call is given ;
And glows once more with Angel-steps
    The path which reaches Heaven.

Our young and gentle friend, whose smile
    Made brighter summer hours,
Amid the frosts of autumn time
    Has left us with the flowers.

No paling of the cheek of bloom
   Forewarned us of decay;
No shadow from the Silent Land
   Fell round our sister's way.

The light of her young life went down,
   As sinks behind the hill
The glory of a setting star,
   Clear, suddenly, and still.

As pure and sweet, her fair brow seemed
   Eternal as the sky;
And like the brook's low song, her voice, —
   A sound which could not die.

And half we deemed she needed not
   The changing of her sphere,
To give to Heaven a Shining One,
   Who walked an Angel here.

The blessing of her quiet life
   Fell on us like the dew;
And good thoughts where her footsteps pressed
   Like fairy blossoms grew.

Sweet promptings unto kindest deeds
   Were in her very look;
We read her face, as one who reads
   A true and holy book:

The measure of a blessed hymn,
   To which our hearts could move;

The breathing of an inward psalm,
    A canticle of love.

We miss her in the place of prayer,
    And by the hearth-fire's light;
We pause beside her door to hear
    Once more her sweet " Good-night ! "

There seems a shadow on the day,
    Her smile no longer cheers;
A dimness on the stars of night,
    Like eyes that look through tears.

Alone unto our Father's will
    One thought hath reconciled;
That He whose love exceedeth ours
    Hath taken home His child.

Fold her, O Father ! in Thine arms,
    And let her henceforth be
A messenger of love between
    Our human hearts and Thee.

Still let her mild rebuking stand
    Between us and the wrong,
And her dear memory serve to make
    Our faith in Goodness strong.

And grant that she who, trembling, here
    Distrusted all her powers,
May welcome to her holier home
    The well-beloved of ours.

1845.

TO RONGE.

This was written after reading the powerful and manly protest of Johannes Ronge against the "pious fraud" of the Bishop of Treves. The bold movement of the young Catholic priest of Prussian Silesia seemed to me full of promise to the cause of political as well as religious liberty in Europe. That it failed was due partly to the faults of the reformer, but mainly to the disagreement of the Liberals of Germany upon a matter of dogma, which prevented them from unity of action. Ronge was born in Silesia in 1813 and died in October, 1887. His autobiography was translated into English and published in London in 1846.

STRIKE home, strong-hearted man! Down to the
      root
Of old oppression sink the Saxon steel.
Thy work is to hew down. In God's name then
Put nerve into thy task. Let other men
Plant, as they may, that better tree whose fruit
The wounded bosom of the Church shall heal.
Be thou the image-breaker. Let thy blows
Fall heavy as the Suabian's iron hand,
On crown or crosier, which shall interpose
Between thee and the weal of Fatherland.
Leave creeds to closet idlers. First of all,
Shake thou all German dream-land with the fall
Of that accursed tree, whose evil trunk
Was spared of old by Erfurt's stalwart monk.
Fight not with ghosts and shadows. Let us hear
The snap of chain-links. Let our gladdened ear
Catch the pale prisoner's welcome, as the light
Follows thy axe-stroke, through his cell of night.
Be faithful to both worlds; nor think to feed
Earth's starving millions with the husks of creed.
Servant of Him whose mission high and holy
Was to the wronged, the sorrowing, and the lowly,

Thrust not his Eden promise from our sphere,
Distant and dim beyond the blue sky's span ;
Like him of Patmos, see it, now and here,
The New Jerusalem comes down to man !
Be warned by Luther's error.   Nor like him,
When the roused Teuton dashes from his limb
The rusted chain of ages, help to bind
His hands for whom thou claim'st the freedom of
          the mind !
  1846.

CHANNING.

The last time I saw Dr. Channing was in the summer of 1841, when, in company with my English friend, Joseph Sturge, so well known for his philanthropic labors and liberal political opinions, I visited him in his summer residence in Rhode Island.   In recalling the impressions of that visit, it can scarcely be necessary to say, that I have no reference to the peculiar religious opinions of a man whose life, beautifully and truly manifested above the atmosphere of sect, is now the world's common legacy.

NOT vainly did old poets tell,
    Nor vainly did old genius paint
God's great and crowning miracle,
    The hero and the saint !

For even in a faithless day
    Can we our sainted ones discern ;
And feel, while with them on the way,
    Our hearts within us burn.

And thus the common tongue and pen
    Which, world-wide, echo Channing's fame,
As one of Heaven's anointed men,
    Have sanctified his name.

In vain shall Rome her portals bar,
  And shut from him her saintly prize,
Whom, in the world's great calendar,
  All men shall canonize.

By Narragansett's sunny bay,
  Beneath his green embowering wood,
To me it seems but yesterday
  Since at his side I stood.

The slopes lay green with summer rains,
  The western wind blew fresh and free,
And glimmered down the orchard lanes
  The white surf of the sea.

With us was one, who, calm and true,
  Life's highest purpose understood,
And, like his blessed Master, knew
  The joy of doing good.

Unlearned, unknown to lettered fame,
  Yet on the lips of England's poor
And toiling millions dwelt his name,
  With blessings evermore.

Unknown to power or place, yet where
  The sun looks o'er the Carib sea,
It blended with the freeman's prayer
  And song of jubilee.

He told of England's sin and wrong,
  The ills her suffering children know,
The squalor of the city's throng,
  The green field's want and woe.

O'er Channing's face the tenderness
　　Of sympathetic sorrow stole,
Like a still shadow, passionless,
　　The sorrow of the soul.

But when the generous Briton told
　　How hearts were answering to his own,
And Freedom's rising murmur rolled
　　Up to the dull-eared throne,

I saw, methought, a glad surprise
　　Thrill through that frail and pain-worn frame,
And, kindling in those deep, calm eyes,
　　A still and earnest flame.

His few, brief words were such as move
　　The human heart, — the Faith-sown seeds
Which ripen in the soil of love
　　To high heroic deeds.

No bars of sect or clime were felt,
　　The Babel strife of tongues had ceased,
And at one common altar knelt
　　The Quaker and the priest.

And not in vain : with strength renewed,
　　And zeal refreshed, and hope less dim,
For that brief meeting, each pursued
　　The path allotted him.

How echoes yet each Western hill
　　And vale with Channing's dying word!
How are the hearts of freemen still
　　By that great warning stirred!

The stranger treads his native soil.
   And pleads, with zeal unfelt before,
The honest right of British toil,
   The claim of England's poor.

Before him time-wrought barriers fall,
   Old fears subside, old hatreds melt,
And, stretching o'er the sea's blue wall,
   The Saxon greets the Celt.

The yeoman on the Scottish lines,
   The Sheffield grinder, worn and grim,
The delver in the Cornwall mines,
   Look up with hope to him.

Swart smiters of the glowing steel,
   Dark feeders of the forge's flame,
Pale watchers at the loom and wheel,
   Repeat his honored name.

And thus the influence of that hour
   Of converse on Rhode Island's strand
Lives in the calm, resistless power
   Which moves our fatherland.

God blesses still the generous thought,
   And still the fitting word He speeds
And Truth, at His requiring taught,
   He quickens into deeds.

Where is the victory of the grave?
   What dust upon the spirit lies?
God keeps the sacred life he gave, —
   The prophet never dies!

1844.

TO MY FRIEND ON THE DEATH OF HIS SISTER.

Sophia Sturge, sister of Joseph Sturge, of Birmingham, the President of the British Complete Suffrage Association, died in the 6th month, 1845. She was the colleague, counsellor, and ever-ready helpmate of her brother in all his vast designs of beneficence. The *Birmingham Pilot* says of her: "Never, perhaps, were the active and passive virtues of the human character more harmoniously and beautifully blended than in this excellent woman."

THINE is a grief, the depth of which another
        May never know;
Yet, o'er the waters, O my stricken brother!
        To thee I go.

I lean my heart unto thee, sadly folding
        Thy hand in mine;
With even the weakness of my soul upholding
        The strength of thine.

I never knew, like thee, the dear departed;
        I stood not by
When, in calm trust, the pure and tranquil-hearted
        Lay down to die.

And on thy ears my words of weak condoling
        Must vainly fall:
The funeral bell which in thy heart is tolling,
        Sounds over all!

I will not mock thee with the poor world's common
        And heartless phrase,

Nor wrong the memory of a sainted woman
  With idle praise.

With silence only as their benediction,
  God's angels come
Where, in the shadow of a great affliction,
  The soul sits dumb!

Yet, would I say what thy own heart approveth:
  Our Father's will,
Calling to Him the dear one whom He loveth,
  Is mercy still.

Not upon thee or thine the solemn angel
  Hath evil wrought:
Her funeral anthem is a glad evangel, —
  The good die not!

God calls our loved ones, but we lose not wholly
  What He hath given;
They live on earth, in thought and deed, as truly
  As in His heaven.

And she is with thee; in thy path of trial
  She walketh yet;
Still with the baptism of thy self-denial
  Her locks are wet.

Up, then, my brother! Lo, the fields of harvest
  Lie white in view!
She lives and loves thee, and the God thou serv-
   est
  To both is true.

Thrust in thy sickle! England's toilworn peasants
    Thy call abide;
And she thou mourn'st, a pure and holy presence,
    Shall glean beside!
1845.

DANIEL WHEELER.

Daniel Wheeler, a minister of the Society of Friends, who
had labored in the cause of his Divine Master in Great Britain,
Russia, and the islands of the Pacific, died in New York in the
spring of 1840, while on a religious visit to this country.

O DEARLY loved!
And worthy of our love! No more
Thy aged form shall rise before
The hushed and waiting worshipper,
In meek obedience utterance giving
To words of truth, so fresh and living,
That, even to the inward sense,
They bore unquestioned evidence
Of an anointed Messenger!
Or, bowing down thy silver hair
In reverent awfulness of prayer,
    The world, its time and sense, shut out
The brightness of Faith's holy trance
Gathered upon thy countenance,
    As if each lingering cloud of doubt,
The cold, dark shadows resting here
In Time's unluminous atmosphere,
    Were lifted by an angel's hand,
And through them on thy spiritual eye
Shone down the blessedness on high,
    The glory of the Better Land!

The oak has fallen !
While, meet for no good work, the vine
May yet its worthless branches twine,
Who knoweth not that with thee fell
A great man in our Israel?
Fallen, while thy loins were girded still,
    Thy feet with Zion's dews still wet,
    And in thy hand retaining yet
The pilgrim's staff and scallop-shell!
Unharmed and safe, where, wild and free,
    Across the Neva's cold morass
The breezes from the Frozen Sea
    With winter's arrowy keenness pass ;
Or where the unwarning tropic gale
Smote to the waves thy tattered sail,
Or where the noon-hour's fervid heat
Against Tahiti's mountains beat ;
    The same mysterious Hand which gave
    Deliverance upon land and wave,
Tempered for thee the blasts which blew
    Ladaga's frozen surface o'er,
And blessed for thee the baleful dew
    Of evening upon Eimeo's shore,
Beneath this sunny heaven of ours,
Midst our soft airs and opening flowers
    Hath given thee a grave !

    His will be done,
Who seeth not as man, whose way
    Is not as ours ! 'T is well with thee !
Nor anxious doubt nor dark dismay
Disquieted thy closing day,
But, evermore, thy soul could say,

" My Father careth still for me ! "
Called from thy hearth and home, — from her,
   The last bud on thy household tree,
The last dear one to minister
   In duty and in love to thee,
From all which nature holdeth dear,
   Feeble with years and worn with pain,
   To seek our distant land again,
Bound in the spirit, yet unknowing
   The things which should befall thee here,
   Whether for labor or for death,
In childlike trust serenely going
   To that last trial of thy faith !

      Oh, far away,
Where never shines our Northern star
   On that dark waste which Balboa saw
From Darien's mountains stretching far,
So strange, heaven-broad, and lone, that there,
With forehead to its damp wind bare,
   He bent his mailéd knee in awe ;
In many an isle whose coral feet
The surges of that ocean beat,
In thy palm shadows, Oahu,
   And Honolulu's silver bay,
Amidst Owyhee's hills of blue,
   And taro-plains of Tooboonai,
Are gentle hearts, which long shall be
Sad as our own at thought of thee,
Worn sowers of Truth's holy seed,
Whose souls in weariness and need
   Were strengthened and refreshed by thine.
For blessèd by our Father's hand
   Was thy deep love and tender care,

Thy ministry and fervent prayer, —
Grateful as Eshcol's clustered vine
To Israel in a weary land!

And they who drew
By thousands round thee, in the hour
  Of prayerful waiting, hushed and deep,
  That He who bade the islands keep
Silence before Him, might renew
  Their strength with His unslumbering power,
They too shall mourn that thou art gone,
  That nevermore thy aged lip
Shall soothe the weak, the erring warn,
Of those who first, rejoicing, heard
Through thee the Gospel's glorious word, —
  Seals of thy true apostleship.
And, if the brightest diadem,
  Whose gems of glory purely burn
  Around the ransomed ones in bliss,
Be evermore reserved for them
  Who here, through toil and sorrow, turn
  Many to righteousness,
May we not think of thee as wearing
That star-like crown of light, and bearing,
Amidst Heaven's white and blissful band,
Th' unfading palm-branch in thy hand;
And joining with a seraph's tongue
In that new song the elders sung,
Ascribing to its blessed Giver
Thanksgiving, love, and praise forever!

Farewell!
And though the ways of Zion mourn
When her strong ones are called away,

Who like thyself have calmly borne
The heat and burden of the day,
Yet He who slumbereth not nor sleepeth
His ancient watch around us keepeth;
Still, sent from His creating hand,
New witnesses for Truth shall stand,
New instruments to sound abroad
The Gospel of a risen Lord;
  To gather to the fold once more
The desolate and gone astray,
The scattered of a cloudy day,
  And Zion's broken walls restore;
And, through the travail and the toil
  Of true obedience, minister
Beauty for ashes, and the oil
  Of joy for mourning, unto her!
So shall her holy bounds increase
With walls of praise and gates of peace:
So shall the Vine, which martyr tears
And blood sustained in other years,
  With fresher life be clothed upon;
And to the world in beauty show
Like the rose-plant of Jericho,
  And glorious as Lebanon!

1847.

TO FREDRIKA BREMER.

It is proper to say that these lines are the joint impromptus of
my sister and myself. They are inserted here as an expression of
our admiration of the gifted stranger whom we have since learned
to love as a friend.

SEERESS of the misty Norland,
    Daughter of the Vikings bold,

Welcome to the sunny Vineland,
　Which thy fathers sought of old !

Soft as flow of Silja's waters,
　When the moon of summer shines,
Strong as Winter from his mountains
　Roaring through the sleeted pines.

Heart and ear, we long have listened
　To thy saga, rune, and song ;
As a household joy and presence
　We have known and loved thee long.

By the mansion's marble mantel,
　Round the log-walled cabin's hearth,
Thy sweet thoughts and northern fancies
　Meet and mingle with our mirth.

And o'er weary spirits keeping
　Sorrow's night-watch, long and chill,
Shine they like thy sun of summer
　Over midnight vale and hill.

We alone to thee are strangers,
　Thou our friend and teacher art ;
Come, and know us as we know thee ;
　Let us meet thee heart to heart !

To our homes and household altars
　We, in turn, thy steps would lead,
As thy loving hand has led us
　O'er the threshold of the Swede.

1849.

TO AVIS KEENE.

ON RECEIVING A BASKET OF SEA-MOSSES.

THANKS for thy gift
      Of ocean flowers,
   Born where the golden drift
   Of the slant sunshine falls
   Down the green, tremulous walls
Of water, to the cool, still coral bowers,
Where, under rainbows of perpetual showers,
      God's gardens of the deep
      His patient angels keep;
Gladdening the dim, strange solitude
   With fairest forms and hues, and thus
   Forever teaching us
The lesson which the many-colored skies,
The flowers, and leaves, and painted butterflies,
The deer's branched antlers, the gay bird that
      flings
The tropic sunshine from its golden wings,
The brightness of the human countenance,
Its play of smiles, the magic of a glance,
      Forevermore repeat,
      In varied tones and sweet,
   That beauty, in and of itself, is good.

O kind and generous friend, o'er whom
   The sunset hues of Time are cast,
   Painting, upon the overpast
   And scattered clouds of noonday sorrow
   The promise of a fairer morrow,
An earnest of the better life to come;

The binding of the spirit broken,
The warning to the erring spoken,
   The comfort of the sad,
The eye to see, the hand to cull
Of common things the beautiful,
   The absent heart made glad
By simple gift or graceful token
Of love it needs as daily food,
All own one Source, and all are good!
Hence, tracking sunny cove and reach,
Where spent waves glimmer up the beach,
And toss their gifts of weed and shell
From foamy curve and combing swell,
No unbefitting task was thine
   To weave these flowers so soft and fair
In unison with His design
   Who loveth beauty everywhere;
And makes in every zone and clime,
   In ocean and in upper air,
" All things beautiful in their time."

For not alone in tones of awe and power
     He speaks to man;
The cloudy horror of the thunder-shower
     His rainbows span;
     And where the caravan
Winds o'er the desert, leaving, as in air
The crane-flock leaves, no trace of passage there,
     He gives the weary eye
The palm-leaf shadow for the hot noon hours,
     And on its branches dry
Calls out the acacia's flowers;
And where the dark shaft pierces down

Beneath the mountain roots,
　Seen by the miner's lamp alone,
　　The star-like crystal shoots;
　　So, where, the winds and waves below,
　　The coral-branchëd gardens grow,
　　His climbing weeds and mosses show,
　　Like foliage, on each stony bough,
　　Of varied hues more strangely gay
　　Than forest leaves in autumn's day; —
　　　Thus evermore,
　　　　On sky, and wave, and shore,
　　An all-pervading beauty seems to say:
　　God's love and power are one; and they,
　　Who, like the thunder of a sultry day,
　　　Smite to restore,
And they, who, like the gentle wind, uplift
The petals of the dew-wet flowers, and drift
　　　Their perfume on the air,
Alike may serve Him, each, with their own gift,
　　Making their lives a prayer!
1850.

THE HILL-TOP.

THE burly driver at my side,
　We slowly climbed the hill,
Whose summit, in the hot noontide,
　Seemed rising, rising still.
At last, our short noon-shadows hid
　The top-stone, bare and brown,
From whence, like Gizeh's pyramid,
　The rough mass slanted down.

I felt the cool breath of the North ;
    Between me and the sun,
O'er deep, still lake, and ridgy earth,
    I saw the cloud-shades run.
Before me, stretched for glistening miles,
    Lay mountain-girdled Squam ;
Like green-winged birds, the leafy isles
    Upon its bosom swam.

And, glimmering through the sun-haze warm,
    Far as the eye could roam,
Dark billows of an earthquake storm
    Beflecked with clouds like foam,
Their vales in misty shadow deep,
    Their rugged peaks in shine,
I saw the mountain ranges sweep
    The horizon's northern line.

There towered Chocorua's peak ; and west,
    Moosehillock's woods were seen,
With many a nameless slide-scarred crest
    And pine-dark gorge between.
Beyond them, like a sun-rimmed cloud,
    The great Notch mountains shone,
Watched over by the solemn-browed
    And awful face of stone !

" A good look-off ! " the driver spake :
    " About this time, last year,
I drove a party to the Lake,
    And stopped, at evening, here.
'T was duskish down below ; but all
    These hills stood in the sun,

Till, dipped behind yon purple wall,
    He left them, one by one.

" A lady, who, from Thornton hill,
    Had held her place outside,
And, as a pleasant woman will,
    Had cheered the long, dull ride,
Besought me, with so sweet a smile,
    That — though I hate delays —
I could not choose but rest awhile, ⌐
    (These women have such ways!)

" On yonder mossy ledge she sat,
    Her sketch upon her knees,
A stray brown lock beneath her hat
    Unrolling in the breeze;
Her sweet face, in the sunset light
    Upraised and glorified, —
I never saw a prettier sight
    In all my mountain ride.

" As good as fair; it seemed her joy
    To comfort and to give;
My poor, sick wife, and cripple boy,
    Will bless her while they live! "
The tremor in the driver's tone
    His manhood did not shame:
"I dare say, sir, you may have known " —
    He named a well-known name.

Then sank the pyramidal mounds,
    The blue lake fled away;

For mountain-scope a parlor's bounds,
  A lighted hearth for day !
From lonely years and weary miles
  The shadows fell apart ;
Kind voices cheered, sweet human smiles
  Shone warm into my heart.

We journeyed on ; but earth and sky
  Had power to charm no more ;
Still dreamed my inward-turning eye
  The dream of memory o'er.
Ah ! human kindness, human love, —
  To few who seek denied ;
Too late we learn to prize above
  The whole round world beside !

1850.

ELLIOTT.

Ebenezer Elliott was to the artisans of England what Burns
was to the peasantry of Scotland. His *Corn-law Rhymes* con-
tributed not a little to that overwhelming tide of popular opinion
and feeling which resulted in the repeal of the tax on bread.
Well has the eloquent author of *The Reforms and Reformers of
Great Britain* said of him, "Not corn-law repealers alone, but all
Britons who moisten their scanty bread with the sweat of the brow,
are largely indebted to his inspiring lay, for the mighty bound
which the laboring mind of England has taken in our day."

HANDS off ! thou tithe-fat plunderer ! play
  No trick of priestcraft here !
Back, puny lordling ! darest thou lay
  A hand on Elliott's bier ?
Alive, your rank and pomp, as dust,
  Beneath his feet he trod :

He knew the locust swarm that cursed
　　The harvest-fields of God.

On these pale lips, the smothered thought
　　Which England's millions feel,
A fierce and fearful splendor caught,
　　As from his forge the steel.
Strong-armed as Thor, a shower of fire
　　His smitten anvil flung;
God's curse, Earth's wrong, dumb Hunger's
　　　ire,
　　He gave them all a tongue!

Then let the poor man's horny hands
　　Bear up the mighty dead,
And labor's swart and stalwart bands
　　Behind as mourners tread.
Leave cant and craft their baptized bounds,
　　Leave rank its minster floor ;
Give England's green and daisied grounds
　　The poet of the poor!

Lay down upon his Sheaf's green verge
　　That brave old heart of oak,
With fitting dirge from sounding forge,
　　And pall of furnace smoke!
Where whirls the stone its dizzy rounds,
　　And axe and sledge are swung,
And, timing to their stormy sounds,
　　His stormy lays are sung.

There let the peasant's step be heard,
　　The grinder chant his rhyme ;

Nor patron's praise nor dainty word
  Befits the man or time.
No soft lament nor dreamer's sigh
  For him whose words were bread ;
The Runic rhyme and spell whereby
  The foodless poor were fed!

Pile up the tombs of rank and pride,
  O England, as thou wilt!
With pomp to nameless worth denied,
  Emblazon titled guilt!
No part or lot in these we claim ;
  But, o'er the sounding wave,
A common right to Elliott's name,
  A freehold in his grave!

1850.

ICHABOD.

This poem was the outcome of the surprise and grief and forecast of evil consequences which I felt on reading the seventh of
March speech of Daniel Webster in support of the " compromise,"
and the Fugitive Slave Law. No partisan or personal enmity dic-
tated it. On the contrary my admiration of the splendid per-
sonality and intellectual power of the great Senator was never
stronger than when I laid down his speech, and, in one of the saddest moments of my life, penned my protest. I saw, as I wrote,
with painful clearness its sure results, — the Slave Power arro-
gant and defiant, strengthened and encouraged to carry out its
scheme for the extension of its baleful system, or the dissolution
of the Union, the guaranties of personal liberty in the free States
broken down, and the whole country made the hunting-ground of
slave-catchers. In the horror of such a vision, so soon fearfully
fulfilled, if one spoke at all, he could only speak in tones of stern
and sorrowful rebuke.

But death softens all resentments, and the consciousness of a

common inheritance of frailty and weakness modifies the severity
of judgment. Years after, in *The Lost Occasion* I gave utterance
to an almost universal regret that the great statesman did not
live to see the flag which he loved trampled under the feet of
Slavery, and, in view of this desecration, make his last days glorious in defence of "Liberty and Union, one and inseparable."

So fallen! so lost! the light withdrawn
    Which once he wore!
The glory from his gray hairs gone
    Forevermore!

Revile him not, the Tempter hath
    A snare for all;
And pitying tears, not scorn and wrath,
    Befit his fall!

Oh, dumb be passion's stormy rage,
    When he who might
Have lighted up and led his age,
    Falls back in night.

Scorn! would the angels laugh, to mark
    A bright soul driven,
Fiend-goaded, down the endless dark,
    From hope and heaven!

Let not the land once proud of him
    Insult him now,
Nor brand with deeper shame his dim,
    Dishonored brow.

But let its humbled sons, instead,
    From sea to lake,

A long lament, as for the dead,
    In sadness make.

Of all we loved and honored, naught
    Save power remains ;
A fallen angel's pride of thought,
    Still strong in chains.

All else is gone ; from those great eyes
    The soul has fled :
When faith is lost, when honor dies,
    The man is dead !

Then, pay the reverence of old days
    To his dead fame ;
Walk backward, with averted gaze,
    And hide the shame !

1850.

THE LOST OCCASION.

SOME die too late and some too soon,
At early morning, heat of noon,
Or the chill evening twilight.   Thou,
Whom the rich heavens did so endow
With eyes of power and Jove's own brow,
With all the massive strength that fills
Thy home-horizon's granite hills,
With rarest gifts of heart and head
From manliest stock inherited,
New England's stateliest type of man,
In port and speech Olympian ;

Whom no one met, at first, but took
A second awed and wondering look
(As turned, perchance, the eyes of Greece
On Phidias' unveiled masterpiece) ;
Whose words in simplest homespun clad,
The Saxon strength of Cædmon's had,
With power reserved at need to reach
The Roman forum's loftiest speech,
Sweet with persuasion, eloquent
In passion, cool in argument,
Or, ponderous, falling on thy foes
As fell the Norse god's hammer blows,
Crushing as if with Talus' flail
Through Error's logic-woven mail,
And failing only when they tried
The adamant of the righteous side, —
Thou, foiled in aim and hope, bereaved
Of old friends, by the new deceived,
Too soon for us, too soon for thee,
Beside thy lonely Northern sea,
Where long and low the marsh-lands spread,
Laid wearily down thy august head.

Thou shouldst have lived to feel below
Thy feet Disunion's fierce upthrow ;
The late-sprung mine that underlaid
Thy sad concessions vainly made.
Thou shouldst have seen from Sumter's wall
The star-flag of the Union fall,
And armed rebellion pressing on
The broken lines of Washington !
No stronger voice than thine had then
Called out the utmost might of men,

To make the Union's charter free
And strengthen law by liberty.
How had that stern arbitrament
To thy gray age youth's vigor lent,
Shaming ambition's paltry prize
Before thy disillusioned eyes;
Breaking the spell about thee wound
Like the green withes that Samson bound;
Redeeming in one effort grand,
Thyself and thy imperilled land!
Ah, cruel fate, that closed to thee,
O sleeper by the Northern sea,
The gates of opportunity!
God fills the gaps of human need,
Each crisis brings its word and deed.
Wise men and strong we did not lack;
But still, with memory turning back,
In the dark hours we thought of thee,
And thy lone grave beside the sea.

Above that grave the east winds blow,
And from the marsh-lands drifting slow
The sea-fog comes, with evermore
The wave-wash of a lonely shore,
And sea-bird's melancholy cry,
As Nature fain would typify
The sadness of a closing scene,
The loss of that which should have been.
But, where thy native mountains bare
Their foreheads to diviner air,
Fit emblem of enduring fame,
One lofty summit keeps thy name.

For thee the cosmic forces did
The rearing of that pyramid,
The prescient ages shaping with
Fire, flood, and frost thy monolith.
Sunrise and sunset lay thereon
With hands of light their benison,
The stars of midnight pause to set
Their jewels in its coronet.
And evermore that mountain mass
Seems climbing from the shadowy pass
To light, as if to manifest
Thy nobler self, thy life at best!

1880.

WORDSWORTH.

WRITTEN ON A BLANK LEAF OF HIS MEMOIRS.

DEAR friends, who read the world aright,
   And in its common forms discern
A beauty and a harmony
   The many never learn!

Kindred in soul of him who found
   In simple flower and leaf and stone
The impulse of the sweetest lays
   Our Saxon tongue has known, —

Accept this record of a life
   As sweet and pure, as calm and good,
As a long day of blandest June
   In green field and in wood.

How welcome to our ears, long pained
   By strife of sect and party noise,
The brook-like murmur of his song
   Of nature's simple joys !

The violet by its mossy stone,
   The primrose by the river's brim,
And chance-sown daffodil, have found
   Immortal life through him.

The sunrise on his breezy lake,
   The rosy tints his sunset brought,
World-seen, are gladdening all the vales
   And mountain-peaks of thought.

Art builds on sand; the works of pride
   And human passion change and fall;
But that which shares the life of God
   With Him surviveth all.

1851.

TO ——.

LINES WRITTEN AFTER A SUMMER DAY'S EXCUR-
SION.

FAIR Nature's priestesses   to whom,
In hieroglyph of bud and bloom,
   Her mysteries are told ;
Who, wise in lore of wood and mead,
The seasons' pictured scrolls can read,
   In lessons manifold !

Thanks for the courtesy, and gay
Good-humor, which on Washing Day
    Our ill-timed visit bore;
Thanks for your graceful oars, which broke
The morning dreams of Artichoke,
    Along his wooded shore!

Varied as varying Nature's ways,
Sprites of the river, woodland fays,
    Or mountain nymphs, ye seem;
Free-limbed Dianas on the green,
Loch Katrine's Ellen, or Undine,
    Upon your favorite stream.

The forms of which the poets told,
The fair benignities of old,
    Were doubtless such as you;
What more than Artichoke the rill
Of Helicon?   Than Pipe-stave hill
    Arcadia's mountain-view?

No sweeter bowers the bee delayed,
In wild Hymettus' scented shade,
    Than those you dwell among;
Snow-flowered azaleas, intertwined
With roses, over banks inclined
    With trembling harebells hung!

A charmèd life unknown to death,
Immortal freshness Nature hath;
    Her fabled fount and glen
Are now and here: Dodona's shrine
Still murmurs in the wind-swept pine, —
    All is that e'er hath been.

The Beauty which old Greece or Rome
Sung, painted, wrought, lies close at home ;
    We need but eye and ear
In all our daily walks to trace
The outlines of incarnate grace,
    The hymns of gods to hear !

1851.

IN PEACE.

A TRACK of moonlight on a quiet lake,
  Whose small waves on a silver-sanded shore
Whisper of peace, and with the low winds make
Such harmonies as keep the woods awake,
And listening all night long for their sweet sake ;
  A green-waved slope of meadow, hovered o'er
By angel-troops of lilies, swaying light
On viewless stems, with folded wings of white ;
A slumberous stretch of mountain-land, far seen
Where the low westering day, with gold and green,
Purple and amber, softly blended, fills
The wooded vales, and melts among the hills ;
A vine-fringed river, winding to its rest
  On the calm bosom of a stormless sea,
Bearing alike upon its placid breast,
With earthly flowers and heavenly stars impressed,
  The hues of time and of eternity :
Such are the pictures which the thought of thee,
O friend, awakeneth, — charming the keen pain
  Of thy departure, and our sense of loss
Requiting with the fullness of thy gain.
  Lo ! on the quiet grave thy life-borne cross,

Dropped only at its side, methinks doth shine,
Of thy beatitude the radiant sign!
  No sob of grief, no wild lament be there,
  To break the Sabbath of the holy air;
But, in their stead, the silent-breathing prayer
Of hearts still waiting for a rest like thine.
O spirit redeemed!   Forgive us, if henceforth,
With sweet and pure similitudes of earth,
  We keep thy pleasant memory freshly green,
Of love's inheritance a priceless part,
  Which Fancy's self, in reverent awe, is seen
To paint, forgetful of the tricks of art,
  With pencil dipped alone in colors of the heart.
  1851.

BENEDICITE.

  GOD'S love and peace be with thee, where
  Soe'er this soft autumnal air
  Lifts the dark tresses of thy hair!

  Whether through city casements comes
  Its kiss to thee, in crowded rooms,
  Or, out among the woodland blooms,

  It freshens o'er thy thoughtful face,
  Imparting, in its glad embrace,
  Beauty to beauty, grace to grace!

  Fair Nature's book together read,
  The old wood-paths that knew our tread,
  The maple shadows overhead, —

The hills we climbed, the river seen
By gleams along its deep ravine, —
All keep thy memory fresh and green.

Where'er I look, where'er I stray,
Thy thought goes with me on my way,
And hence the prayer I breathe to-day;

O'er lapse of time and change of scene,
The weary waste which lies between
Thyself and me, my heart I lean.

Thou lack'st not Friendship's spell-word, nor
The half-unconscious power to draw
All hearts to thine by Love's sweet law.

With these good gifts of God is cast
Thy lot, and many a charm thou hast
To hold the blessed angels fast.

If, then, a fervent wish for thee
The gracious heavens will heed from me,
What should, dear heart, its burden be?

The sighing of a shaken reed, —
What can I more than meekly plead
The greatness of our common need?

God's love, — unchanging, pure, and true, —
The Paraclete white-shining through
His peace, — the fall of Hermon's dew!

With such a prayer, on this sweet day,
As thou mayst hear and I may say,
I greet thee, dearest, far away!
1851.

KOSSUTH.

It can scarcely be necessary to say that there are elements in the character and passages in the history of the great Hungarian statesman and orator, which necessarily command the admiration of those, even, who believe that no political revolution was ever worth the price of human blood.

TYPE of two mighty continents! — combining
　The strength of Europe with the warmth and
　　　glow
Of Asian song and prophecy, — the shining
　Of Orient splendors over Northern snow!
Who shall receive him? Who, unblushing, speak
Welcome to him, who, while he strove to break
The Austrian yoke from Magyar necks, smote off
At the same blow the fetters of the serf,
Rearing the altar of his Fatherland
　On the firm base of freedom, and thereby
Lifting to Heaven a patriot's stainless hand,
　Mocked not the God of Justice with a lie!
Who shall be Freedom's mouthpiece? Who shall
　　　give
Her welcoming cheer to the great fugitive?
Not he who, all her sacred trusts betraying,
　Is scourging back to slavery's hell of pain
　The swarthy Kossuths of our land again!
Not he whose utterance now from lips designed
The bugle-march of Liberty to wind,

And call her hosts beneath the breaking light,
The keen reveille of her morn of fight,
  Is but the hoarse note of the blood-hound's bay-
      ing,
The wolf's long howl behind the bondman's flight!
Oh for the tongue of him who lies at rest
  In Quincy's shade of patrimonial trees,
Last of the Puritan tribunes and the best,
  To lend a voice to Freedom's sympathies,
And hail the coming of the noblest guest
The Old World's wrong has given the New World
     of the West!

1851.

TO MY OLD SCHOOLMASTER.

AN EPISTLE NOT AFTER THE MANNER OF HORACE.

These lines were addressed to my worthy friend Joshua Coffin,
teacher, historian, and antiquarian. He was one of the twelve
persons who with William Lloyd Garrison formed the first anti-
slavery society in New England.

OLD friend, kind friend! lightly down
Drop time's snow-flakes on thy crown!
Never be thy shadow less,
Never fail thy cheerfulness;
Care, that kills the cat, may plough
Wrinkles in the miser's brow,
Deepen envy's spiteful frown,
Draw the mouths of bigots down,
Plague ambition's dream, and sit
Heavy on the hypocrite,
Haunt the rich man's door, and ride
In the gilded coach of pride; —

Let the fiend pass! — what can he
Find to do with such as thee?
Seldom comes that evil guest
Where the conscience lies at rest,
And brown health and quiet wit
Smiling on the threshold sit.

I, the urchin unto whom,
In that smoked and dingy room,
Where the district gave thee rule
O'er its ragged winter school,
Thou didst teach the mysteries
Of those weary A B C's, —
Where, to fill the every pause
Of thy wise and learned saws,
Through the cracked and crazy wall
Came the cradle-rock and squall,
And the goodman's voice, at strife
With his shrill and tipsy wife, —
Luring us by stories old,
With a comic unction told,
More than by the eloquence
Of terse birchen arguments
(Doubtful gain, I fear), to look
With complacence on a book! —
Where the genial pedagogue
Half forgot his rogues to flog,
Citing tale or apologue,
Wise and merry in its drift
As was Phædrus' twofold gift,
Had the little rebels known it,
Risum et prudentiam monet!
I, — the man of middle years,
In whose sable locks appears

Many a warning fleck of gray, —
Looking back to that far day,
And thy primal lessons, feel
Grateful smiles my lips unseal,
As, remembering thee, I blend
Olden teacher, present friend,
Wise with antiquarian search,
In the scrolls of State and Church:
Named on history's title-page,
Parish-clerk and justice sage;
For the ferule's wholesome awe
Wielding now the sword of law.

Threshing Time's neglected sheaves,
Gathering up the scattered leaves
Which the wrinkled sibyl cast
Careless from her as she passed, —
Twofold citizen art thou,
Freeman of the past and now.
He who bore thy name of old
Midway in the heavens did hold
Over Gibeon moon and sun;
Thou hast bidden them backward run;
Of to-day the present ray
Flinging over yesterday!

Let the busy ones deride
What I deem of right thy pride:
Let the fools their treadmills grind,
Look not forward nor behind,
Shuffle in and wriggle out,
Veer' with every breeze about,
Turning like a windmill sail,
Or a dog that seeks his tail;

Let them laugh to see thee fast
Tabernacled in the Past,
Working out with eye and lip,
Riddles of old penmanship,
Patient as Belzoni there
Sorting out, with loving care,
Mummies of dead questions stripped
From their sevenfold manuscript !

Dabbling, in their noisy way,
In the puddles of to-day,
Little know they of that vast
Solemn ocean of the past,
On whose margin, wreck-bespread,
Thou art walking with the dead,
Questioning the stranded years,
Waking smiles, by turns, and tears,
As thou callest up again
Shapes the dust has long o'erlain, —
Fair-haired woman, bearded man,
Cavalier and Puritan ;
In an age whose eager view
Seeks but present things, and new,
Mad for party, sect and gold,
Teaching reverence for the old.

On that shore, with fowler's tact,
Coolly bagging fact on fact,
Naught amiss to thee can float,
Tale, or song, or anecdote ;
Village gossip, centuries old,
Scandals by our grandams told,
What the pilgrim's table spread,

Where he lived, and whom he wed,
Long-drawn bill of wine and beer
For his ordination cheer,
Or the flip that wellnigh made
Glad his funeral cavalcade;
Weary prose, and poet's lines,
Flavored by their age, like wines,
Eulogistic of some quaint,
Doubtful, puritanic saint;
Lays that quickened husking jigs,
Jests that shook grave periwigs,
When the parson had his jokes
And his glass, like other folks;
Sermons that, for mortal hours,
Taxed our fathers' vital powers,
As the long nineteenthlies poured
Downward from the sounding-board,
And, for fire of Pentecost,
Touched their beards December's frost.

Time is hastening on, and we
What our fathers are shall be, —
Shadow-shapes of memory!
Joined to that vast multitude
Where the great are but the good,
And the mind of strength shall prove
Weaker than the heart of love;
Pride of graybeard wisdom less
Than the infant's guilelessness,
And his song of sorrow more
Than the crown the Psalmist wore!
Who shall then, with pious zeal,
At our moss-grown thresholds kneel,

From a stained and stony page
Reading to a careless age,
With a patient eye like thine,
Prosing tale and limping line,
Names and words the hoary rime
Of the Past has made sublime?
Who shall work for us as well
The antiquarian's miracle?
Who to seeming life recall
Teacher grave and pupil small?
Who shall give to thee and me
Freeholds in futurity?

Well, whatever lot be mine,
Long and happy days be thine,
Ere thy full and honored age
Dates of time its latest page!
Squire for master, State for school,
Wisely lenient, live and rule;
Over grown-up knave and rogue
Play the watchful pedagogue;
Or, while pleasure smiles on duty,
At the call of youth and beauty,
Speak for them the spell of law
Which shall bar and bolt withdraw,
And the flaming sword remove
From the Paradise of Love.
Still, with undimmed eyesight, pore
Ancient tome and record o'er;
Still thy week-day lyrics croon,
Pitch in church the Sunday tune,
Showing something, in thy part,
Of the old Puritanic art,
Singer after Sternhold's heart!

In thy pew, for many a year,
Homilies from Oldbug hear,[3]
Who to wit like that of South,
And the Syrian's golden mouth,
Doth the homely pathos add
Which the pilgrim preachers had;
Breaking, like a child at play,
Gilded idols of the day,
Cant of knave and pomp of fool
Tossing with his ridicule,
Yet, in earnest or in jest,
Ever keeping truth abreast.
And, when thou art called, at last,
To thy townsmen of the past,
Not as stranger shalt thou come;
Thou shalt find thyself at home
With the little and the big,
Woollen cap and periwig,
Madam in her high-laced ruff,
Goody in her home-made stuff, —
Wise and simple, rich and poor,
Thou hast known them all before!

1851.

THE CROSS.

Richard Dillingham, a young member of the Society of Friends,
died in the Nashville penitentiary, where he was confined for the
act of aiding the escape of fugitive slaves.

" THE cross, if rightly borne, shall be
No burden, but support to thee;"[4]
So, moved of old time for our sake,
The holy monk of Kempen spake.

Thou brave and true one ! upon whom
Was laid the cross of martyrdom,
How didst thou, in thy generous youth,
Bear witness to this blessed truth !

Thy cross of suffering and of shame
A staff within thy hands became,
In paths where faith alone could see
The Master's steps supporting thee.

Thine was the seed-time ; God alone
Beholds the end of what is sown ;
Beyond our vision, weak and dim,
The harvest-time is hid with Him.

Yet, unforgotten where it lies,
That seed of generous sacrifice,
Though seeming on the desert cast,
Shall rise with bloom and fruit at last.
1852.

THE HERO.

The hero of the incident related in this poem was Dr. Samuel
Gridley Howe, the well-known philanthropist, who when a young
man volunteered his aid in the Greek struggle for independence.

" OH for a knight like Bayard,
    Without reproach or fear ;
  My light glove on his casque of steel,
    My love-knot on his spear !

" Oh for the white plume floating
    Sad Zutphen's field above, —

The lion heart in battle,
  The woman's heart in love!

" Oh that man once more were manly,
    Woman's pride, and not her scorn:
  That once more the pale young mother
    Dared to boast 'a man is born'!

" But, now life's slumberous current
    No sun-bowed cascade wakes;
  No tall, heroic manhood
    The level dulness breaks.

" Oh for a knight like Bayard,
    Without reproach or fear!
  My light glove on his casque of steel,
    My love-knot on his spear!"

Then I said, my own heart throbbing
    To the time her proud pulse beat,
" Life hath its regal natures yet,
    True, tender, brave, and sweet!

" Smile not, fair unbeliever!
    One man, at least, I know,
  Who might wear the crest of Bayard
    Or Sidney's plume of snow.

" Once, when over purple mountains
    Died away the Grecian sun,
  And the far Cyllenian ranges
    Paled and darkened, one by one, —

" Fell the Turk, a bolt of thunder,
    Cleaving all the quiet sky,
And against his sharp steel lightnings
    Stood the Suliote but to die.

" Woe for the weak and halting!
    The crescent blazed behind
A curving line of sabres,
    Like fire before the wind!

" Last to fly, and first to rally,
    Rode he of whom I speak,
When, groaning in his bridle-path,
    Sank down a wounded Greek.

" With the rich Albanian costume
    Wet with many a ghastly stain,
Gazing on earth and sky as one
    Who might not gaze again!

" He looked forward to the mountains,
    Back on foes that never spare,
Then flung him from his saddle,
    And placed the stranger there.

" ' Allah! hu!' Through flashing sabres,
    Through a stormy hail of lead,
The good Thessalian charger
    Up the slopes of olives sped.

" Hot spurred the turbaned riders;
    He almost felt their breath,

Where a mountain stream rolled darkly down
    Between the hills and death.

" One brave and manful struggle, —
    He gained the solid land,
And the cover of the mountains,
    And the carbines of his band ! "

" It was very great and noble,"
    Said the moist-eyed listener then,
" But one brave deed makes no hero ;
    Tell me what he since hath been ! "

" Still a brave and generous manhood,
    Still an honor without stain,
In the prison of the Kaiser,
    By the barricades of Seine.

" But dream not helm and harness
    The sign of valor true ;
Peace hath higher tests of manhood
    Than battle ever knew.

" Wouldst know him now?   Behold him,
    The Cadmus of the blind,
Giving the dumb lip language,
    The idiot-clay a mind.

" Walking his round of duty
    Serenely day by day,
With the strong man's hand of labor
    And childhood's heart of play.

" True as the knights of story,
    Sir Lancelot and his peers,
Brave in his calm endurance
    As they in tilt of spears.

" As waves in stillest waters,
    As stars in noonday skies,
All that wakes to noble action
    In his noon of calmness lies.

" Wherever outraged Nature
    Asks word or action brave,
Wherever struggles labor,
    Wherever groans a slave, —

" Wherever rise the peoples,
    Wherever sinks a throne,
The throbbing heart of Freedom finds
    An answer in his own.

" Knight of a better era,
    Without reproach or fear!
Said I not well that Bayards
    And Sidneys still are here ? "

1853.

RANTOUL.

No more fitting inscription could be placed on the tombstone of
Robert Rantoul than this: " He died at his post in Congress, and
his last words were a protest in the name of Democracy against
the Fugitive-Slave Law."

ONE day, along the electric wire
    His manly word for Freedom sped;

We came next morn : that tongue of fire
  Said only, " He who spake is dead ! "

Dead ! while his voice was living yet,
  In echoes round the pillared dome !
Dead ! while his blotted page lay wet
  With themes of state and loves of home !

Dead ! in that crowning grace of time,
  That triumph of life's zenith hour !
Dead ! while we watched his manhood's prime
  Break from the slow bud into flower !

Dead ! he so great, and strong, and wise,
  While the mean thousands yet drew breath ;
How deepened, through that dread surprise,
  The mystery and the awe of death !

From the high place whereon our votes
  Had borne him, clear, calm, earnest, fell
His first words, like the prelude notes
  Of some great anthem yet to swell.

We seemed to see our flag unfurled,
  Our champion waiting in his place
For the last battle of the world,
  The Armageddon of the race.

Through him we hoped to speak the word
  Which wins the freedom of a land ;
And lift, for human right, the sword
  Which dropped from Hampden's dying hand.

For he had sat at Sidney's feet,
 And walked with Pym and Vane apart;
And, through the centuries, felt the beat
 Of Freedom's march in Cromwell's heart.

He knew the paths the worthies held,
 Where England's best and wisest trod;
And, lingering, drank the springs that welled
 Beneath the touch of Milton's rod.

No wild enthusiast of the right,
 Self-poised and clear, he showed alway
The coolness of his northern night,
 The ripe repose of autumn's day.

His steps were slow, yet forward still
 He pressed where others paused or failed;
The calm star clomb with constant will,
 The restless meteor flashed and paled!

Skilled in its subtlest wile, he knew
 And owned the higher ends of Law;
Still rose majestic on his view
 The awful Shape the schoolman saw.

Her home the heart of God; her voice
 The choral harmonics whereby
The stars, through all their spheres, rejoice,
 The rhythmic rule of earth and sky!

We saw his great powers misapplied
 To poor ambitions; yet, through all,
We saw him take the weaker side,
 And right the wronged, and free the thrall.

Now, looking o'er the frozen North,
   For one like him in word and act,
To call her old, free spirit forth,
   And give her faith the life of fact, —

To break her party bonds of shame,
   And labor with the zeal of him
To make the Democratic name
   Of Liberty the synonyme, —

We sweep the land from hill to strand,
   We seek the strong, the wise, the brave,
And, sad of heart, return to stand
   In silence by a new-made grave!

There, where his breezy hills of home
   Look out upon his sail-white seas,
The sounds of winds and waters come,
   And shape themselves to words like these:

" Why, murmuring, mourn that he, whose power
   Was lent to Party over-long,
Heard the still whisper at the hour
   He set his foot on Party wrong?

" The human life that closed so well
   No lapse of folly now can stain:
The lips whence Freedom's protest fell
   No meaner thought can now profane.

" Mightier than living voice his grave
   That lofty protest utters o'er;
Through roaring wind and smiting wave
   It speaks his hate of wrong once more.

" Men of the North ! your weak regret
  Is wasted here ; arise and pay
To freedom and to him your debt,
  By following where he led the way ! "
1853.

WILLIAM FORSTER.

William Forster, of Norwich, England, died in East Tennessee,
in the 1st month, 1854, while engaged in presenting to the gover-
nors of the States of this Union the address of his religious society
on the evils of slavery.   He was the relative and coadjutor of the
Buxtons, Gurneys, and Frys ; and his whole life, extending almost to threescore and ten years, was a pure and beautiful example of Christian benevolence.   He had travelled over Europe, and
visited most of its sovereigns, to plead against the slave-trade and
slavery ; and had twice before made visits to this country, under
impressions of religious duty.   He was the father of the Right
Hon. William Edward Forster.   He visited my father's house
in Haverhill during his first tour in the United States.

THE years are many since his hand
    Was laid upon my head,
Too weak and young to understand
    The serious words he said.

Yet often now the good man's look
    Before me seems to swim,
As if some inward feeling took
    The outward guise of him.

As if, in passion's heated war,
    Or near temptation's charm,
Through him the low-voiced monitor
    Forewarned me of the harm.

Stranger and pilgrim ! from that day
    Of meeting, first and last,

Wherever Duty's pathway lay,
  His reverent steps have passed.

The poor to feed, the lost to seek,
  To proffer life to death,
Hope to the erring, — to the weak
  The strength of his own faith.

To plead the captive's right; remove
  The sting of hate from Law;
And soften in the fire of love
  The hardened steel of War.

He walked the dark world, in the mild,
  Still guidance of the Light;
In tearful tenderness a child,
  A strong man in the right.

From what great perils, on his way,
  He found, in prayer, release;
Through what abysmal shadows lay
  His pathway unto peace,

God knoweth : we could only see
  The tranquil strength he gained;
The bondage lost in liberty,
  The fear in love unfeigned.

And I, — my youthful fancies grown
  The habit of the man,
Whose field of life by angels sown
  The wilding vines o'erran, —

Low bowed in silent gratitude,
    My manhood's heart enjoys
That reverence for the pure and good
    Which blessed the dreaming boy's.

Still shines the light of holy lives
    Like star-beams over doubt ;
Each sainted memory, Christlike, drives
    Some dark possession out.

O friend ! O brother ! not in vain
    Thy life so calm and true,
The silver dropping of the rain,
    The fall of summer dew !

How many burdened hearts have prayed
    Their lives like thine might be !
But more shall pray henceforth for aid
    To lay them down like thee.

With weary hand, yet steadfast will,
    In old age as in youth,
Thy Master found thee sowing still
    The good seed of His truth.

As on thy task-field closed the day
    In golden-skied decline,
His angel met thee on the way,
    And lent his arm to thine.

Thy latest care for man, — thy last
    Of earthly thought a prayer, —
Oh, who thy mantle, backward cast,
    Is worthy now to wear ?

Methinks the mound which marks thy bed
  Might bless our land and save,
As rose, of old, to life the dead
  Who touched the prophet's grave !

1854.

TO CHARLES SUMNER.

If I have seemed more prompt to censure wrong
  Than praise the right ; if seldom to thine ear
  My voice hath mingled with the exultant cheer
Borne upon all our Northern winds along ;
If I have failed to join the fickle throng
In wide-eyed wonder, that thou standest strong
In victory, surprised in thee to find
Brougham's scathing power with Canning's grace
      combined ;
That he, for whom the ninefold Muses sang,
From their twined arms a giant athlete sprang,
Barbing the arrows of his native tongue
With the spent shafts Latona's archer flung,
To smite the Python of our land and time,
Fell as the monster born of Crissa's slime,
Like the blind bard who in Castalian springs
Tempered the steel that clove the crest of kings,
And on the shrine of England's freedom laid
The gifts of Cumæ and of Delphi's shade, —
Small need hast thou of words of praise from me.
  Thou knowest my heart, dear friend, and well
      canst guess
  That, even though silent, I have not the less
Rejoiced to see thy actual life agree
With the large future which I shaped for thee,
When, years ago, beside the summer sea,

White in the moon, we saw the long waves fall
Baffled and broken from the rocky wall,
That, to the menace of the brawling flood,
Opposed alone its massive quietude,
Calm as a fate; with not a leaf nor vine
Nor birch-spray trembling in the still moonshine,
Crowning it like God's peace. I sometimes
    think
  That night-scene by the sea prophetical,
(For Nature speaks in symbols and in signs,
And through her pictures human fate divines),
That rock, wherefrom we saw the billows sink
  In murmuring rout, uprising clear and tall
In the white light of heaven, the type of one
Who, momently by Error's host assailed,
Stands strong as Truth, in greaves of granite
    mailed;
  And, tranquil-fronted, listening over all
The tumult, hears the angels say, Well done!
  1854.

BURNS.

ON RECEIVING A SPRIG OF HEATHER IN BLOSSOM.

No more these simple flowers belong
  To Scottish maid and lover;
Sown in the common soil of song,
  They bloom the wide world over.

In smiles and tears, in sun and showers,
  The minstrel and the heather,
The deathless singer and the flowers
  He sang of live together.

Wild heather-bells and Robert Burns!
  The moorland flower and peasant!
How, at their mention, memory turns
  Her pages old and pleasant!

The gray sky wears again its gold
  And purple of adorning,
And manhood's noonday shadows hold
  The dews of boyhood's morning.

The dews that washed the dust and soil
  From off the wings of pleasure,
The sky, that flecked the ground of toil
  With golden threads of leisure.

I call to mind the summer day,
  The early harvest mowing,
The sky with sun and clouds at play,
  And flowers with breezes blowing.

I hear the blackbird in the corn,
  The locust in the haying;
And, like the fabled hunter's horn,
  Old tunes my heart is playing.

How oft that day, with fond delay,
  I sought the maple's shadow,
And sang with Burns the hours away,
  Forgetful of the meadow!

Bees hummed, birds twittered, overhead
  I heard the squirrels leaping,
The good dog listened while I read,
  And wagged his tail in keeping.

I watched him while in sportive mood
    I read " *The Twa Dogs'* " story,
And half believed he understood
    The poet's allegory.

Sweet day, sweet songs! The golden hours
    Grew brighter for that singing,
From brook and bird and meadow flowers
    A dearer welcome bringing.

New light on home-seen Nature beamed,
    New glory over Woman;
And daily life and duty seemed
    No longer poor and common.

I woke to find the simple truth
    Of fact and feeling better
Than all the dreams that held my youth
    A still repining debtor:

That Nature gives her handmaid, Art,
    The themes of sweet discoursing;
The tender idyls of the heart
    In every tongue rehearsing.

Why dream of lands of gold and pearl,
    Of loving knight and lady,
When farmer boy and barefoot girl
    Were wandering there already?

I saw through all familiar things
    The romance underlying;
The joys and griefs that plume the wings
    Of Fancy skyward flying.

I saw the same blithe day return,
 The same sweet fall of even,
That rose on wooded Craigie-burn,
 And sank on crystal Devon.

I matched with Scotland's heathery hills
 The sweetbrier and the clover;
With Ayr and Doon, my native rills,
 Their wood-hymns chanting over.

O'er rank and pomp, as he had seen,
 I saw the Man uprising;
No longer common or unclean,
 The child of God's baptizing!

With clearer eyes I saw the worth
 Of life among the lowly;
The Bible at his Cotter's hearth
 Had made my own more holy.

And if at times an evil strain,
 To lawless love appealing,
Broke in upon the sweet refrain
 Of pure and healthful feeling,

It died upon the eye and ear,
 No inward answer gaining;
No heart had I to see or hear
 The discord and the staining.

Let those who never erred forget
 His worth, in vain bewailings;
Sweet Soul of Song! I own my debt
 Uncancelled by his failings!

Lament who will the ribald line
   Which tells his lapse from duty,
How kissed the maddening lips of wine
   Or wanton ones of beauty;

But think, while falls that shade between
   The erring one and Heaven,
That he who loved like Magdalen,
   Like her may be forgiven.

Not his the song whose thunderous chime
   Eternal echoes render;
The mournful Tuscan's haunted rhyme,
   And Milton's starry splendor!

But who his human heart has laid
   To Nature's bosom nearer?
Who sweetened toil like him, or paid
   To love a tribute dearer?

Through all his tuneful art, how strong
   The human feeling gushes!
The very moonlight of his song
   Is warm with smiles and blushes!

Give lettered pomp to teeth of Time,
   So "Bonnie Doon" but tarry;
Blot out the Epic's stately rhyme,
   But spare his Highland Mary!

1854.

TO GEORGE B. CHEEVER.

So spake Esaias : so, in words of flame,
Tekoa's prophet-herdsman smote with blame
The traffickers in men, and put to shame,
    All earth and heaven before,
The sacerdotal robbers of the poor.

All the dread Scripture lives for thee again,
To smite like lightning on the hands profane
Lifted to bless the slave-whip and the chain.
    Once more the old Hebrew tongue
Bends with the shafts of God a bow new-strung!

Take up the mantle which the prophets wore ;
Warn with their warnings, show the Christ once
      more
Bound, scourged, and crucified in His blameless
      poor ;
    And shake above our land
The unquenched bolts that blazed in Hosea's
      hand!

Not vainly shalt thou cast upon our years
The solemn burdens of the Orient seers,
And smite with truth a guilty nation's ears.
    Mightier was Luther's word
Than Seckingen's mailed arm or Hutton's
      sword!

1858.

TO JAMES T. FIELDS.

ON A BLANK LEAF OF " POEMS PRINTED, NOT PUB-
LISHED."

WELL thought! who would not rather hear
　The songs to Love and Friendship sung
　Than those which move the stranger's tongue,
And feed his unselected ear?

Our social joys are more than fame;
　Life withers in the public look.
　Why mount the pillory of a book,
Or barter comfort for a name?

Who in a house of glass would dwell,
　With curious eyes at every pane?
　To ring him in and out again,
Who wants the public crier's bell?

To see the angel in one's way,
　Who wants to play the ass's part, —
　Bear on his back the wizard Art,
And in his service speak or bray?

And who his manly locks would shave,
　And quench the eyes of common sense,
　To share the noisy recompense
That mocked the shorn and blinded slave?

The heart has needs beyond the head,
　And, starving in the plenitude
　Of strange gifts, craves its common food, —
Our human nature's daily bread.

We are but men : no gods are we,
  To sit in mid-heaven, cold and bleak,
  Each separate, on his painful peak,
Thin-cloaked in self-complacency !

Better his lot whose axe is swung
  In Wartburg woods, or that poor girl's
  Who by the Ilm her spindle whirls
And sings the songs that Luther sung,

Than his who, old, and cold, and vain,
  At Weimar sat, a demigod,
  And bowed with Jove's imperial nod
His votaries in and out again !

Ply, Vanity, thy wingëd feet !
  Ambition, hew thy rocky stair !
  Who envies him who feeds on air
The icy splendor of his seat ?

I see your Alps, above me, cut
  The dark, cold sky ; and dim and lone
  I see ye sitting, — stone on stone, —
With human senses dulled and shut.

I could not reach you, if I would,
  Nor sit among your cloudy shapes ;
  And (spare the fable of the grapes
And fox) I would not if I could.

Keep to your lofty pedestals !
  The safer plain below I choose :
  Who never wins can rarely lose,
Who never climbs as rarely falls.

Let such as love the eagle's scream
    Divide with him his home of ice :
    For me shall gentler notes suffice, —
The valley-song of bird and stream ;

The pastoral bleat, the drone of bees,
    The flail-beat chiming far away,
    The cattle-low, at shut of day,
The voice of God in leaf and breeze !

Then lend thy hand, my wiser friend,
    And help me to the vales below,
    (In truth, I have not far to go,)
Where sweet with flowers the fields extend.
1858.

THE MEMORY OF BURNS.

Read at the Boston celebration of the hundredth anniversary
of the birth of Robert Burns, 25th 1st mo., 1859.   In my absence
these lines were read by Ralph Waldo Emerson.

How sweetly come the holy psalms
    From saints and martyrs down,
The waving of triumphal palms
    Above the thorny crown !
The choral praise, the chanted prayers
    From harps by angels strung,
The hunted Cameron's mountain airs,
    The hymns that Luther sung !

Yet, jarring not the heavenly notes,
    The sounds of earth are heard,

As through the open minster floats
  The song of breeze and bird!
Not less the wonder of the sky
  That daisies bloom below;
The brook sings on, though loud and high
  The cloudy organs blow!

And, if the tender ear be jarred
  That, haply, hears by turns
The saintly harp of Olney's bard,
  The pastoral pipe of Burns,
No discord mars His perfect plan
  Who gave them both a tongue;
For he who sings the love of man
  The love of God hath sung!

To-day be every fault forgiven
  Of him in whom we joy!
We take, with thanks, the gold of Heaven
  And leave the earth's alloy.
Be ours his music as of spring,
  His sweetness as of flowers,
The songs the bard himself might sing
  In holier ears than ours.

Sweet airs of love and home, the hum
  Of household melodies,
Come singing, as the robins come
  To sing in door-yard trees.
And, heart to heart, two nations lean,
  No rival wreaths to twine,
But blending in eternal green
  The holly and the pine!

IN REMEMBRANCE OF JOSEPH STURGE.

IN the fair land o'erwatched by Ischia's mountains,
    Across the charmëd bay
Whose blue waves keep with Capri's silver foun-
    tains
    Perpetual holiday,

A king lies dead, his wafer duly eaten,
    His gold-bought masses given ;
And Rome's great altar smokes with gums to
    sweeten
    Her foulest gift to Heaven.

And while all Naples thrills with mute thanks-
    giving,
    The court of England's queen
For the dead monster so abhorred while living
    In mourning garb is seen.

With a true sorrow God rebukes that feigning ;
    By lone Edgbaston's side
Stands a great city in the sky's sad raining,
    Bareheaded and wet-eyed !

Silent for once the restless hive of labor,
    Save the low funeral tread,
Or voice of craftsman whispering to his neighbor
    The good deeds of the dead.

For him no minster's chant of the immortals
    Rose from the lips of sin ;

No mitred priest swung back the heavenly por-
        tals
    To let the white soul in.

But Age and Sickness framed their tearful faces
    In the low hovel's door,
And prayers went up from all the dark by-places
    And Ghettos of the poor.

The pallid toiler and the negro chattel,
    The vagrant of the street,
The human dice wherewith in games of battle
    The lords of earth compete,

Touched with a grief that needs no outward drap-
        ing,
    All swelled the long lament,
Of grateful hearts, instead of marble, shaping
    His viewless monument!

For never yet, with ritual pomp and splendor,
    In the long heretofore,
A heart more loyal, warm, and true, and tender,
    Has England's turf closed o'er.

And if there fell from out her grand old steeples
    No crash of brazen wail,
The murmurous woe of kindreds, tongues, and
        peoples
    Swept in on every gale.

It came from Holstein's birchen-belted meadows,
    And from the tropic calms

Of Indian islands in the sun-smit shadows
    Of Occidental palms ;

From the locked roadsteads of the Bothnian peas-
      ants,
    And harbors of the Finn,
Where war's worn victims saw his gentle pres-
    ence
    Come sailing, Christ-like, in,

To seek the lost, to build the old waste places,
    To link the hostile shores
Of severing seas, and sow with England's daisies
    The moss of Finland's moors.

Thanks for the good man's beautiful example,
    Who in the vilest saw
Some sacred crypt or altar of a temple
    Still vocal with God's law ;

And heard with tender ear the spirit sighing
    As from its prison cell,
Praying for pity, like the mournful crying
    Of Jonah out of hell.

Not his the golden pen's or lip's persuasion,
    But a fine sense of right,
And Truth's directness, meeting each occasion
    Straight as a line of light.

His faith and works, like streams that intermin-
      gle,
    In the same channel ran:

The crystal clearness of an eye kept single
    Shamed all the frauds of man.

The very gentlest of all human natures
    He joined to courage strong,
And love outreaching unto all God's creatures
    With sturdy hate of wrong.

Tender as woman, manliness and meekness
    In him were so allied
That they who judged him by his strength or weak-
        ness
    Saw but a single side.

Men failed, betrayed him, but his zeal seemed nour-
        ished
    By failure and by fall;
Still a large faith in human-kind he cherished,
    And in God's love for all.

And now he rests: his greatness and his sweet-
        ness
    No more shall seem at strife,
And death has moulded into calm completeness
    The statue of his life.

Where the dews glisten and the songbirds warble,
    His dust to dust is laid,
In Nature's keeping, with no pomp of marble
    To shame his modest shade.

The forges glow, the hammers all are ringing;
    Beneath its smoky veil,

Hard by, the city of his love is swinging
    Its clamorous iron flail.

But round his grave are quietude and beauty,
    And the sweet heaven above, —
The fitting symbols of a life of duty
    Transfigured into love!
1859.

BROWN OF OSSAWATOMIE.

JOHN BROWN of Ossawatomie spake on his dying
    day :
" I will not have to shrive my soul a priest in Slav-
    ery's pay.
But let some poor slave-mother whom I have
    striven to free,
With her children, from the gallows-stair put up a
    prayer for me ! "

John Brown of Ossawatomie, they led him out to
    die ;
And lo! a poor slave-mother with her little child
    pressed nigh.
Then the bold, blue eye grew tender, and the old
    harsh face grew mild,
As he stooped between the jeering ranks and kissed
    the negro's child !

The shadows of his stormy life that moment fell
    apart ;
And they who blamed the bloody hand forgave the
    loving heart.

That kiss from all its guilty means redeemed the
      good intent,
And round the grisly fighter's hair the martyr's
      aureole bent !

Perish with him the folly that seeks through evil
      good !
Long live the generous purpose unstained with
      human blood !
Not the raid of midnight terror, but the thought
      which underlies ;
Not the borderer's pride of daring, but the Chris-
      tian's sacrifice.

Nevermore may yon Blue Ridges the Northern
      rifle hear,
Nor see the light of blazing homes flash on the
      negro's spear.
But let the free-winged angel Truth their guarded
      passes scale,
To teach that right is more than might, and justice
      more than mail !

So vainly shall Virginia set her battle in array ;
In vain her trampling squadrons knead the winter
      snow with clay.
She may strike the pouncing eagle, but she dares
      not harm the dove ;
And every gate she bars to Hate shall open wide
      to Love !

    1859.

NAPLES.

INSCRIBED TO ROBERT C. WATERSTON, OF BOSTON.

Helen Waterston died at Naples in her eighteenth year, and lies
buried in the Protestant cemetery there. The stone over her
grave bears the lines,

> Fold her, O Father, in Thine arms,
> And let her henceforth be
> A messenger of love between
> Our human hearts and Thee.

I GIVE thee joy! — I know to thee
  The dearest spot on earth must be
Where sleeps thy loved one by the summer sea ;

  Where, near her sweetest poet's tomb,
  The land of Virgil gave thee room
To lay thy flower with her perpetual bloom.

  I know that when the sky shut down
  Behind thee on the gleaming town,
On Baiæ's baths and Posilippo's crown ;

  And, through thy tears, the mocking day
  Burned Ischia's mountain lines away,
And Capri melted in its sunny bay ;

  Through thy great farewell sorrow shot
  The sharp pang of a bitter thought
That slaves must tread around that holy spot.

  Thou knewest not the land was blest
  In giving thy beloved rest,
Holding the fond hope closer to her breast

That every sweet and saintly grave
Was freedom's prophecy, and gave
The pledge of Heaven to sanctify and save.

That pledge is answered.   To thy ear
The unchained city sends its cheer,
And, tuned to joy, the muffled bells of fear

Ring Victor in.   The land sits free
And happy by the summer sea,
And Bourbon Naples now is Italy!

She smiles above her broken chain
The languid smile that follows pain,
Stretching her cramped limbs to the sun again.

Oh, joy for all, who hear her call
From gray Camaldoli's convent-wall
And Elmo's towers to freedom's carnival!

A new life breathes among her vines
And olives, like the breath of pines
Blown downward from the breezy Apennines.

Lean, O my friend, to meet that breath,
Rejoice as one who witnesseth
Beauty from ashes rise, and life from death!

Thy sorrow shall no more be pain,
Its tears shall fall in sunlit rain,
Writing the grave with flowers: " Arisen again! "
1860.

A MEMORIAL.

Moses Austin Cartland, a dear friend and relation, who led a
faithful life as a teacher and died in the summer of 1863.

OH, thicker, deeper, darker growing,
　　The solemn vista to the tomb
Must know henceforth another shadow,
　　And give another cypress room.

In love surpassing that of brothers,
　　We walked, O friend, from childhood's day;
And, looking back o'er fifty summers,
　　Our footprints track a common way.

One in our faith, and one our longing
　　To make the world within our reach
Somewhat the better for our living,
　　And gladder for our human speech.

Thou heard'st with me the far-off voices,
　　The old beguiling song of fame,
But life to thee was warm and present,
　　And love was better than a name.

To homely joys and loves and friendships
　　Thy genial nature fondly clung;
And so the shadow on the dial
　　Ran back and left thee always young.

And who could blame the generous weakness
　　Which, only to thyself unjust,
So overprized the worth of others,
　　And dwarfed thy own with self-distrust?

All hearts grew warmer in the presence
  Of one who, seeking not his own,
Gave freely for the love of giving,
  Nor reaped for self the harvest sown.

Thy greeting smile was pledge and prelude
  Of generous deeds and kindly words;
In thy large heart were fair guest-chambers,
  Open to sunrise and the birds!

The task was thine to mould and fashion
  Life's plastic newness into grace:
To make the boyish heart heroic,
  And light with thought the maiden's face.

O'er all the land, in town and prairie,
  With bended heads of mourning, stand
The living forms that owe their beauty
  And fitness to thy shaping hand.

Thy call has come in ripened manhood,
  The noonday calm of heart and mind,
While I, who dreamed of thy remaining
  To mourn me, linger still behind:

Live on, to own, with self-upbraiding,
  A debt of love still due from me, —
The vain remembrance of occasions,
  Forever lost, of serving thee.

It was not mine among thy kindred
  To join the silent funeral prayers,
But all that long sad day of summer
  My tears of mourning dropped with theirs.

All day the sea-waves sobbed with sorrow,
  The birds forgot their merry trills:
All day I heard the pines lamenting
  With thine upon thy homestead hills.

Green be those hillside pines forever,
  And green the meadowy lowlands be,
And green the old memorial beeches,
  Name-carven in the woods of Lee!

Still let them greet thy life companions
  Who thither turn their pilgrim feet,
In every mossy line recalling
  A tender memory sadly sweet.

O friend! if thought and sense avail not
  To know thee henceforth as thou art,
That all is well with thee forever
  I trust the instincts of my heart.

Thine be the quiet habitations,
  Thine the green pastures, blossom-sown,
And smiles of saintly recognition,
  As sweet and tender as thy own.

Thou com'st not from the hush and shadow
  To meet us, but to thee we come,
With thee we never can be strangers,
  And where thou art must still be home.
1863.

BRYANT ON HIS BIRTHDAY.

Mr. Bryant's seventieth birthday, November 3, 1864, was celebrated by a festival to which these verses were sent.

WE praise not now the poet's art,
   The rounded beauty of his song;
Who weighs him from his life apart
   Must do his nobler nature wrong.

Not for the eye, familiar grown
   With charms to common sight denied, —
The marvellous gift he shares alone
   With him who walked on Rydal-side;

Not for rapt hymn nor woodland lay,
   Too grave for smiles, too sweet for tears;
We speak his praise who wears to-day
   The glory of his seventy years.

When Peace brings Freedom in her train,
   Let happy lips his songs rehearse;
His life is now his noblest strain,
   His manhood better than his verse!

Thank God! his hand on Nature's keys
   Its cunning keeps at life's full span;
But, dimmed and dwarfed, in times like these,
   The poet seems beside the man!

So be it! let the garlands die,
   The singer's wreath, the painter's meed,

Let our names perish, if thereby
Our country may be saved and freed!
1864.

THOMAS STARR KING.

Published originally as a prelude to the posthumous volume of
selections edited by Richard Frothingham.

THE great work laid upon his twoscore years
Is done, and well done. If we drop our tears,
Who loved him as few men were ever loved,
We mourn no blighted hope nor broken plan
With him whose life stands rounded and approved
In the full growth and stature of a man.
Mingle, O bells, along the Western slope,
With your deep toll a sound of faith and hope!
Wave cheerily still, O banner, half-way down,
From thousand-masted bay and steepled town!
Let the strong organ with its loftiest swell
Lift the proud sorrow of the land, and tell
That the brave sower saw his ripened grain.
O East and West! O morn and sunset twain
No more forever! — has he lived in vain
Who, priest of Freedom, made ye one, and told
Your bridal service from his lips of gold?
1864.

LINES ON A FLY-LEAF.

I NEED not ask thee, for my sake,
To read a book which well may make

Its way by native force of wit
Without my manual sign to it.
Its piquant writer needs from me
No gravely masculine guaranty,
And well might laugh her merriest laugh
At broken spears in her behalf ;
Yet, spite of all the critics tell,
I frankly own I like her well.
It may be that she wields a pen
Too sharply nibbed for thin-skinned men,
That her keen arrows search and try
The armor joints of dignity,
And, though alone for error meant,
Sing through the air irreverent.
I blame her not, the young athlete
Who plants her woman's tiny feet,
And dares the chances of debate
Where bearded men might hesitate,
Who, deeply earnest, seeing well
The ludicrous and laughable,
Mingling in eloquent excess
Her anger and her tenderness,
And, chiding with a half-caress,
Strives, less for her own sex than ours,
With principalities and powers,
And points us upward to the clear
Sunned heights of her new atmosphere.

Heaven mend her faults ! — I will not pause
To weigh and doubt and peck at flaws,
Or waste my pity when some fool
Provokes her measureless ridicule.
Strong-minded is she ?   Better so
Than dulness set for sale or show.

A household folly, capped and belled
In fashion's dance of puppets held,
Or poor pretence of womanhood,
Whose formal, flavorless platitude
Is warranted from all offence
Of robust meaning's violence.
Give me the wine of thought whose bead
Sparkles along the page I read, —
Electric words in which I find
The tonic of the northwest wind;
The wisdom which itself allies
To sweet and pure humanities,
Where scorn of meanness, hate of wrong,
Are underlaid by love as strong;
The genial play of mirth that lights
Grave themes of thought, as when, on nights
Of summer-time, the harmless blaze
Of thunderless heat-lightning plays,
And tree and hill-top resting dim
And doubtful on the sky's vague rim,
Touched by that soft and lambent gleam,
Start sharply outlined from their dream.

Talk not to me of woman's sphere,
Nor point with Scripture texts a sneer,
Nor wrong the manliest saint of all
By doubt, if he were here, that Paul
Would own the heroines who have lent
Grace to truth's stern arbitrament,
Foregone the praise to woman sweet,
And cast their crowns at Duty's feet;
Like her, who by her strong Appeal
Made Fashion weep and Mammon feel,

Who, earliest summoned to withstand
The color-madness of the land,
Counted her life-long losses gain,
And made her own her sisters' pain;
Or her who, in her greenwood shade,
Heard the sharp call that Freedom made,
And, answering, struck from Sappho's lyre
Of love the Tyrtæan carmen's fire:
Or that young girl, — Domrémy's maid
Revived a nobler cause to aid, —
Shaking from warning finger-tips
The doom of her apocalypse;
Or her, who world-wide entrance gave
To the log-cabin of the slave,
Made all his want and sorrow known,
And all earth's languages his own.

1866.

GEORGE L. STEARNS.

No man rendered greater service to the cause of freedom than
Major Stearns in the great struggle between invading slave-hold-
ers and the free settlers of Kansas.

He has done the work of a true man, —
  Crown him, honor him, love him.
Weep over him, tears of woman,
  Stoop manliest brows above him!

O dusky mothers and daughters,
  Vigils of mourning keep for him!
Up in the mountains, and down by the waters,
  Lift up your voices and weep for him!

For the warmest of hearts is frozen,
    The freest of hands is still ;
And the gap in our picked and chosen
    The long years may not fill.

No duty could overtask him,
    No need his will outrun ;
Or ever our lips could ask him,
    His hands the work had done.

He forgot his own soul for others,
    Himself to his neighbor lending ;
He found the Lord in his suffering brothers,
    And not in the clouds descending.

So the bed was sweet to die on,
    Whence he saw the doors wide swung
Against whose bolted iron
    The strength of his life was flung.

And he saw ere his eye was darkened
    The sheaves of the harvest-bringing,
And knew while his ear yet hearkened
    The voice of the reapers singing.

Ah, well ! The world is discreet ;
    There are plenty to pause and wait ;
But here was a man who set his feet
    Sometimes in advance of fate ;

Plucked off the old bark when the inner
    Was slow to renew it,
And put to the Lord's work the sinner
    When saints failed to do it.

Never rode to the wrong's redressing
  A worthier paladin.
Shall he not hear the blessing,
  " Good and faithful, enter in ! "

1867.

GARIBALDI.

In trance and dream of old, God's prophet saw
  The casting down of thrones. Thou, watching
    lone
  The hot Sardinian coast-line, hazy-hilled,
  Where, fringing round Caprera's rocky zone
With foam, the slow waves gather and withdraw,
  Behold'st the vision of the seer fulfilled,
  And hear'st the sea-winds burdened with a
    sound
Of falling chains, as, one by one, unbound,
The nations lift their right hands up and swear
  Their oath of freedom. From the chalk-white
    wall
Of England, from the black Carpathian range,
  Along the Danube and the Theiss, through all
  The passes of the Spanish Pyrenees,
And from the Seine's thronged banks, a murmur
    strange
  And glad floats to thee o'er thy summer seas
On the salt wind that stirs thy whitening hair, —
  The song of freedom's bloodless victories !
Rejoice, O Garibaldi ! Though thy sword
Failed at Rome's gates, and blood seemed vainly
    poured

Where, in Christ's name, the crownëd infidel
Of France wrought murder with the arms of hell
   On that sad mountain slope whose ghostly dead,
Unmindful of the gray exorcist's ban,
Walk, unappeased, the chambered Vatican,
   And draw the curtains of Napoleon's bed!
God's providence is not blind, but, full of eyes,
It searches all the refuges of lies;
And in His time and way, the accursed things
   Before whose evil feet thy battle-gage
   Has clashed defiance from hot youth to age
Shall perish.   All men shall be priests and kings,
   One royal brotherhood, one church made free
   By love, which is the law of liberty!
1869.

TO LYDIA MARIA CHILD,

ON READING HER POEM IN "THE STANDARD."

Mrs. Child wrote her lines, beginning, "Again the trees are
clothed in vernal green," May 24, 1859, on the first anniversary
of Ellis Gray Loring's death, but did not publish them for some
years afterward, when I first read them, or I could not have
made the reference which I did to the extinction of slavery.

THE sweet spring day is glad with music,
   But through it sounds a sadder strain;
The worthiest of our narrowing circle
   Sings Loring's dirges o'er again.

O woman greatly loved!   I join thee
   In tender memories of our friend;

With thee across the awful spaces
  The greeting of a soul I send!

What cheer hath he?   How is it with him?
  Where lingers he this weary while?
Over what pleasant fields of Heaven
  Dawns the sweet sunrise of his smile?

Does he not know our feet are treading
  The earth hard down on Slavery's grave?
That, in our crowning exultations,
  We miss the charm his presence gave?

Why on this spring air comes no whisper
  From him to tell us all is well?
Why to our flower-time comes no token
  Of lily and of asphodel?

I feel the unutterable longing,
  Thy hunger of the heart is mine;
I reach and grope for hands in darkness,
  My ear grows sharp for voice or sign.

Still on the lips of all we question
  The finger of God's silence lies;
Will the lost hands in ours be folded?
  Will the shut eyelids ever rise?

O friend! no proof beyond this yearning,
  This outreach of our hearts, we need;
God will not mock the hope He giveth,
  No love He prompts shall vainly plead.

Then let us stretch our hands in darkness,
　　And call our loved ones o'er and o'er;
Some day their arms shall close about us,
　　And the old voices speak once more.

No dreary splendors wait our coming
　　Where rapt ghost sits from ghost apart;
Homeward we go to Heaven's thanksgiving,
　　The harvest-gathering of the heart.

1870.

THE SINGER.

This poem was written on the death of Alice Cary. Her sister
Phœbe, heart-broken by her loss, followed soon after. Noble and
richly gifted, lovely in person and character, they left behind
them only friends and admirers.

YEARS since (but names to me before),
Two sisters sought at eve my door;
Two song-birds wandering from their nest,
A gray old farm-house in the West.

How fresh of life the younger one,
Half smiles, half tears, like rain in sun!
Her gravest mood could scarce displace
The dimples of her nut-brown face.

Wit sparkled on her lips not less
For quick and tremulous tenderness;
And, following close her merriest glance,
Dreamed through her eyes the heart's ro-
　　mance.

Timid and still, the elder had
Even then a smile too sweetly sad;
The crown of pain that all must wear
Too early pressed her midnight hair.

Yet ere the summer eve grew long,
Her modest lips were sweet with song;
A memory haunted all her words
Of clover-fields and singing birds.

Her dark, dilating eyes expressed
The broad horizons of the west;
Her speech dropped prairie flowers; the gold
Of harvest wheat about her rolled.

Fore-doomed to song she seemed to me:
I queried not with destiny:
I knew the trial and the need,
Yet, all the more, I said, God speed!

What could I other than I did?
Could I a singing-bird forbid?
Deny the wind-stirred leaf? Rebuke
The music of the forest brook?

She went with morning from my door,
But left me richer than before;
Thenceforth I knew her voice of cheer,
The welcome of her partial ear.

Years passed: through all the land her **name**
A pleasant household word became:
All felt behind the singer stood
A sweet and gracious womanhood.

Her life was earnest work, not play;
Her tired feet climbed a weary way;
And even through her lightest strain
We heard an undertone of pain.

Unseen of her her fair fame grew,
The good she did she rarely knew,
Unguessed of her in life the love
That rained its tears her grave above.

When last I saw her, full of peace,
She waited for her great release;
And that old friend so sage and bland,
Our later Franklin, held her hand.

For all that patriot bosoms stirs
Had moved that woman's heart of hers,
And men who toiled in storm and sun
Found her their meet companion.

Our converse, from her suffering bed
To healthful themes of life she led:
The out-door world of bud and bloom
And light and sweetness filled her room.

Yet evermore an underthought
Of loss to come within us wrought,
And all the while we felt the strain
Of the strong will that conquered pain.

God giveth quietness at last!
The common way that all have passed
She went, with mortal yearnings fond,
To fuller life and love beyond.

Fold the rapt soul in your embrace,
My dear ones!   Give the singer place
To you, to her, — I know not where, —
I lift the silence of a prayer.

For only thus our own we find;
The gone before, the left behind,
All mortal voices die between;
The unheard reaches the unseen.

Again the blackbirds sing; the streams
Wake, laughing, from their winter dreams,
And tremble in the April showers
The tassels of the maple flowers.

But not for her has spring renewed
The sweet surprises of the wood;
And bird and flower are lost to her
Who was their best interpreter!

What to shut eyes has God revealed?
What hear the ears that death has sealed?
What undreamed beauty passing show
Requites the loss of all we know?

O silent land, to which we move,
Enough if there alone be love,
And mortal need can ne'er outgrow
What it is waiting to bestow!

O white soul! from that far-off shore
Float some sweet song the waters o'er,

Our faith confirm, our fears dispel,
With the old voice we loved so well!
1871.

HOW MARY GREW.

These lines were in answer to an invitation to hear a lecture of
Mary Grew, of Philadelphia, before the Boston Radical Club.
The reference in the last stanza is to an essay on Sappho by
T. W. Higginson, read at the club the preceding month.

WITH wisdom far beyond her years,
And graver than her wondering peers,
So strong, so mild, combining still
The tender heart and queenly will,
To conscience and to duty true,
So, up from childhood, Mary Grew!

Then in her gracious womanhood
She gave her days to doing good.
She dared the scornful laugh of men,
The hounding mob, the slanderer's pen.
She did the work she found to do, —
A Christian heroine, Mary Grew!

The freed slave thanks her; blessing comes
To her from women's weary homes;
The wronged and erring find in her
Their censor mild and comforter.
The world were safe if but a few
Could grow in grace as Mary Grew!

So, New Year's Eve, I sit and say,
By this low wood-fire, ashen gray;

Just wishing, as the night shuts down,
That I could hear in Boston town,
In pleasant Chestnut Avenue,
From her own lips, how Mary Grew!

And hear her graceful hostess tell
The silver-voicëd oracle
Who lately through her parlors spoke
As through Dodona's sacred oak,
A wiser truth than any told
By Sappho's lips of ruddy gold, —
The way to make the world anew,
Is just to grow — as Mary Grew!

1871.

SUMNER.

"I am not one who has disgraced beauty of sentiment by deformity of conduct, or the maxims of a freeman by the actions of a slave; but, by the grace of God, I have kept my life unsullied." — MILTON's *Defence of the People of England.*

O MOTHER STATE! the winds of March
   Blew chill o'er Auburn's Field of God,
Where, slow, beneath a leaden arch
   Of sky, thy mourning children trod.

And now, with all thy woods in leaf,
   Thy fields in flower, beside thy dead
Thou sittest, in thy robes of grief,
   A Rachel yet uncomforted!

And once again the organ swells,
   Once more the flag is half-way hung,

And yet again the mournful bells
    In all thy steeple-towers are rung.

And I, obedient to thy will,
    Have come a simple wreath to lay,
Superfluous, on a grave that still
    Is sweet with all the flowers of May.

I take, with awe, the task assigned ;
    It may be that my friend might miss,
In his new sphere of heart and mind,
    Some token from my hand in this.

By many a tender memory moved,
    Along the past my thought I send ;
The record of the cause he loved
    Is the best record of its friend.

No trumpet sounded in his ear,
    He saw not Sinai's cloud and flame,
But never yet to Hebrew seer
    A clearer voice of duty came. .

God said : "Break thou these yokes ; undo
    These heavy burdens.   I ordain
A work to last thy whole life through,
    A ministry of strife and pain.

" Forego thy dreams of lettered ease,
    Put thou the scholar's promise by,
The rights of man are more than these."
    He heard, and answered : " Here am I ! "

He set his face against the blast,
   His feet against the flinty shard,
Till the hard service grew, at last,
   Its own exceeding great reward.

Lifted like Saul's above the crowd,
   Upon his kingly forehead fell
The first sharp bolt of Slavery's cloud,
   Launched at the truth he urged so well.

Ah! never yet, at rack or stake,
   Was sorer loss made Freedom's gain,
Than his, who suffered for her sake
   The beak-torn Titan's lingering pain!

The fixed star of his faith, through all
   Loss, doubt, and peril, shone the same;
As through a night of storm, some tall,
   Strong lighthouse lifts its steady flame.

Beyond the dust and smoke he saw
   The sheaves of Freedom's large increase,
The holy fanes of equal law,
   The New Jerusalem of peace.

The weak might fear, the worldling mock,
   The faint and blind of heart regret;
All knew at last th' eternal rock
   On which his forward feet were set.

The subtlest scheme of compromise
   Was folly to his purpose bold;
The strongest mesh of party lies
   Weak to the simplest truth he told.

One language held his heart and lip,
    Straight onward to his goal he trod,
And proved the highest statesmanship
    Obedience to the voice of God.

No wail was in his voice, — none heard,
    When treason's storm-cloud blackest grew,
The weakness of a doubtful word ;
    His duty, and the end, he knew.

The first to smite, the first to spare ;
    When once the hostile ensigns fell,
He stretched out hands of generous care
    To lift the foe he fought so well.

For there was nothing base or small
    Or craven in his soul's broad plan ;
Forgiving all things personal,
    He hated only wrong to man.

The old traditions of his State,
    The memories of her great and good,
Took from his life a fresher date,
    And in himself embodied stood.

How felt the greed of gold and place,
    The venal crew that schemed and planned,
The fine scorn of that haughty face,
    The spurning of that bribeless hand !

If than Rome's tribunes statelier
    He wore his senatorial robe,
His lofty port was all for her,
    The one dear spot on all the globe.

If to the master's plea he gave
  The vast contempt his manhood felt,
He saw a brother in the slave, —
  With man as equal man he dealt.

Proud was he?   If his presence kept
  Its grandeur wheresoe'er he trod,
As if from Plutarch's gallery stepped
  The hero and the demigod,

None failed, at least, to reach his ear,
  Nor want nor woe appealed in vain;
The homesick soldier knew his cheer,
  And blessed him from his ward of pain.

Safely his dearest friends may own
  The slight defects he never hid,
The surface-blemish in the stone
  Of the tall, stately pyramid.

Suffice it that he never brought
  His conscience to the public mart;
But lived himself the truth he taught,
  White-souled, clean-handed, pure of heart.

What if he felt the natural pride
  Of power in noble use, too true
With thin humilities to hide
  The work he did, the lore he knew?

Was he not just?   Was any wronged
  By that assured self-estimate?
He took but what to him belonged,
  Unenvious of another's state.

Well might he heed the words he spake,
　And scan with care the written page
Through which he still shall warm and wake
　The hearts of men from age to age.

Ah! who shall blame him now because
　He solaced thus his hours of pain!
Should not the o'erworn thresher pause,
　And hold to light his golden grain?

No sense of humor dropped its oil
　On the hard ways his purpose went;
Small play of fancy lightened toil;
　He spake alone the thing he meant.

He loved his books, the Art that hints
　A beauty veiled behind its own,
The graver's line, the pencil's tints,
　The chisel's shape evoked from stone.

He cherished, void of selfish ends,
　The social courtesies that bless
And sweeten life, and loved his friends
　With most unworldly tenderness.

But still his tired eyes rarely learned
　The glad relief by Nature brought;
Her mountain ranges never turned
　His current of persistent thought.

The sea rolled chorus to his speech
　Three-banked like Latium's tall trireme,
With laboring oars; the grove and beach
　Were Forum and the Academe.

The sensuous joy from all things fair
    His strenuous bent of soul repressed,
And left from youth to silvered hair
    Few hours for pleasure, none for rest.

For all his life was poor without,
    O Nature, make the last amends!
Train all thy flowers his grave about,
    And make thy singing-birds his friends!

Revive again, thou summer rain,
    The broken turf upon his bed!
Breathe, summer wind, thy tenderest strain
    Of low, sweet music overhead!

With calm and beauty symbolize
    The peace which follows long annoy,
And lend our earth-bent, mourning eyes,
    Some hint of his diviner joy.

For safe with right and truth he is,
    As God lives he must live alway;
There is no end for souls like his,
    No night for children of the day!

Nor cant nor poor solicitudes
    Made weak his life's great argument;
Small leisure his for frames and moods
    Who followed Duty where she went.

The broad, fair fields of God he saw
    Beyond the bigot's narrow bound;
The truths he moulded into law
    In Christ's beatitudes he found.

His state-craft was the Golden Rule,
  His right of vote a sacred trust;
Clear, over threat and ridicule,
  All heard his challenge: "Is it just?"

And when the hour supreme had come,
  Not for himself a thought he gave;
In that last pang of martyrdom,
  His care was for the half-freed slave.

Not vainly dusky hands upbore,
  In prayer, the passing soul to heaven
Whose mercy to His suffering poor
  Was service to the Master given.

Long shall the good State's annals tell,
  Her children's children long be taught,
How, praised or blamed, he guarded well
  The trust he neither shunned nor sought.

If for one moment turned thy face,
  O Mother, from thy son, not long
He waited calmly in his place
  The sure remorse which follows wrong.

Forgiven be the State he loved
  The one brief lapse, the single blot;
Forgotten be the stain removed,
  Her righted record shows it not!

The lifted sword above her shield
  With jealous care shall guard his fame;
The pine-tree on her ancient field
  To all the winds shall speak his name.

The marble image of her son
   Her loving hands shall yearly crown,
And from her pictured Pantheon
   His grand, majestic face look down.

O State so passing rich before,
   Who now shall doubt thy highest claim?
The world that counts thy jewels o'er
   Shall longest pause at Sumner's name!

1874.

THIERS.

I.

FATE summoned, in gray-bearded age, to act
A history stranger than his written fact,
   Him who portrayed the splendor and the gloom
Of that great hour when throne and altar fell
With long death-groan which still is audible.
   He, when around the walls of Paris rung
   The Prussian bugle like the blast of doom,
And every ill which follows unblest war
Maddened all France from Finistère to Var,
   The weight of fourscore from his shoulders
     flung,
And guided Freedom in the path he saw
Lead out of chaos into light and law,
Peace, not imperial, but republican,
And order pledged to all the Rights of Man.

II.

Death called him from a need as imminent
As that from which the Silent William went

When powers of evil, like the smiting seas
On Holland's dikes, assailed her liberties.
Sadly, while yet in doubtful balance hung
The weal and woe of France, the bells were rung
For her lost leader.   Paralyzed of will,
Above his bier the hearts of men stood still.
Then, as if set to his dead lips, the horn
Of Roland wound once more to rouse and warn,
The old voice.filled the air !   His last brave word
Not vainly France to all her boundaries stirred.
Strong as in life, he still for Freedom wrought,
As the dead Cid at red Toloso fought.
  1877.

FITZ–GREENE HALLECK.

AT THE UNVEILING OF HIS STATUE.

AMONG their graven shapes to whom
    Thy civic wreaths belong,
O city of his love, make room
    For one whose gift was song.

Not his the soldier's sword to wield,
    Nor his the helm of state,
Nor glory of the stricken field,
    Nor triumph of debate.

In common ways, with common men,
    He served his race and time
As well as if his clerkly pen
    Had never danced to rhyme.

If, in the thronged and noisy mart,
  The Muses found their son,
Could any say his tuneful art
  A duty left undone?

He toiled and sang; and year by year
  Men found their homes more sweet,
And through a tenderer atmosphere
  Looked down the brick-walled street.

The Greek's wild onset Wall Street knew;
  The Red King walked Broadway;
And Alnwick Castle's roses blew
  From Palisades to Bay.

Fair City by the Sea! upraise
  His veil with reverent hands;
And mingle with thy own the praise
  And pride of other lands.

Let Greece his fiery lyric breathe
  Above her hero-urns;
And Scotland, with her holly, wreathe
  The flower he culled for Burns.

Oh, stately stand thy palace walls,
  Thy tall ships ride the seas;
To-day thy poet's name recalls
  A prouder thought than these.

Not less thy pulse of trade shall beat,
  Nor less thy tall fleets swim,
That shaded square and dusty street
  Are classic ground through him.

Alive, he loved, like all who sing,
    The echoes of his song;
Too late the tardy meed we bring,
    The praise delayed so long.

Too late, alas! Of all who knew
    The living man, to-day
Before his unveiled face, how few
    Make bare their locks of gray!

Our lips of praise must soon be dumb,
    Our grateful eyes be dim;
O brothers of the days to come,
    Take tender charge of him!

New hands the wires of song may sweep,
    New voices challenge fame;
But let no moss of years o'ercreep
    The lines of Halleck's name.

1877.

WILLIAM FRANCIS BARTLETT.

Oh, well may Essex sit forlorn
    Beside her sea-blown shore;
Her well beloved, her noblest born,
    Is hers in life no more!

No lapse of years can render less
    Her memory's sacred claim;
No fountain of forgetfulness
    Can wet the lips of Fame.

A grief alike to wound and heal,
    A thought to soothe and pain,
The sad, sweet pride that mothers feel
    To her must still remain.

Good men and true she has not lacked,
    And brave men yet shall be ;
The perfect flower, the crowning fact,
    Of all her years was he !

As Galahad pure, as Merlin sage,
    What worthier knight was found
To grace in Arthur's golden age
    The fabled Table Round ?

A voice, the battle's trumpet-note,
    To welcome and restore ;
A hand, that all unwilling smote,
    To heal and build once more !

A soul of fire, a tender heart
    Too warm for hate, he knew
The generous victor's graceful part
    To sheathe the sword he drew.

When Earth, as if on evil dreams,
    Looks back upon her wars,
And the white light of Christ outstreams
    From the red disk of Mars,

His fame who led the stormy van
    Of battle well may cease,
But never that which crowns the man
    Whose victory was Peace.

Mourn, Essex, on thy sea-blown shore
   Thy beautiful and brave,
Whose failing hand the olive bore,
   Whose dying lips forgave!

Let age lament the youthful chief,
   And tender eyes be dim;
The tears are more of joy than grief
   That fall for one like him!

1878.

BAYARD TAYLOR.

I.

"AND where now, Bayard, will thy footsteps
      tend?"
   My sister asked our guest one winter's day.
   Smiling he answered in the Friends' sweet way
Common to both: "Wherever thou shalt send!
What wouldst thou have me see for thee?"   She
      laughed,
   Her dark eyes dancing in the wood-fire's glow:
   "Loffoden isles, the Kilpis, and the low,
Unsetting sun on Finmark's fishing-craft."
"All these and more I soon shall see for thee!"
   He answered cheerily: and he kept his pledge
   On Lapland snows, the North Cape's windy
      wedge,
And Tromsö freezing in its winter sea.
   He went and came. But no man knows the
      track
   Of his last journey, and he comes not back!

II.

He brought us wonders of the new and old ;
  We shared all climes with him. The Arab's
    tent
  To him its story-telling secret lent.
And, pleased, we listened to the tales he told.
His task, beguiled with songs that shall endure,
  In manly, honest thoroughness he wrought ;
  From humble home-lays to the heights of thought
Slowly he climbed, but every step was sure.
How, with the generous pride that friendship hath,
  We, who so loved him, saw at last the crown
  Of civic honor on his brows pressed down,
Rejoiced, and knew not that the gift was death.
  And now for him, whose praise in deafened ears
  Two nations speak, we answer but with tears !

III.

O Vale of Chester ! trod by him so oft,
  Green as thy June turf keep his memory.   Let
  Nor wood, nor dell, nor storied stream forget,
Nor winds that blow round lonely Cedarcroft ;
Let the home voices greet him in the far,
  Strange land that holds him ; let the messages
  Of love pursue him o'er the chartless seas
And unmapped vastness of his unknown star !
Love's language, heard beyond the loud discourse
  Of perishable fame, in every sphere
  Itself interprets ; and its utterance here
Somewhere in God's unfolding universe
  Shall reach our traveller, softening the surprise
  Of his rapt gaze on unfamiliar skies !
1879.

OUR AUTOCRAT.

Read at the breakfast given in honor of Dr. Holmes by the publishers of the *Atlantic Monthly*, December 3, 1879.

HIS laurels fresh from song and lay,
　　Romance, art, science, rich in all,
And young of heart, how dare we say
　　We keep his seventieth festival?

No sense is here of loss or lack;
　　Before his sweetness and his light
The dial holds its shadow back,
　　The charmèd hours delay their flight.

His still the keen analysis
　　Of men and moods, electric wit,
Free play of mirth, and tenderness
　　To heal the slightest wound from it.

And his the pathos touching all
　　Life's sins and sorrows and regrets,
Its hopes and fears, its final call
　　And rest beneath the violets.

His sparkling surface scarce betrays
　　The thoughtful tide beneath it rolled,
The wisdom of the latter days,
　　And tender memories of the old.

What shapes and fancies, grave or gay,
　　Before us at his bidding come!
The Treadmill tramp, the One-Horse Shay,
　　The dumb despair of Elsie's doom!

The tale of Avis and the Maid,
  The plea for lips that cannot speak,
The holy kiss that Iris laid
  On Little Boston's pallid cheek!

Long may he live to sing for us
  His sweetest songs at evening time,
And, like his Chambered Nautilus,
  To holier heights of beauty climb !

Though now unnumbered guests surround
  The table that he rules at will,
Its Autocrat, however crowned,
  Is but our friend and comrade still.

The world may keep his honored name,
  The wealth of all his varied powers;
A stronger claim has love than fame,
  And he himself is only ours !

WITHIN THE GATE.

L. M. C.

I have more fully expressed my admiration and regard for
Lydia Maria Child in the biographical introduction which I wrote
for the volume of *Letters*, published after her death.

WE sat together, last May-day, and talked
  Of the dear friends who walked
Beside us, sharers of the hopes and fears
  Of five and forty years,

Since first we met in Freedom's hope forlorn,
    And heard her battle-horn
Sound through the valleys of the sleeping North,
    Calling her children forth,

And youth pressed forward with hope-lighted eyes,
    And age, with forecast wise
Of the long strife before the triumph won,
    Girded his armor on.

Sadly, as name by name we called the roll,
    We heard the dead-bells toll
For the unanswering many, and we knew
    The living were the few.

And we, who waited our own call before
    The inevitable door,
Listened and looked, as all have done, to win
    Some token from within.

No sign we saw, we heard no voices call ;
    The impenetrable wall
Cast down its shadow, like an awful doubt,
    On all who sat without.

Of many a hint of life beyond the veil,
    And many a ghostly tale
Wherewith the ages spanned the gulf between
    The seen and the unseen,

Seeking from omen, trance, and dream to gain
    Solace to doubtful pain,
And touch, with groping hands, the garment hem
    Of truth sufficing them,

We talked; and, turning from the sore unrest
    Of an all-baffling quest,
We thought of holy lives that from us passed
    Hopeful unto the last,

As if they saw beyond the river of death,
    Like Him of Nazareth,
The many mansions of the Eternal days
    Lift up their gates of praise.

And, hushed to silence by a reverent awe,
    Methought, O friend, I saw
In thy true life of word, and work, and thought
    The proof of all we sought.

Did we not witness in the life of thee
    Immortal prophecy?
And feel, when with thee, that thy footsteps trod
    An everlasting road?

Not for brief days thy generous sympathies,
    Thy scorn of selfish ease;
Not for the poor prize of an earthly goal
    Thy strong uplift of soul.

Than thine was never turned a fonder heart
    To nature and to art
In fair-formed Hellas in her golden prime,
    Thy Philothea's time.

Yet, loving beauty, thou couldst pass it by,
    And for the poor deny
Thyself, and see thy fresh, sweet flower of fame
    Wither in blight and blame.

Sharing His love who holds in His embrace
    The lowliest of our race,
Sure the Divine economy must be
    Conservative of thee !

For truth must live with truth, self-sacrifice
    Seek out its great allies ;
Good must find good by gravitation sure,
    And love with love endure.

And so, since thou hast passed within the gate
    Whereby awhile I wait,
I give blind grief and blinder sense the lie :
    Thou hast not lived to die !

1881.

IN MEMORY.

JAMES T. FIELDS.

As a guest who may not stay
Long and sad farewells to say
Glides with smiling face away,

Of the sweetness and the zest
Of thy happy life possessed
Thou hast left us at thy best.

Warm of heart and clear of brain,
Of thy sun-bright spirit's wane
Thou hast spared us all the pain.

Now that thou hast gone away,
What is left of one to say
Who was open as the day?

What is there to gloss or shun?
Save with kindly voices none
Speak thy name beneath the sun.

Safe thou art on every side,
Friendship nothing finds to hide,
Love's demand is satisfied.

Over manly strength and worth,
At thy desk of toil, or hearth,
Played the lambent light of mirth, —

Mirth that lit, but never burned;
All thy blame to pity turned;
Hatred thou hadst never learned.

Every harsh and vexing thing
At thy home-fire lost its sting;
Where thou wast was always spring.

And thy perfect trust in good,
Faith in man and womanhood,
Chance and change and time withstood.

Small respect for cant and whine,
Bigot's zeal and hate malign,
Had that sunny soul of thine.

But to thee was duty's claim
Sacred, and thy lips became
Reverent with one holy Name.

Therefore, on thy unknown way,
Go in God's peace! We who stay
But a little while delay.

Keep for us, O friend, where'er
Thou art waiting, all that here
Made thy earthly presence dear;

Something of thy pleasant past
On a ground of wonder cast,
In the stiller waters glassed!

Keep the human heart of thee;
Let the mortal only be
Clothed in immortality.

And when fall our feet as fell
Thine upon the asphodel,
Let thy old smile greet us well;

Proving in a world of bliss
What we fondly dream in this, —
Love is one with holiness!

1881.

WILSON.

Read at the Massachusetts Club on the seventieth anniversary
of the birthday of Vice-President Wilson, February 16, 1882.

THE lowliest born of all the land,
He wrung from Fate's reluctant hand
   The gifts which happier boyhood claims;
And, tasting on a thankless soil
The bitter bread of unpaid toil,
   He fed his soul with noble aims.

And Nature, kindly provident,
To him the future's promise lent;
   The powers that shape man's destinies,
Patience and faith and toil, he knew,
The close horizon round him grew,
   Broad with great possibilities.

By the low hearth-fire's fitful blaze
He read of old heroic days,
   The sage's thought, the patriot's speech;
Unhelped, alone, himself he taught,
His school the craft at which he wrought,
   His lore the book within his reach.

He felt his country's need; he knew
The work her children had to do;
   And when, at last, he heard the call
In her behalf to serve and dare,
Beside his senatorial chair
   He stood the unquestioned peer of all.

Beyond the accident of birth
He proved his simple manhood's worth;
    Ancestral pride and classic grace
Confessed the large-brained artisan,
So clear of sight, so wise in plan
    And counsel, equal to his place.

With glance intuitive he saw
Through all disguise of form and law,
    And read men like an open book;
Fearless and firm, he never quailed
Nor turned aside for threats, nor failed
    To do the thing he undertook.

How wise, how brave, he was, how well
He bore himself, let history tell
    While waves our flag o'er land and sea,
No black thread in its warp or weft;
He found dissevered States, he left
    A grateful Nation, strong and free!

THE POET AND THE CHILDREN.

LONGFELLOW.

WITH a glory of winter sunshine
    Over his locks of gray,
In the old historic mansion
    He sat on his last birthday;

With his books and his pleasant pictures,
    And his household and his kin,
While a sound as of myriads singing
    From far and near stole in.

It came from his own fair city,
  From the prairie's boundless plain,
From the Golden Gate of sunset,
  And the cedarn woods of Maine.

And his heart grew warm within him,
  And his moistening eyes grew dim,
For he knew that his country's children
  Were singing the songs of him :

The lays of his life's glad morning,
  The psalms of his evening time,
Whose echoes shall float forever
  On the winds of every clime.

All their beautiful consolations,
  Sent forth like birds of cheer,
Came flocking back to his windows,
  And sang in the Poet's ear.

Grateful, but solemn and tender,
  The music rose and fell
With a joy akin to sadness
  And a greeting like farewell.

With a sense of awe he listened
  To the voices sweet and young;
The last of earth and the first of heaven
  Seemed in the songs they sung.

And waiting a little longer
  For the wonderful change to come,
He heard the Summoning Angel,
  Who calls God's children home !

And to him in a holier welcome
　　Was the mystical meaning given
Of the words of the blessed Master:
　　" Of such is the kingdom of heaven! "

1882.

A WELCOME TO LOWELL.

TAKE our hands, James Russell Lowell,
　　Our hearts are all thy own;
To-day we bid thee welcome
　　Not for ourselves alone.

In the long years of thy absence
　　Some of us have grown old,
And some have passed the portals
　　Of the Mystery untold;

For the hands that cannot clasp thee,
　　For the voices that are dumb,
For each and all I bid thee
　　A grateful welcome home!

For Cedarcroft's sweet singer
　　To the nine-fold Muses dear;
For the Seer the winding Concord
　　Paused by his door to hear;

For him, our guide and Nestor,
　　Who the march of song began,
The white locks of his ninety years
　　Bared to thy winds, Cape Ann!

For him who, to the music
   Her pines and hemlocks played,
Set the old and tender story
   Of the lorn Acadian maid ;

For him, whose voice for freedom
   Swayed friend and foe at will,
Hushed is the tongue of silver,
   The golden lips are still !

For her whose life of duty
   At scoff and menace smiled,
Brave as the wife of Roland,
   Yet gentle as a Child.

And for him the three-hilled city
   Shall hold in memory long,
Whose name is the hint and token
   Of the pleasant Fields of Song !

For the old friends unforgotten,
   For the young thou hast not known,
I speak their heart-warm greeting ;
   Come back and take thy own !

From England's royal farewells,
   And honors fitly paid,
Come back, dear Russell Lowell,
   To Elmwood's waiting shade !

Come home with all the garlands
   That crown of right thy head.

I speak for comrades living,
I speak for comrades dead!
AMESBURY, *6th mo.*, 1885.

AN ARTIST OF THE BEAUTIFUL.

GEORGE FULLER.

HAUNTED of Beauty, like the marvellous youth
Who sang Saint Agnes' Eve! How passing fair
Her shapes took color in thy homestead air!
How on thy canvas even her dreams were truth!
Magician! who from commonest elements
Called up divine ideals, clothed upon
By mystic lights soft blending into one
Womanly grace and child-like innocence.
Teacher! thy lesson was not given in vain.
Beauty is goodness; ugliness is sin;
Art's place is sacred: nothing foul therein
May crawl or tread with bestial feet profane.
If rightly choosing is the painter's test,
Thy choice, O master, ever was the best.
1885.

MULFORD.

Author of *The Nation* and *The Republic of God.*

UNNOTED as the setting of a star
He passed; and sect and party scarcely knew
When from their midst a sage and seer with-
drew
To fitter audience, where the great dead are

In God's republic of the heart and mind,
Leaving no purer, nobler soul behind.
1886.

TO A CAPE ANN SCHOONER.

LUCK to the craft that bears this name of mine,
Good fortune follow with her golden spoon
The glazëd hat and tarry pantaloon;
And wheresoe'er her keel shall cut the brine,
Cod, hake and haddock quarrel for her line.
Shipped with her crew, whatever wind may blow,
Or tides delay, my wish with her shall go,
Fishing by proxy.   Would that it might show
At need her course, in lack of sun and star,
Where icebergs threaten, and the sharp reefs
    are;
Lift the blind fog on Anticosti's lee
And Avalon's rock; make populous the sea
Round Grand Manan with eager finny swarms,
Break the long calms, and charm away the
    storms.
OAK KNOLL, 23 *3rd mo.*, 1886.

SAMUEL J. TILDEN.

GREYSTONE, AUG. 4, 1886.

ONCE more, O all-adjusting Death!
    The nation's Pantheon opens wide;
Once more a common sorrow saith
    A strong, wise man has died.

Faults doubtless had he.   Had we not
    Our own, to question and asperse
The worth we doubted or forgot
    Until beside his hearse?

Ambitious, cautious, yet the man
    To strike down fraud with resolute hand;
A patriot, if a partisan,
    He loved his native land.

So let the mourning bells be rung,
    The banner droop its folds half way,
And while the public pen and tongue
    Their fitting tribute pay,

Shall we not vow above his bier
    To set our feet on party lies,
And wound no more a living ear
    With words that Death denies?

1886.

OCCASIONAL POEMS

EVA.

Suggested by Mrs. Stowe's tale of *Uncle Tom's Cabin*, and written when the characters in the tale were realities by the fireside of countless American homes.

DRY the tears for holy Eva,
With the blessed angels leave her;
Of the form so soft and fair
Give to earth the tender care.

For the golden locks of Eva
Let the sunny south-land give her
Flowery pillow of repose,
Orange-bloom and budding rose.

In the better home of Eva
Let the shining ones receive her,
With the welcome-voicëd psalm,
Harp of gold and waving palm!

All is light and peace with Eva;
There the darkness cometh never;
Tears are wiped, and fetters fall,
And the Lord is all in all.

Weep no more for happy Eva,
Wrong and sin no more shall grieve her;
Care and pain and weariness
Lost in love so measureless.

Gentle Eva, loving Eva,
Child confessor, true believer,
Listener at the Master's knee,
" Suffer such to come to me."

Oh, for faith like thine, sweet Eva,
Lighting all the solemn river,
And the blessings of the poor
Wafting to the heavenly shore!

1852.

A LAY OF OLD TIME.

Written for the Essex County Agricultural Fair, and sung at
the banquet at Newburyport, October 2, 1856.

ONE morning of the first sad Fall,
  Poor Adam and his bride
Sat in the shade of Eden's wall —
  But on the outer side.

She, blushing in her fig-leaf suit
  For the chaste garb of old;
He, sighing o'er his bitter fruit
  For Eden's drupes of gold.

Behind them, smiling in the morn,
  Their forfeit garden lay,
Before them, wild with rock and thorn,
  The desert stretched away.

They heard the air above them fanned,
    A light step on the sward,
And lo! they saw before them stand
    The angel of the Lord!

"Arise," he said, " why look behind,
    When hope is all before,
And patient hand and willing mind,
    Your loss may yet restore?

" I leave with you a spell whose power
    Can make the desert glad,
And call around you fruit and flower
    As fair as Eden had.

"I clothe your hands with power to lift
    The curse from off your soil;
Your very doom shall seem a gift,
    Your loss a gain through Toil.

" Go, cheerful as yon humming-bees,
    To labor as to play."
White glimmering over Eden's trees
    The angel passed away.

The pilgrims of the world went forth
    Obedient to the word,
And found where'er they tilled the earth
    A garden of the Lord!

The thorn-tree cast its evil fruit
    And blushed with plum and pear,
And seeded grass and trodden root
    Grew sweet beneath their care.

We share our primal parents' fate,
    And, in our turn and day,
Look back on Eden's sworded gate
    As sad and lost as they.

But still for us his native skies
    The pitying Angel leaves,
And leads through Toil to Paradise
    New Adams and new Eves!

A SONG OF HARVEST.

For the Agricultural and Horticultural Exhibition at Amesbury and Salisbury, September 28, 1858.

THIS day, two hundred years ago,
    The wild grape by the river's side,
And tasteless groundnut trailing low,
    The table of the woods supplied.

Unknown the apple's red and gold,
    The blushing tint of peach and pear;
The mirror of the Powow told
    No tale of orchards ripe and rare.

Wild as the fruits he scorned to till,
    These vales the idle Indian trod;
Nor knew the glad, creative skill,
    The joy of him who toils with God.

O Painter of the fruits and flowers!
    We thank Thee for thy wise design

Whereby these human hands of ours
  In Nature's garden work with Thine.

And thanks that from our daily need
  The joy of simple faith is born;
That he who smites the summer weed,
  May trust Thee for the autumn corn.

Give fools their gold, and knaves their power;
  Let fortune's bubbles rise and fall;
Who sows a field, or trains a flower,
  Or plants a tree, is more than all.

For he who blesses most is blest;
  And God and man shall own his worth
Who toils to leave as his bequest
  An added beauty to the earth.

And, soon or late, to all that sow,
  The time of harvest shall be given;
The flower shall bloom, the fruit shall grow,
  If not on earth, at last in heaven.

KENOZA LAKE.

This beautiful lake in East Haverhill was the "Great Pond" of the writer's boyhood. In 1859 a movement was made for improving its shores as a public park. At the opening of the park, August 31, 1859, the poem which gave it the name of Kenoza (in the Indian language signifying Pickerel) was read.

As Adam did in Paradise,
  To-day the primal right we claim:
Fair mirror of the woods and skies,
  We give to thee a name.

Lake of the pickerel! — let no more
   The echoes answer back, " Great Pond,"
But sweet Kenoza, from thy shore
   And watching hills beyond,

Let Indian ghosts, if such there be
   Who ply unseen their shadowy lines,
Call back the ancient name to thee,
   As with the voice of pines.

The shores we trod as barefoot boys,
   The nutted woods we wandered through,
To friendship, love, and social joys
   We consecrate anew.

Here shall the tender song be sung,
   And memory's dirges soft and low,
And wit shall sparkle on the tongue,
   And mirth shall overflow,

Harmless as summer lightning plays
   From a low, hidden cloud by night,
A light to set the hills ablaze,
   But not a bolt to smite.

In sunny South and prairied West
   Are exiled hearts remembering still,
As bees their hive, as birds their nest,
   The homes of Haverhill.

They join us in our rites to-day ;
   And, listening, we may hear, erelong,
From inland lake and ocean bay,
   The echoes of our song.

Kenoza! o'er no sweeter lake
   Shall morning break or noon-cloud sail, —
No fairer face than thine shall take
   The sunset's golden veil.

Long be it ere the tide of trade
   Shall break with harsh-resounding din
The quiet of thy banks of shade,
   And hills that fold thee in.

Still let thy woodlands hide the hare,
   The shy loon sound his trumpet-note,
Wing-weary from his fields of air,
   The wild-goose on thee float.

Thy peace rebuke our feverish stir,
   Thy beauty our deforming strife;
Thy woods and waters minister
   The healing of their life.

And sinless Mirth, from care released,
   Behold, unawed, thy mirrored sky,
Smiling as smiled on Cana's feast
   The Master's loving eye.

And when the summer day grows dim,
   And light mists walk thy mimic sea,
Revive in us the thought of Him
   Who walked on Galilee!

FOR AN AUTUMN FESTIVAL.

THE Persian's flowery gifts, the shrine
    Of fruitful Ceres, charm no more ;
The woven wreaths of oak and pine
    Are dust along the Isthmian shore.

But beauty hath its homage still,
    And nature holds us still in debt ;
And woman's grace and household skill,
    And manhood's toil, are honored yet.

And we, to-day, amidst our flowers
    And fruits, have come to own again
The blessings of the summer hours,
    The early and the latter rain ;

To see our Father's hand once more
    Reverse for us the plenteous horn
Of autumn, filled and running o'er
    With fruit, and flower, and golden corn !

Once more the liberal year laughs out
    O'er richer stores than gems or gold ;
Once more with harvest-song and shout
    Is Nature's bloodless triumph told.

Our common mother rests and sings,
    Like Ruth, among her garnered sheaves ;
Her lap is full of goodly things,
    Her brow is bright with autumn leaves.

Oh, favors every year made new!
  Oh, gifts with rain and sunshine sent!
The bounty overruns our due,
  The fulness shames our discontent.

We shut our eyes, the flowers bloom on;
  We murmur, but the corn-ears fill,
We choose the shadow, but the sun
  That casts it shines behind us still.

God gives us with our rugged soil
  The power to make it Eden-fair,
And richer fruits to crown our toil
  Than summer-wedded islands bear.

Who murmurs at his lot to-day?
  Who scorns his native fruit and bloom?
Or sighs for dainties far away,
  Beside the bounteous board of home?

Thank Heaven, instead, that Freedom's arm
  Can change a rocky soil to gold, —
That brave and generous lives can warm
  A clime with northern ices cold.

And let these altars, wreathed with flowers
  And piled with fruits, awake again
Thanksgivings for the golden hours,
  The early and the latter rain!

1859.

THE QUAKER ALUMNI.

Read at the Friends' School Anniversary, Providence, R. I., 6th
mo., 1860.

FROM the well-springs of Hudson, the sea-cliffs of
    Maine,
Grave men, sober matrons, you gather again ;
And, with hearts warmer grown as your heads grow
    more cool,
Play over the old game of going to school.

All your strifes and vexations, your whims and
    complaints,
(You were not saints yourselves, if the children of
    saints !)
All your petty self-seekings and rivalries done,
Round the dear Alma Mater your hearts beat as
    one !

How widely soe'er you have strayed from the fold,
Though your "thee" has grown "you," and your
    drab blue and gold,
To the old friendly speech and the garb's sober
    form,
Like the heart of Argyle to the tartan, you warm.

But, the first greetings over, you glance round the
    hall ;
Your hearts call the roll, but they answer not all :
Through the turf green above them the dead can-
    not hear ;
Name by name, in the silence, falls sad as a
    tear !

In love, let us trust, they were summoned so
    soon
From the morning of life, while we toil through its
    noon;
They were frail like ourselves, they had needs like
    our own,
And they rest as we rest in God's mercy alone.

Unchanged by our changes of spirit and frame,
Past, now, and henceforward the Lord is the
    same;
Though we sink in the darkness, His arms break
    our fall,
And in death as in life, He is Father of all!

We are older: our footsteps, so light in the play
Of the far-away school-time, move slower to-day; —
Here a beard touched with frost, there a bald,
    shining crown,
And beneath the cap's border gray mingles with
    brown.

But faith should be cheerful, and trust should be
    glad,
And our follies and sins, not our years, make us
    sad.
Should the heart closer shut as the bonnet grows
    prim,
And the face grow in length as the hat grows in
    brim?

Life is brief, duty grave; but, with rain-folded
    wings,
Of yesterday's sunshine the grateful heart sings;

And we, of all others, have reason to pay
The tribute of thanks, and rejoice on our way;

For the counsels that turned from the follies of
    youth;
For the beauty of patience, the whiteness of
    truth;
For the wounds of rebuke, when love tempered its
    edge;
For the household's restraint, and the discipline's
    hedge;

For the lessons of kindness vouchsafed to the
    least
Of the creatures of God, whether human or beast,
Bringing hope to the poor, lending strength to the
    frail,
In the lanes of the city, the slave-hut, and jail;

For a womanhood higher and holier, by all
Her knowledge of good, than was Eve ere her
    fall, —
Whose task-work of duty moves lightly as play,
Serene as the moonlight and warm as the day;

And, yet more, for the faith which embraces the
    whole,
Of the creeds of the ages the life and the soul,
Wherein letter and spirit the same channel run,
And man has not severed what God has made
    one!

For a sense of the Goodness revealed everywhere,
As sunshine impartial, and free as the air;

For a trust in humanity, Heathen or Jew,
And a hope for all darkness the Light shineth
      through.

Who scoffs at our birthright? — the words of the
      seers,
And the songs of the bards in the twilight of
      years,
All the foregleams of wisdom in santon and sage,
In prophet and priest, are our true heritage.

The Word which the reason of Plato discerned;
The truth, as whose symbol the Mithra-fire burned;
The soul of the world which the Stoic but guessed,
In the Light Universal the Quaker confessed!

No honors of war to our worthies belong;
Their plain stem of life never flowered into song;
But the fountains they opened still gush by the
      way,
And the world for their healing is better to-day.

He who lies where the minster's groined arches
      curve down
To the tomb-crowded transept of England's re-
      nown,
The glorious essayist, by genius enthroned,
Whose pen as a sceptre the Muses all owned, —

Who through the world's pantheon walked in his
      pride,
Setting new statues up, thrusting old ones aside,
And in fiction the pencils of history dipped,
To gild o'er or blacken each saint in his crypt, —

How vainly he labored to sully with blame
The white bust of Penn, in the niche of his fame!
Self-will is self-wounding, perversity blind:
On himself fell the stain for the Quaker designed!

For the sake of his true-hearted father before
     him;
For the sake of the dear Quaker mother that bore
     him;
For the sake of his gifts, and the works that out-
     live him,
And his brave words for freedom, we freely for-
     give him!

There are those who take note that our numbers
     are small, —
New Gibbons who write our decline and our fall;
But the Lord of the seed-field takes care of His
     own,
And the world shall yet reap what our sowers have
     sown.

The last of the sect to his fathers may go,
Leaving only his coat for some Barnum to show;
But the truth will outlive him, and broaden with
     years,
Till the false dies away, and the wrong disappears.

Nothing fails of its end. Out of sight sinks the
     stone,
In the deep sea of time, but the circles sweep on,
Till the low-rippled murmurs along the shores run,
And the dark and dead waters leap glad in the
     sun.

Meanwhile shall we learn, in our ease, to forget
To the martyrs of Truth and of Freedom our
debt? —
Hide their words out of sight, like the garb that
they wore,
And for Barclay's Apology offer one more?

Shall we fawn round the priestcraft that glutted
the shears,
And festooned the stocks with our grandfathers'
ears?
Talk of Woolman's unsoundness? count Penn
heterodox?
And take Cotton Mather in place of George Fox?

Make our preachers war-chaplains? quote Scrip-
ture to take
The hunted slave back, for Onesimus' sake?
Go to burning church-candles, and chanting in
choir,
And on the old meeting-house stick up a spire?

No! the old paths we 'll keep until better are
shown,
Credit good where we find it, abroad or our own;
And while " Lo here " and " Lo there " the multi-
tude call,
Be true to ourselves, and do justice to all.

The good round about us we need not refuse,
Nor talk of our Zion as if we were Jews;
But why shirk the badge which our fathers have
worn,
Or beg the world's pardon for having been born?

We need not pray over the Pharisee's prayer,
Nor claim that our wisdom is Benjamin's share;
Truth to us and to others is equal and one:
Shall we bottle the free air, or hoard up the sun?

Well know we our birthright may serve but to
    show
How the meanest of weeds in the richest soil grow;
But we need not disparage the good which we hold;
Though the vessels be earthen, the treasure is gold!

Enough and too much of the sect and the name.
What matters our label, so truth be our aim?
The creed may be wrong, but the life may be true,
And hearts beat the same under drab coats or blue.

So the man be a man, let him worship, at will,
In Jerusalem's courts, or on Gerizim's hill.
When she makes up her jewels, what cares yon
    good town
For the Baptist of Wayland, the Quaker of Brown?

And this green, favored island, so fresh and sea-
    blown,
When she counts up the worthies her annals have
    known,
Never waits for the pitiful gaugers of sect
To measure her love, and mete out her respect.

Three shades at this moment seem walking her
    strand,
Each with head halo-crowned, and with palms in
    his hand, —

Wise Berkeley, grave Hopkins, and, smiling serene
On prelate and puritan, Channing is seen.

One holy name bearing, no longer they need
Credentials of party, and pass-words of creed :
The new song they sing hath a threefold accord,
And they own one baptism, one faith, and one
      Lord !

But the golden sands run out : occasions like these
Glide swift into shadow, like sails on the seas :
While we sport with the mosses and pebbles ashore,
They lessen and fade, and we see them no more.

Forgive me, dear friends, if my vagrant thoughts
      seem
Like a school-boy's who idles and plays with his
      theme.
Forgive the light measure whose changes display
The sunshine and rain of our brief April day.

There are moments in life when the lip and the
      eye
Try the question of whether to smile or to cry ;
And scenes and reunions that prompt like our
      own
The tender in feeling, the playful in tone.

I, who never sat down with the boys and the girls
At the feet of your Slocums, and Cartlands, and
      Earles, —
By courtesy only permitted to lay
On your festival's altar my poor gift, to-day, —

I would joy in your joy : let me have a friend's
    part
In the warmth of your welcome of hand and of
    heart, —
On your play-ground of boyhood unbend the brow's
    care,
And shift the old burdens our shoulders must bear.

Long live the good School ! giving out year by
    year
Recruits to true manhood and womanhood dear :
Brave boys, modest maidens, in beauty sent forth,
The living epistles and proof of its worth !

In and out let the young life as steadily flow
As in broad Narragansett the tides come and go ;
And its sons and its daughters in prairie and
    town
Remember its honor, and guard its renown.

Not vainly the gift of its founder was made ;
Not prayerless the stones of its corner were laid :
The blessing of Him whom in secret they sought
Has owned the good work which the fathers have
    wrought.

To Him be the glory forever !   We bear
To the Lord of the Harvest our wheat with the
    tare.
What we lack in our work may He find in our will,
And winnow in mercy our good from the ill !

OUR RIVER.

FOR A SUMMER FESTIVAL AT " THE LAURELS " ON
THE MERRIMAC.

Jean Pierre Brissot, the famous leader of the Girondist party
in the French Revolution, when a young man travelled exten-
sively in the United States. He visited the valley of the Merrimac, and speaks in terms of admiration of the view from Moulton's hill opposite Amesbury. The " Laurel Party " so called,
was composed of ladies and gentlemen in the lower valley of the
Merrimac, and invited friends and guests in other sections of the
country. Its thoroughly enjoyable annual festivals were held in
the early summer on the pine-shaded, laurel-blossomed slopes of
the Newbury side of the river opposite Pleasant Valley in Amesbury. The several poems called out by these gatherings are here
printed in sequence.

ONCE more on yonder laurelled height
    The summer flowers have budded ;
Once more with summer's golden light
    The vales of home are flooded ;
And once more, by the grace of Him
    Of every good the Giver,
We sing upon its wooded rim
    The praises of our river :

Its pines above, its waves below,
    The west-wind down it blowing,
As fair as when the young Brissot
    Beheld it seaward flowing, —
And bore its memory o'er the deep,
    To soothe a martyr's sadness,
And fresco, in his troubled sleep,
    His prison-walls with gladness.

We know the world is rich with streams
  Renowned in song and story,
Whose music murmurs through our dreams
  Of human love and glory :
We know that Arno's banks are fair,
  And Rhine has castled shadows,
And, poet-tuned, the Doon and Ayr
  Go singing down their meadows.

But while, unpictured and unsung
  By painter or by poet,
Our river waits the tuneful tongue
  And cunning hand to show it, —
We only know the fond skies lean
  Above it, warm with blessing,
And the sweet soul of our Undine
  Awakes to our caressing.

No fickle sun-god holds the flocks
  That graze its shores in keeping ;
No icy kiss of Dian mocks
  The youth beside it sleeping :
Our Christian river loveth most
  The beautiful and human ;
The heathen streams of Naiads boast,
  But ours of man and woman.

The miner in his cabin hears
  The ripple we are hearing ;
It whispers soft to homesick ears
  Around the settler's clearing :
In Sacramento's vales of corn,
  Or Santee's bloom of cotton,

Our river by its valley-born
  Was never yet forgotten.

The drum rolls loud, the bugle fills
  The summer air with clangor;
The war-storm shakes the solid hills
  Beneath its tread of anger;
Young eyes that last year smiled in ours
  Now point the rifle's barrel,
And hands then stained with fruits and flowers
  Bear redder stains of quarrel.

But blue skies smile, and flowers bloom on,
  And rivers still keep flowing,
The dear God still his rain and sun
  On good and ill bestowing.
His pine-trees whisper, "Trust and wait!"
  His flowers are prophesying
That all we dread of change or fate
  His love is underlying.

And thou, O Mountain-born! — no more
  We ask the wise Allotter
Than for the firmness of thy shore,
  The calmness of thy water,
The cheerful lights that overlay
  Thy rugged slopes with beauty,
To match our spirits to our day
  And make a joy of duty.

1861.

REVISITED.

Read at "The Laurels," on the Merrimac, 6th month, 1865.

THE roll of drums and the bugle's wailing
  Vex the air of our vales no more ;
The spear is beaten to hooks of pruning,
  The share is the sword the soldier wore !

Sing soft, sing low, our lowland river,
  Under thy banks of laurel bloom ;
Softly and sweet, as the hour beseemeth,
  Sing us the songs of peace and home.

Let all the tenderer voices of nature
  Temper the triumph and chasten mirth,
Full of the infinite love and pity
  For fallen martyr and darkened hearth.

But to Him who gives us beauty for ashes,
  And the oil of joy for mourning long,
Let thy hills give thanks, and all thy waters
  Break into jubilant waves of song !

Bring us the airs of hills and forests,
  The sweet aroma of birch and pine,
Give us a waft of the north-wind laden
  With sweetbrier odors and breath of kine !

Bring us the purple of mountain sunsets,
  Shadows of clouds that rake the hills,
The green repose of thy Plymouth meadows,
  The gleam and ripple of Campton rills.

Lead us away in shadow and sunshine,
   Slaves of fancy, through all thy miles,
The winding ways of Pemigewasset,
   And Winnipesaukee's hundred isles.

Shatter in sunshine over thy ledges,
   Laugh in thy plunges from fall to fall;
Play with thy fringes of elms, and darken
   Under the shade of the mountain wall.

The cradle-song of thy hillside fountains
   Here in thy glory and strength repeat;
Give us a taste of thy upland music,
   Show us the dance of thy silver feet.

Into thy dutiful life of uses
   Pour the music and weave the flowers;
With the song of birds and bloom of meadows
   Lighten and gladden thy heart and ours.

Sing on! bring down, O lowland river,
   The joy of the hills to the waiting sea;
The wealth of the vales, the pomp of mountains,
   The breath of the woodlands, bear with thee.

Here, in the calm of thy seaward valley,
   Mirth and labor shall hold their truce;
Dance of water and mill of grinding,
   Both are beauty and both are use.

Type of the Northland's strength and glory,
   Pride and hope of our home and race, —
Freedom lending to rugged labor
   Tints of beauty and lines of grace.

Once again, O beautiful river,
　　Hear our greetings and take our thanks;
Hither we come, as Eastern pilgrims
　　Throng to the Jordan's sacred banks.

For though by the Master's feet untrodden,
　　Though never His word has stilled thy waves,
Well for us may thy shores be holy,
　　With Christian altars and saintly graves.

And well may we own thy hint and token
　　Of fairer valleys and streams than these,
Where the rivers of God are full of water,
　　And full of sap are His healing trees!

"THE LAURELS."

At the twentieth and last anniversary.

FROM these wild rocks I look to-day
　　O'er leagues of dancing waves, and see
The far, low coast-line stretch away
　　To where our river meets the sea.

The light wind blowing off the land
　　Is burdened with old voices; through
Shut eyes I see how lip and hand
　　The greeting of old days renew.

O friends whose hearts still keep their prime,
　　Whose bright example warms and cheers,
Ye teach us how to smile at Time,
　　And set to music all his years!

I thank you for sweet summer days,
  For pleasant memories lingering long,
For joyful meetings, fond delays,
  And ties of friendship woven strong.

As for the last time, side by side,
  You tread the paths familiar grown,
I reach across the severing tide,
  And blend my farewells with your own.

Make room, O river of our home!
  For other feet in place of ours,
And in the summers yet to come,
  Make glad another Feast of Flowers!

Hold in thy mirror, calm and deep,
  The pleasant pictures thou hast seen;
Forget thy lovers not, but keep
  Our memory like thy laurels green.

ISLES OF SHOALS, *7th mo.*, 1870.

JUNE ON THE MERRIMAC.

O DWELLERS in the stately towns,
  What come ye out to see?
This common earth, this common sky,
  This water flowing free?

As gayly as these kalmia flowers
  Your door-yard blossoms spring;
As sweetly as these wild-wood birds
  Your cagëd minstrels sing.

You find but common bloom and green,
  The rippling river's rune,
The beauty which is everywhere
  Beneath the skies of June;

The Hawkswood oaks, the storm-torn plumes
  Of old pine-forest kings,
Beneath whose century-woven shade
  Deer Island's mistress sings.

And here are pictured Artichoke,
  And Curson's bowery mill;
And Pleasant Valley smiles between
  The river and the hill.

You know full well these banks of bloom,
  The upland's wavy line,
And how the sunshine tips with fire
  The needles of the pine.

Yet, like some old remembered psalm,
  Or sweet, familiar face,
Not less because of commonness
  You love the day and place.

And not in vain in this soft air
  Shall hard-strung nerves relax,
Not all in vain the o'erworn brain
  Forego its daily tax.

The lust of power, the greed of gain
  Have all the year their own;
The haunting demons well may let
  Our one bright day alone.

Unheeded let the newsboy call,
   Aside the ledger lay :
The world will keep its treadmill step
   Though we fall out to-day.

The truants of life's weary school,
   Without excuse from thrift
We change for once the gains of toil
   For God's unpurchased gift.

From ceilëd rooms, from silent books,
   From crowded car and town,
Dear Mother Earth, upon thy lap,
   We lay our tired heads down.

Cool, summer wind, our heated brows;
   Blue river, through the green
Of clustering pines, refresh the eyes
   Which all too much have seen.

For us these pleasant woodland ways
   Are thronged with memories old,
Have felt the grasp of friendly hands
   And heard love's story told.

A sacred presence overbroods
   The earth whereon we meet ;
These winding forest-paths are trod
   By more than mortal feet.

Old friends called from us by the voice
   Which they alone could hear,
From mystery to mystery,
   From life to life, draw near.

More closely for the sake of them
  Each other's hands we press ;
Our voices take from them a tone
  Of deeper tenderness.

Our joy is theirs, their trust is ours,
  Alike below, above,
Or here or there, about us fold
  The arms of one great love !

We ask to-day no countersign,
  No party names we own ;
Unlabelled, individual,
  We bring ourselves alone.

What cares the unconventioned wood
  For pass-words of the town ?
The sound of fashion's shibboleth
  The laughing waters drown.

Here cant forgets his dreary tone,
  And care his face forlorn ;
The liberal air and sunshine laugh
  The bigot's zeal to scorn.

From manhood's weary shoulder falls
  His load of selfish cares ;
And woman takes her rights as flowers
  And brooks and birds take theirs.

The license of the happy woods,
  The brook's release are ours ;
The freedom of the unshamed wind
  Among the glad-eyed flowers.

Yet here no evil thought finds place,
　Nor foot profane comes in ;
Our grove, like that of Samothrace,
　Is set apart from sin.

We walk on holy ground ; above
　A sky more holy smiles ;
The chant of the beatitudes
　Swells down these leafy aisles.

Thanks to the gracious Providence
　That brings us here once more ;
For memories of the good behind
　And hopes of good before !

And if, unknown to us, sweet days
　Of June like this must come,
Unseen of us these laurels clothe
　The river-banks with bloom ;

And these green paths must soon be trod
　By other feet than ours,
Full long may annual pilgrims come
　To keep the Feast of Flowers ;

The matron be a girl once more,
　The bearded man a boy,
And we, in heaven's eternal June,
　Be glad for earthly joy !

1876.

HYMN

FOR THE OPENING OF THOMAS STARR KING'S HOUSE OF
WORSHIP, 1864.

The poetic and patriotic preacher, who had won fame in the
East, went to California in 1860 and became a power on the Pacific coast. It was not long after the opening of the house of
worship built for him that he died.

Amidst these glorious works of Thine,
The solemn minarets of the pine,
And awful Shasta's icy shrine, —

Where swell Thy hymns from wave and gale,
And organ-thunders never fail,
Behind the cataract's silver veil, —

Our puny walls to Thee we raise,
Our poor reed-music sounds Thy praise:
Forgive, O Lord, our childish ways!

For, kneeling on these altar-stairs,
We urge Thee not with selfish prayers,
Nor murmur at our daily cares.

Before Thee, in an evil day,
Our country's bleeding heart we lay,
And dare not ask Thy hand to stay;

But, through the war-cloud, pray to Thee
For union, but a union free,
With peace that comes of purity!

That Thou wilt bare Thy arm to save
And, smiting through this Red Sea wave,
Make broad a pathway for the slave!

For us, confessing all our need,
We trust nor rite nor word nor deed,
Nor yet the broken staff of creed.

Assured alone that Thou art good
To each, as to the multitude,
Eternal Love and Fatherhood, —

Weak, sinful, blind, to Thee we kneel,
Stretch dumbly forth our hands, and feel
Our weakness is our strong appeal.

So, by these Western gates of Even
We wait to see with Thy forgiven
The opening Golden Gate of Heaven!

Suffice it now.   In time to be
Shall holier altars rise to Thee, —
Thy Church our broad humanity!

White flowers of love its walls shall climb,
Soft bells of peace shall ring its chime,
Its days shall all be holy time.

A sweeter song shall then be heard, —
The music of the world's accord
Confessing Christ, the Inward Word!

That song shall swell from shore to shore,
One hope, one faith, one love, restore
The seamless robe that Jesus wore.

HYMN

FOR THE HOUSE OF WORSHIP AT GEORGETOWN,
ERECTED IN MEMORY OF A MOTHER.

The giver of the house was the late George Peabody, of London.

THOU dwellest not, O Lord of all !
   In temples which thy children raise ;
Our work to thine is mean and small,
   And brief to thy eternal days.

Forgive the weakness and the pride,
   If marred thereby our gift may be,
For love, at least, has sanctified
   The altar that we rear to thee.

The heart and not the hand has wrought
   From sunken base to tower above
The image of a tender thought,
   The memory of a deathless love !

And though should never sound of speech
   Or organ echo from its wall,
Its stones would pious lessons teach,
   Its shade in benedictions fall.

Here should the dove of peace be found,
   And blessings and not curses given ;

Nor strife profane, nor hatred wound,
　　The mingled loves of earth and heaven.

Thou, who didst soothe with dying breath
　　The dear one watching by Thy cross,
Forgetful of the pains of death
　　In sorrow for her mighty loss,

In memory of that tender claim,
　　O Mother-born, the offering take,
And make it worthy of Thy name,
　　And bless it for a mother's sake!

1868.

A SPIRITUAL MANIFESTATION.

Read at the President's Levee, Brown University, 29th 6th month, 1870.

To-DAY the plant by Williams set
　　Its summer bloom discloses;
The wilding sweetbrier of his prayers
　　Is crowned with cultured roses.

Once more the Island State repeats
　　The lesson that he taught her,
And binds his pearl of charity
　　Upon her brown-locked daughter.

Is 't fancy that he watches still
　　His Providence plantations?
That still the careful Founder takes
　　A part on these occasions?

Methinks I see that reverend form,
  Which all of us so well know:
He rises up to speak; he jogs
  The presidential elbow.

" Good friends," he says, " you reap a field
  I sowed in self-denial,
For toleration had its griefs
  And charity its trial.

" Great grace, as saith Sir Thomas More,
  To him must needs be given
Who heareth heresy and leaves
  The heretic to Heaven!

" I hear again the snuffled tones,
  I see in dreary vision
Dyspeptic dreamers, spiritual bores,
  And prophets with a mission.

" Each zealot thrust before my eyes
  His Scripture-garbled label;
All creeds were shouted in my ears
  As with the tongues of Babel.

" Scourged at one cart-tail, each denied
  The hope of every other;
Each martyr shook his branded fist
  At the conscience of his brother!

" How cleft the dreary drone of man
  The shriller pipe of woman,
As Gorton led his saints elect,
  Who held all things in common!

" Their gay robes trailed in ditch and swamp,
    And torn by thorn and thicket,
The dancing-girls of Merry Mount
    Came dragging to my wicket.

" Shrill Anabaptists, shorn of ears ;
    Gray witch-wives, hobbling slowly ;
And Antinomians, free of law,
    Whose very sins were holy.

" Hoarse ranters, crazed Fifth Monarchists,
    Of stripes and bondage braggarts,
Pale Churchmen, with singed rubrics snatched
    From Puritanic fagots.

" And last, not least, the Quakers came,
    With tongues still sore from burning,
The Bay State's dust from off their feet
    Before my threshold spurning ;

" A motley host, the Lord's *débris*,
    Faith's odds and ends together ;
Well might I shrink from guests with lungs
    Tough as their breeches leather :

" If, when the hangman at their heels
    Came, rope in hand to catch them,
I took the hunted outcasts in,
    I never sent to fetch them.

" I fed, but spared them not a whit ;
    I gave to all who walked in,
Not clams and succotash alone,
    But stronger meat of doctrine.

" I proved the prophets false, I pricked
　　The bubble of perfection,
And clapped upon their inner light
　　The snuffers of election.

" And looking backward on my times,
　　This credit I am taking ;
I kept each sectary's dish apart,
　　No spiritual chowder making.

" Where now the blending signs of sect
　　Would puzzle their assorter,
The dry-shod Quaker kept the land,
　　The Baptist held the water.

" A common coat now serves for both,
　　The hat's no more a fixture ;
And which was wet and which was dry,
　　Who knows in such a mixture ?

" Well !　He who fashioned Peter's dream
　　To bless them all is able ;
And bird and beast and creeping thing
　　Make clean upon His table !

" I walked by my own light ; but when
　　The ways of faith divided,
Was I to force unwilling feet
　　To tread the path that I did ?

" I touched the garment-hem of truth,
　　Yet saw not all its splendor ;
I knew enough of doubt to feel
　　For every conscience tender.

" God left men free of choice, as when
  His Eden-trees were planted;
Because they chose amiss, should I
  Deny the gift He granted?

" So, with a common sense of need,
  Our common weakness feeling,
I left them with myself to God
  And His all-gracious dealing!

" I kept His plan whose rain and sun
  To tare and wheat are given;
And if the ways to hell were free,
  I left them free to heaven!"

Take heart with us, O man of old,
  Soul-freedom's brave confessor,
So love of God and man wax strong,
  Let sect and creed be lesser.

The jarring discords of thy day
  In ours one hymn are swelling;
The wandering feet, the severed paths,
  All seek our Father's dwelling.

And slowly learns the world the truth
  That makes us all thy debtor, —
That holy life is more than rite,
  And spirit more than letter;

That they who differ pole-wide serve
  Perchance the common Master,
And other sheep He hath than they
  Who graze one narrow pasture!

For truth's worst foe is he who claims
    To act as God's avenger,
And deems, beyond his sentry-beat,
    The crystal walls in danger!

Who sets for heresy his traps
    Of verbal quirk and quibble,
And weeds the garden of the Lord
    With Satan's borrowed dibble.

To-day our hearts like organ keys
    One Master's touch are feeling;
The branches of a common Vine
    Have only leaves of healing.

Co-workers, yet from varied fields,
    We share this restful nooning;
The Quaker with the Baptist here
    Believes in close communing.

Forgive, dear saint, the playful tone,
    Too light for thy deserving;
Thanks for thy generous faith in man,
    Thy trust in God unswerving.

Still echo in the hearts of men
    The words that thou hast spoken;
No forge of hell can weld again
    The fetters thou hast broken.

The pilgrim needs a pass no more
    From Roman or Genevan;
Thought-free, no ghostly tollman keeps
    Henceforth the road to Heaven!

CHICAGO.

The great fire at Chicago was on 8-10 October, 1871.

MEN said at vespers : " All is well ! "
In one wild night the city fell ;
Fell shrines of prayer and marts of gain
Before the fiery hurricane.

On threescore spires had sunset shone,
Where ghastly sunrise looked on none.
Men clasped each other's hands, and said :
" The City of the West is dead ! "

Brave hearts who fought, in slow retreat,
The fiends of fire from street to street,
Turned, powerless, to the blinding glare,
The dumb defiance of despair.

A sudden impulse thrilled each wire
That signalled round that sea of fire ;
Swift words of cheer, warm heart-throbs came ;
In tears of pity died the flame !

From East, from West, from South and North,
The messages of hope shot forth,
And, underneath the severing wave,
The world, full-handed, reached to save.

Fair seemed the old ; but fairer still
The new, the dreary void shall fill
With dearer homes than those o'erthrown,
For love shall lay each corner-stone.

Rise, stricken city! from thee throw
The ashen sackcloth of thy woe;
And build, as to Amphion's strain,
To songs of cheer thy walls again!

How shrivelled in thy hot distress
The primal sin of selfishness!
How instant rose, to take thy part,
The angel in the human heart!

Ah! not in vain the flames that tossed
Above thy dreadful holocaust;
The Christ again has preached through thee
The Gospel of Humanity!

Then lift once more thy towers on high,
And fret with spires the western sky,
To tell that God is yet with us,
And love is still miraculous!

1871.

KINSMAN.

Died at the Island of Panay (Philippine group), aged nineteen
years.

WHERE ceaseless Spring her garland twines,
    As sweetly shall the loved one rest,
As if beneath the whispering pines
    And maple shadows of the West.

Ye mourn, O hearts of home! for him,
    But, haply, mourn ye not alone;
For him shall far-off eyes be dim,
    And pity speak in tongues unknown.

There needs no graven line to give
 The story of his blameless youth ;
All hearts shall throb intuitive,
 And nature guess the simple truth.

The very meaning of his name
 Shall many a tender tribute win ;
The stranger own his sacred claim,
 And all the world shall be his kin.

And there, as here, on main and isle,
 The dews of holy peace shall fall,
The same sweet heavens above him smile,
 And God's dear love be over all !

1874.

THE GOLDEN WEDDING OF LONGWOOD.

Longwood, not far from Bayard Taylor's birthplace in Kennett Square, Pennsylvania, was the home of my esteemed friends John and Hannah Cox, whose golden wedding was celebrated in 1874.

WITH fifty years between you and your well-kept
  wedding vow,
The Golden Age, old friends of mine, is not a fable
  now.

And, sweet as has life's vintage been through all
  your pleasant past,
Still, as at Cana's marriage-feast, the best wine is
  the last !

Again before me, with your names, fair Chester's
  landscape comes,
Its meadows, woods, and ample barns, and quaint,
  stone-builded homes.

The smooth-shorn vales, the wheaten slopes, the
    boscage green and soft,
Of which their poet sings so well from towered
    Cedarcroft.

And lo! from all the country-side come neighbors,
    kith and kin;
From city, hamlet, farm-house old, the wedding
    guests come in.

And they who, without scrip or purse, mob-hunted,
    travel-worn,
In Freedom's age of martyrs came, as victors now
    return.

Older and slower, yet the same, files in the long
    array,
And hearts are light and eyes are glad, though
    heads are badger-gray.

The fire-tried men of Thirty-eight who saw with
    me the fall,
Midst roaring flames and shouting mob, of Penn-
    sylvania Hall;

And they of Lancaster who turned the cheeks of
    tyrants pale,
Singing of freedom through the grates of Moya-
    monsing jail!

And haply with them, all unseen, old comrades,
    gone before,
Pass, silently as shadows pass, within your open
    door, —

The eagle face of Lindley Coates, brave Garrett's
daring zeal,
The Christian grace of Pennock, the steadfast
heart of Neal.

Ah me! beyond all power to name, the worthies
tried and true,
Grave men, fair women, youth and maid, pass by
in hushed review.

Of varying faiths, a common cause fused all their
hearts in one.
God give them now, whate'er their names, the
peace of duty done!

How gladly would I tread again the old-remem-
bered places,
Sit down beside your hearth once more and look
in the dear old faces!

And thank you for the lessons your fifty years are
teaching,
For honest lives that louder speak than half our
noisy preaching;

For your steady faith and courage in that dark and
evil time,
When the Golden Rule was treason, and to feed
the hungry, crime;

For the poor slave's house of refuge when the
hounds were on his track,
And saint and sinner, church and state, joined
hands to send him back.

Blessings upon you! — What you did for each sad,
    suffering one,
So homeless, faint, and naked, unto our Lord was
    done!

Fair fall on Kennett's pleasant vales and Long-
    wood's bowery ways
The mellow sunset of your lives, friends of my
    early days.

May many more of quiet years be added to your
    sum,
And, late at last, in tenderest love, the beckoning
    angel come.

Dear hearts are here, dear hearts are there, alike
    below, above;
Our friends are now in either world, and love is
    sure of love.

    1874.

HYMN

FOR THE OPENING OF PLYMOUTH CHURCH, ST. PAUL,
MINNESOTA.

ALL things are Thine: no gift have we,
Lord of all gifts, to offer Thee;
And hence with grateful hearts to-day,
Thy own before Thy feet we lay.

Thy will was in the builders' thought;
Thy hand unseen amidst us wrought;
Through mortal motive, scheme and plan,
Thy wise eternal purpose ran.

No lack Thy perfect fulness knew;
For human needs and longings grew
This house of prayer, this home of rest,
In the fair garden of the West.

In weakness and in want we call
On Thee for whom the heavens are small;
Thy glory is Thy children's good,
Thy joy Thy tender Fatherhood.

O Father! deign these walls to bless,
Fill with Thy love their emptiness,
And let their door a gateway be
To lead us from ourselves to Thee!

1872.

LEXINGTON.

1775.

No Berserk thirst of blood had they,
  No battle-joy was theirs, who set
  Against the alien bayonet
Their homespun breasts in that old day.

Their feet had trodden peaceful ways;
  They loved not strife, they dreaded pain;
  They saw not, what to us is plain,
That God would make man's wrath his praise.

No seers were they, but simple men;
  Its vast results the future hid:
  The meaning of the work they did
Was strange and dark and doubtful then.

Swift as their summons came they left
  The plough mid-furrow standing still,
  The half-ground corn grist in the mill,
The spade in earth, the axe in cleft.

They went where duty seemed to call,
  They scarcely asked the reason why;
  They only knew they could but die,
And death was not the worst of all!

Of man for man the sacrifice,
  All that was theirs to give, they gave.
  The flowers that blossomed from their grave
Have sown themselves beneath all skies.

Their death-shot shook the feudal tower,
  And shattered slavery's chain as well;
  On the sky's dome, as on a bell,
Its echo struck the world's great hour.

That fateful echo is not dumb:
  The nations listening to its sound
  Wait, from a century's vantage-ground,
The holier triumphs yet to come, —

The bridal time of Law and Love,
  The gladness of the world's release,
  When, war-sick, at the feet of Peace
The hawk shall nestle with the dove! —

The golden age of brotherhood
  Unknown to other rivalries
  Than of the mild humanities,
And gracious interchange of good,

When closer strand shall lean to strand,
  Till meet, beneath saluting flags,
  The eagle of our mountain-crags,
The lion of our Motherland!
1875.

THE LIBRARY.

Sung at the opening of the Haverhill Library, November 11, 1875.

"LET there be light!" God spake of old,
  And over chaos dark and cold,
  And through the dead and formless frame
Of nature, life and order came.

Faint was the light at first that shone
  On giant fern and mastodon,
  On half-formed plant and beast of prey,
And man as rude and wild as they.

Age after age, like waves, o'erran
  The earth, uplifting brute and man;
  And mind, at length, in symbols dark
Its meanings traced on stone and bark.

On leaf of palm, on sedge-wrought roll,
  On plastic clay and leathern scroll,
  Man wrote his thoughts; the ages passed,
And lo! the Press was found at last!

Then dead souls woke; the thoughts of men
  Whose bones were dust revived again;
  The cloister's silence found a tongue,
Old prophets spake, old poets sung.

And here, to-day, the dead look down,
The kings of mind again we crown ;
We hear the voices lost so long,
The sage's word, the sibyl's song.

Here Greek and Roman find themselves
Alive along these crowded shelves ;
And Shakespeare treads again his stage,
And Chaucer paints anew his age.

As if some Pantheon's marbles broke
Their stony trance, and lived and spoke,
Life thrills along the alcoved hall,
The lords of thought await our call!

"I WAS A STRANGER, AND YE TOOK ME IN."

An incident in St. Augustine, Florida.

'NEATH skies that winter never knew
  The air was full of light and balm,
And warm and soft the Gulf wind blew
  Through orange bloom and groves of palm.

A stranger from the frozen North,
  Who sought the fount of health in vain,
Sank homeless on the alien earth,
  And breathed the languid air with pain.

God's angel came! The tender shade
  Of pity made her blue eye dim ;
Against her woman's breast she laid
  The drooping, fainting head of him.

She bore him to a pleasant room,
  Flower-sweet and cool with salt sea air,
And watched beside his bed, for whom
  His far-off sisters might not care.

She fanned his feverish brow and smoothed
  Its lines of pain with tenderest touch.
With holy hymn and prayer she soothed
  The trembling soul that feared so much.

Through her the peace that passeth sight
  Came to him, as he lapsed away
As one whose troubled dreams of night
  Slide slowly into tranquil day.

The sweetness of the Land of Flowers
  Upon his lonely grave she laid:
The jasmine dropped its golden showers,
  The orange lent its bloom and shade.

And something whispered in her thought,
  More sweet than mortal voices be:
" The service thou for him hast wrought
  O daughter! hath been done for me."
1875.

CENTENNIAL HYMN.

Written for the opening of the International Exhibition, Phila-
delphia, May 10, 1876. The music for the hymn was written by
John K. Paine, and may be found in *The Atlantic Monthly* for
June, 1876.

I.

OUR fathers' God! from out whose hand
The centuries fall like grains of sand,

We meet to-day, united, free,
And loyal to our land and Thee,
To thank Thee for the era done,
And trust Thee for the opening one.

II.

Here, where of old, by Thy design,
The fathers spake that word of Thine
Whose echo is the glad refrain
Of rended bolt and falling chain,
To grace our festal time, from all
The zones of earth our guests we call.

III.

Be with us while the New World greets
The Old World thronging all its streets,
Unveiling all the triumphs won
By art or toil beneath the sun;
And unto common good ordain
This rivalship of hand and brain.

IV.

Thou, who hast here in concord furled
The war flags of a gathered world,
Beneath our Western skies fulfil
The Orient's mission of good-will,
And, freighted with love's Golden Fleece,
Send back its Argonauts of peace.

V.

For art and labor met in truce,
For beauty made the bride of use,
We thank Thee; but, withal, we crave
The austere virtues strong to save,

The honor proof to place or gold,
The manhood never bought nor sold !

VI.

Oh make Thou us, through centuries long,
In peace secure, in justice strong ;
Around our gift of freedom draw
The safeguards of Thy righteous law :
And, cast in some diviner mould,
Let the new cycle shame the old !

AT SCHOOL–CLOSE.

BOWDOIN STREET, BOSTON, 1877.

THE end has come, as come it must
    To all things ; in these sweet June days
The teacher and the scholar trust
    Their parting feet to separate ways.

They part : but in the years to be
    Shall pleasant memories cling to each,
As shells bear inland from the sea
    The murmur of the rhythmic beach.

One knew the joy the sculptor knows
    When, plastic to his lightest touch,
His clay-wrought model slowly grows
    To that fine grace desired so much.

So daily grew before her eyes
    The living shapes whereon she wrought,

Strong, tender, innocently wise,
　The child's heart with the woman's thought.

And one shall never quite forget
　The voice that called from dream and play,
The firm but kindly hand that set
　Her feet in learning's pleasant way, —

The joy of Undine soul-possessed,
　The wakening sense, the strange delight
That swelled the fabled statue's breast
　And filled its clouded eyes with sight!

O Youth and Beauty, loved of all!
　Ye pass from girlhood's gate of dreams;
In broader ways your footsteps fall,
　Ye test the truth of all that seems.

Her little realm the teacher leaves,
　She breaks her wand of power apart,
While, for your love and trust, she gives
　The warm thanks of a grateful heart.

Hers is the sober summer noon
　Contrasted with your morn of spring,
The waning with the waxing moon,
　The folded with the outspread wing.

Across the distance of the years
　She sends her God-speed back to you;
She has no thought of doubts or fears :
　Be but yourselves, be pure, be true,

And prompt in duty ; heed the deep,
  Low voice of conscience; through the ill
And discord round about you, keep
  Your faith in human nature still.

Be gentle : unto griefs and needs,
  Be pitiful as woman should,
And, spite of all the lies of creeds,
  Hold fast the truth that God is good.

Give and receive ; go forth and bless
  The world that needs the hand and heart
Of Martha's helpful carefulness
  No less than Mary's better part.

So shall the stream of time flow by
  And leave each year a richer good,
And matron loveliness outvie
  The nameless charm of maidenhood.

And, when the world shall link your names
  With gracious lives and manners fine,
The teacher shall assert her claims,
  And proudly whisper, " These were mine ! "

HYMN OF THE CHILDREN.

Sung at the anniversary of the Children's Mission, Boston, 1878.

THINE are all the gifts, O God !
  Thine the broken bread ;
Let the naked feet be shod,
  And the starving fed.

Let Thy children, by Thy grace,
　　Give as they abound,
Till the poor have breathing-space,
　　And the lost are found.

Wiser than the miser's hoards
　　Is the giver's choice ;
Sweeter than the song of birds
　　Is the thankful voice.

Welcome smiles on faces sad
　　As the flowers of spring ;
Let the tender hearts be glad
　　With the joy they bring.

Happier for their pity's sake
　　Make their sports and plays,
And from lips of childhood take
　　Thy perfected praise !

THE LANDMARKS.

This poem was read at a meeting of citizens of Boston having
for its object the preservation of the Old South Church famous in
Colonial and Revolutionary history.

I.

THROUGH the streets of Marblehead
Fast the red-winged terror sped ;

Blasting, withering, on it came,
With its hundred tongues of flame,

Where St. Michael's on its way
Stood like chained Andromeda,

Waiting on the rock, like her,
Swift doom or deliverer!

Church that, after sea-moss grew
Over walls no longer new,

Counted generations five,
Four entombed and one alive;

Heard the martial thousand tread
Battleward from Marblehead;

Saw within the rock-walled bay
Treville's lilied pennons play,

And the fisher's dory met
By the barge of Lafayette,

Telling good news in advance
Of the coming fleet of France!

Church to reverend memories dear,
Quaint in desk and chandelier;

Bell, whose century-rusted tongue
Burials tolled and bridals rung;

Loft, whose tiny organ kept
Keys that Snetzler's hand had swept;

Altar, o'er whose tablet old
Sinai's law its thunders rolled!

Suddenly the sharp cry came:
" Look! St. Michael's is aflame!"

Round the low tower wall the fire
Snake-like wound its coil of ire.

Sacred in its gray respect
From the jealousies of sect,

" Save it," seemed the thought of all,
" Save it, though our roof-trees fall!"

Up the tower the young men sprung;
One, the bravest, outward swung

By the rope, whose kindling strands
Smoked beneath the holder's hands,

Smiting down with strokes of power
Burning fragments from the tower.

Then the gazing crowd beneath
Broke the painful pause of breath;

Brave men cheered from street to street,
With home's ashes at their feet;

Houseless women kerchiefs waved:
" Thank the Lord! St. Michael's saved!"

II.

In the heart of Boston town
Stands the church of old renown,

From whose walls the impulse went
Which set free a continent;

From whose pulpit's oracle
Prophecies of freedom fell;

And whose steeple-rocking din
Rang the nation's birth-day in!

Standing at this very hour
Perilled like St. Michael's tower,

Held not in the clasp of flame,
But by mammon's grasping claim.

Shall it be of Boston said
She is shamed by Marblehead?

City of our pride! as there,
Hast thou none to do and dare?

Life was risked for Michael's shrine;
Shall not wealth be staked for thine?

Woe to thee, when men shall search
Vainly for the Old South Church;

When from Neck to Boston Stone,
All thy pride of place is gone;

When from Bay and railroad car,
Stretched before them wide and far,

Men shall only see a great
Wilderness of brick and slate,

Every holy spot o'erlaid
By the commonplace of trade!

City of our love! to thee
Duty is but destiny.

True to all thy record saith,
Keep with thy traditions faith;

Ere occasion 's overpast,
Hold its flowing forelock fast;

Honor still the precedents
Of a grand munificence;

In thy old historic way
Give, as thou didst yesterday

At the South-land's call, or on
Need's demand from fired St. John.

Set thy Church's muffled bell
Free the generous deed to tell.

Let thy loyal hearts rejoice
In the glad, sonorous voice,

Ringing from the brazen mouth
Of the bell of the Old South, —

Ringing clearly, with a will,
" What she was is Boston still ! "

1879.

GARDEN.

A hymn for the American Horticultural Society, 1882.

O PAINTER of the fruits and flowers,
    We own Thy wise design,
Whereby these human hands of ours
    May share the work of Thine !

Apart from Thee we plant in vain
    The root and sow the seed ;
Thy early and Thy later rain,
    Thy sun and dew we need.

Our toil is sweet with thankfulness,
    Our burden is our boon ;
The curse of Earth's gray morning is
    The blessing of its noon.

Why search the wide world everywhere
    For Eden's unknown ground ?
That garden of the primal pair
    May nevermore be found.

But, blest by Thee, our patient toil
    May right the ancient wrong,

And give to every clime and soil
   The beauty lost so long.

Our homestead flowers and fruited trees
   May Eden's orchard shame ;
We taste the tempting sweets of these
   Like Eve, without her blame.

And, North and South and East and West,
   The pride of every zone,
The fairest, rarest, and the best
   May all be made our own.

Its earliest shrines the young world sought
   In hill-groves and in bowers,
The fittest offerings thither brought
   Were Thy own fruits and flowers.

And still with reverent hands we cull
   Thy gifts each year renewed;
The good is always beautiful,
   The beautiful is good.

A GREETING.

Read at Harriet Beecher Stowe's seventieth anniversary, June
14, 1882, at a garden party at ex-Governor Claflin's in Newton-
ville, Mass.

THRICE welcome from the Land of Flowers
And golden-fruited orange bowers
To this sweet, green-turfed June of ours !
To her who, in our evil time,
Dragged into light the nation's crime

With strength beyond the strength of men,
And, mightier than their swords, her pen!
To her who world-wide entrance gave
To the log-cabin of the slave;
Made all his wrongs and sorrows known,
And all earth's languages his own, —
North, South, and East and West, made all
The common air electrical,
Until the o'ercharged bolts of heaven
Blazed down, and every chain was riven!

Welcome from each and all to her
Whose Wooing of the Minister
Revealed the warm heart of the man
Beneath the creed-bound Puritan,
And taught the kinship of the love
Of man below and God above;
To her whose vigorous pencil-strokes
Sketched into life her Oldtown Folks;
Whose fireside stories, grave or gay,
In quaint Sam Lawson's vagrant way,
With old New England's flavor rife,
Waifs from her rude idyllic life,
Are racy as the legends old
By Chaucer or Boccaccio told;
To her who keeps, through change of place
And time, her native strength and grace,
Alike where warm Sorrento smiles,
Or where, by birchen-shaded isles,
Whose summer winds have shivered o'er
The icy drift of Labrador,
She lifts to light the priceless Pearl
Of Harpswell's angel-beckoned girl!

To her at threescore years and ten
Be tributes of the tongue and pen;
Be honor, praise, and heart-thanks given,
The loves of earth, the hopes of heaven!

Ah, dearer than the praise that stirs
The air to-day, our love is hers!
She needs no guaranty of fame
Whose own is linked with Freedom's name.
Long ages after ours shall keep
Her memory living while we sleep;
The waves that wash our gray coast lines,
The winds that rock the Southern pines,
Shall sing of her; the unending years
Shall tell her tale in unborn ears.
And when, with sins and follies past,
Are numbered color-hate and caste,
White, black, and red shall own as one
The noblest work by woman done.

GODSPEED.

Written on the occasion of a voyage made by my friends Annie
Fields and Sarah Orne Jewett.

OUTBOUND, your bark awaits you.   Were I one
    Whose prayer availeth much, my wish should be
    Your favoring trade-wind and consenting sea.
By sail or steed was never love outrun,
And, here or there, love follows her in whom
    All graces and sweet charities unite,
    The old Greek beauty set in holier light;

And her for whom New England's byways bloom,
Who walks among us welcome as the Spring,
   Calling up blossoms where her light feet stray.
   God keep you both, make beautiful your way,
Comfort, console, and bless ; and safely bring,
Ere yet I make upon a vaster sea
The unreturning voyage, my friends to me.
  1882.

WINTER ROSES.

In reply to a flower gift from Mrs. Putnam's school at Jamaica
Plain.

    My garden roses long ago
      Have perished from the leaf-strewn walks ;
    Their pale, fair sisters smile no more
      Upon the sweet-brier stalks.

    Gone with the flower-time of my life,
      Spring's violets, summer's blooming pride,
    And Nature's winter and my own
      Stand, flowerless, side by side.

    So might I yesterday have sung ;
      To-day, in bleak December's noon,
    Come sweetest fragrance, shapes, and hues,
      The rosy wealth of June !

    Bless the young hands that culled the gift,
      And bless the hearts that prompted it ;
    If undeserved it comes, at least
      It seems not all unfit.

Of old my Quaker ancestors
    Had gifts of forty stripes save one;
To-day as many roses crown
    The gray head of their son.

And with them, to my fancy's eye,
    The fresh-faced givers smiling come,
And nine and thirty happy girls
    Make glad a lonely room.

They bring the atmosphere of youth;
    The light and warmth of long ago
Are in my heart, and on my cheek
    The airs of morning blow.

O buds of girlhood, yet unblown,
    And fairer than the gift ye chose,
For you may years like leaves unfold
    The heart of Sharon's rose!

1883.

THE REUNION.

Read September 10, 1885, to the surviving students of Haverhill Academy in 1827–1830.

THE gulf of seven and fifty years
    We stretch our welcoming hands across;
    The distance but a pebble's toss
Between us and our youth appears.

For in life's school we linger on
    The remnant of a once full list;
    Conning our lessons, undismissed,
With faces to the setting sun.

And some have gone the unknown way,
  And some await the call to rest;
  Who knoweth whether it is best
For those who went or those who stay?

And yet despite of loss and ill,
  If faith and love and hope remain,
  Our length of days is not in vain,
And life is well worth living still.

Still to a gracious Providence
  The thanks of grateful hearts are due,
  For blessings when our lives were new,
For all the good vouchsafed us since.

The pain that spared us sorer hurt,
  The wish denied, the purpose crossed,
  And pleasure's fond occasions lost,
Were mercies to our small desert.

'T is something that we wander back,
  Gray pilgrims, to our ancient ways,
  And tender memories of old days
Walk with us by the Merrimac;

That even in life's afternoon
  A sense of youth comes back again,
  As through this cool September rain
The still green woodlands dream of June.

The eyes grown dim to present things
  Have keener sight for bygone years,
  And sweet and clear, in deafening ears,
The bird that sang at morning sings.

Dear comrades, scattered wide and far,
    Send from their homes their kindly word,
    And dearer ones, unseen, unheard,
Smile on us from some heavenly star.

For life and death with God are one,
    Unchanged by seeming change His care
    And love are round us here and there;
He breaks no thread His hand has spun.

Soul touches soul, the muster roll
    Of life eternal has no gaps;
    And after half a century's lapse
Our school-day ranks are closed and whole.

Hail and farewell! We go our way;
    Where shadows end, we trust in light;
    The star that ushers in the night
Is herald also of the day!

NORUMBEGA HALL.

Norumbega Hall at Wellesley College, named in honor of
Eben Norton Horsford, who has been one of the most munificent
patrons of that noble institution, and who had just published an
essay claiming the discovery of the site of the somewhat myth-
ical city of Norumbega, was opened with appropriate ceremonies,
in April, 1886. The following sonnet was written for the occasion, and was read by President Alice E. Freeman, to whom it
was addressed.

Nor on Penobscot's wooded bank the spires
Of the sought City rose, nor yet beside
The winding Charles, nor where the daily tide
Of Naumkeag's haven rises and retires,

The vision tarried ; but somewhere we knew
The beautiful gates must open to our quest,
Somewhere that marvellous City of the West
Would lift its towers and palace domes in view,
And, lo ! at last its mystery is made known —
Its only dwellers maidens fair and young,
Its Princess such as England's Laureate sung ;
And safe from capture, save by love alone,
It lends its beauty to the lake's green shore,
And Norumbega is a myth no more.

THE BARTHOLDI STATUE.

1886.

THE land, that, from the rule of kings,
    In freeing us, itself made free,
Our Old World Sister, to us brings
    Her sculptured Dream of Liberty :

Unlike the shapes on Egypt's sands
    Uplifted by the toil-worn slave,
On Freedom's soil with freemen's hands
    We rear the symbol free hands gave.

O France, the beautiful ! to thee
    Once more a debt of love we owe :
In peace beneath thy Colors Three,
    We hail a later Rochambeau !

Rise, stately Symbol ! holding forth
    Thy light and hope to all who sit
In chains and darkness !   Belt the earth
    With watch-fires from thy torch uplit !

Reveal the primal mandate still
  Which Chaos heard and ceased to be,
Trace on mid-air th' Eternal Will
  In signs of fire: " Let man be free ! "

Shine far, shine free, a guiding light
  To Reason's ways and Virtue's aim,
A lightning-flash the wretch to smite
  Who shields his license with thy name !

ONE OF THE SIGNERS.

Written for the unveiling of the statue of Josiah Bartlett at Amesbury, Mass., July 4, 1888. Governor Bartlett, who was a native of the town, was a signer of the Declaration of Independence. Amesbury or Ambresbury, so called from the " anointed stones " of the great Druidical temple near it, was the seat of one of the earliest religious houses in Britain. The tradition that the guilty wife of King Arthur fled thither for protection forms one of the finest passages in Tennyson's *Idyls of the King*.

O STORIED vale of Merrimac
  Rejoice through all thy shade and shine,
And from his century's sleep call back
  A brave and honored son of thine.

Unveil his effigy between
  The living and the dead to-day;
The fathers of the Old Thirteen
  Shall witness bear as spirits may.

Unseen, unheard, his gray compeers
  The shades of Lee and Jefferson,
Wise Franklin reverend with his years
  And Carroll, lord of Carrollton !

Be thine henceforth a pride of place
  Beyond thy namesake's over-sea,
Where scarce a stone is left to trace
  The Holy House of Amesbury.

A prouder memory lingers round
  The birthplace of thy true man here
Than that which haunts the refuge found
  By Arthur's mythic Guinevere.

The plain deal table where he sat
  And signed a nation's title-deed
Is dearer now to fame than that
  Which bore the scroll of Runnymede.

Long as, on Freedom's natal morn,
  Shall ring the Independence bells,
Give to thy dwellers yet unborn
  The lesson which his image tells.

For in that hour of Destiny,
  Which tried the men of bravest stock,
He knew the end alone must be
  A free land or a traitor's block.

Among those picked and chosen men
  Than his, who here first drew his breath,
No firmer fingers held the pen
  Which wrote for liberty or death.

Not for their hearths and homes alone,
  But for the world their work was done;
On all the winds their thought has flown
  Through all the circuit of the sun.

We trace its flight by broken chains,
   By songs of grateful Labor still;
To-day, in all her holy fanes,
   It rings the bells of freed Brazil.

O hills that watched his boyhood's home,
   O earth and air that nursed him, give,
In this memorial semblance, room
   To him who shall its bronze outlive!

And thou, O Land he loved, rejoice
   That in the countless years to come,
Whenever Freedom needs a voice,
   These sculptured lips shall not be dumb!

THE TENT ON THE BEACH

It can scarcely be necessary to name as the two companions whom I reckoned with myself in this poetical picnic, Fields the lettered magnate, and Taylor the free cosmopolite. The long line of sandy beach which defines almost the whole of the New Hampshire sea-coast is especially marked near its southern extremity, by the salt-meadows of Hampton. The Hampton River winds through these meadows, and the reader may, if he choose, imagine my tent pitched near its mouth, where also was the scene of the *Wreck of Rivermouth*. The green bluff to the northward is Great Boar's Head; southward is the Merrimac, with Newburyport lifting its steeples above brown roofs and green trees on its banks.

I WOULD not sin, in this half-playful strain, —
   Too light perhaps for serious years, though born
Of the enforced leisure of slow pain, —
   Against the pure ideal which has drawn
My feet to follow its far-shining gleam.
A simple plot is mine: legends and runes
Of credulous days, old fancies that have lain
Silent from boyhood taking voice again,
Warmed into life once more, even as the tunes
That, frozen in the fabled hunting-horn,
Thawed into sound : — a winter fireside dream
Of dawns and sunsets by the summer sea,
Whose sands are traversed by a silent throng
Of voyagers from that vaster mystery
Of which it is an emblem ; — and the dear
Memory of one who might have tuned my song
To sweeter music by her delicate ear.

1st mo., 1867.

WHEN heats as of a tropic clime
  Burned all our inland valleys through,
Three friends, the guests of summer time,
  Pitched their white tent where sea-winds blew.
Behind them, marshes, seamed and crossed
With narrow creeks, and flower-embossed,
Stretched to the dark oak wood, whose leafy arms
Screened from the stormy East the pleasant inland
    farms.

At full of tide their bolder shore
  Of sun-bleached sand the waters beat;
At ebb, a smooth and glistening floor
  They touched with light, receding feet.
Northward a green bluff broke the chain
Of sand-hills; southward stretched a plain
Of salt grass, with a river winding down,
Sail-whitened, and beyond the steeples of the town,

Whence sometimes, when the wind was light
  And dull the thunder of the beach,
They heard the bells of morn and night
  Swing, miles away, their silver speech.
Above low scarp and turf-grown wall
They saw the fort-flag rise and fall;
And, the first star to signal twilight's hour,
The lamp-fire glimmer down from the tall light-
    house tower.

They rested there, escaped awhile
  From cares that wear the life away,
To eat the lotus of the Nile
  And drink the poppies of Cathay, —

To fling their loads of custom down,
Like drift-weed, on the sand-slopes brown,
And in the sea waves drown the restless pack
Of duties, claims, and needs that barked upon their
    track.

One, with his beard scarce silvered, bore
    A ready credence in his looks,
A lettered magnate, lording o'er
    An ever-widening realm of books.
In him brain-currents, near and far,
Converged as in a Leyden jar;
The old, dead authors thronged him round about,
And Elzevir's gray ghosts from leathern graves
    looked out.

He knew each living pundit well,
    Could weigh the gifts of him or her,
And well the market value tell
    Of poet and philosopher.
But if he lost, the scenes behind,
Somewhat of reverence vague and blind,
Finding the actors human at the best,
No readier lips than his the good he saw confessed.

His boyhood fancies not outgrown,
    He loved himself the singer's art;
Tenderly, gently, by his own
    He knew and judged an author's heart.
No Rhadamanthine brow of doom
Bowed the dazed pedant from his room;
And bards, whose name is legion, if denied,
Bore off alike intact their verses and their pride.

Pleasant it was to roam about
   The lettered world as he had done,
And see the lords of song without
   Their singing robes and garlands on.
With Wordsworth paddle Rydal mere,
Taste rugged Elliott's home-brewed beer,
And with the ears of Rogers, at fourscore,
Hear Garrick's buskined tread and Walpole's wit
     once more.

And one there was, a dreamer born,
   Who, with a mission to fulfil,
Had left the Muses' haunts to turn
   The crank of an opinion-mill,
Making his rustic reed of song
A weapon in the war with wrong,
Yoking his fancy to the breaking-plough
That beam-deep turned the soil for truth to spring
     and grow.

Too quiet seemed the man to ride
   The wingèd Hippogriff Reform ;
Was his a voice from side to side
   To pierce the tumult of the storm ?
A silent, shy, peace-loving man,
He seemed no fiery partisan
To hold his way against the public frown,
The ban of Church and State, the fierce mob's
     hounding down.

For while he wrought with strenuous will
   The work his hands had found to do,
He heard the fitful music still
   Of winds that out of dream-land blew.

The din about him could not drown
What the strange voices whispered down;
Along his task-field weird processions swept,
The visionary pomp of stately phantoms stepped

The common air was thick with dreams, —
He told them to the toiling crowd;
Such music as the woods and streams
Sang in his ear he sang aloud;
In still, shut bays, on windy capes,
He heard the call of beckoning shapes,
And, as the gray old shadows prompted him,
To homely moulds of rhyme he shaped their legends grim.

He rested now his weary hands,
And lightly moralized and laughed,
As, tracing on the shifting sands
A burlesque of his paper-craft,
He saw the careless waves o'errun
His words, as time before had done,
Each day's tide-water washing clean away,
Like letters from the sand, the work of yesterday.

And one, whose Arab face was tanned
By tropic sun and boreal frost,
So travelled there was scarce a land
Or people left him to exhaust,
In idling mood had from him hurled
The poor squeezed orange of the world,
And in the tent-shade, as beneath a palm,
Smoked, cross-legged like a Turk, in Oriental calm.

The very waves that washed the sand
  Below him, he had seen before
Whitening the Scandinavian strand
  And sultry Mauritanian shore.
From ice-rimmed isles, from summer seas
Palm-fringed, they bore him messages;
He heard the plaintive Nubian songs again,
And mule-bells tinkling down the mountain-paths
    of Spain.

His memory round the ransacked earth
  On Puck's long girdle slid at ease;
And, instant, to the valley's girth
  Of mountains, spice isles of the seas,
Faith flowered in minster stones, Art's guess
At truth and beauty, found access;
Yet loved the while, that free cosmopolite,
Old friends, old ways, and kept his boyhood's
    dreams in sight.

Untouched as yet by wealth and pride,
  That virgin innocence of beach:
No shingly monster, hundred-eyed,
  Stared its gray sand-birds out of reach;
Unhoused, save where, at intervals,
The white tents showed their canvas walls,
Where brief sojourners, in the cool, soft air,
Forgot their inland heats, hard toil, and year-long
    care.

Sometimes along the wheel-deep sand
  A one-horse wagon slowly crawled,
Deep laden with a youthful band,
  Whose look some homestead old recalled;

Brother perchance, and sisters twain,
   And one whose blue eyes told, more plain
Than the free language of her rosy lip,
Of the still dearer claim of love's relationship.

With cheeks of russet-orchard tint,
   The light laugh of their native rills,
The perfume of their garden's mint,
   The breezy freedom of the hills,
They bore, in unrestrained delight,
The motto of the Garter's knight,
Careless as if from every gazing thing
Hid by their innocence, as Gyges by his ring.

The clanging sea-fowl came and went,
   The hunter's gun in the marshes rang;
At nightfall from a neighboring tent
   A flute-voiced woman sweetly sang.
Loose-haired, barefooted, hand-in-hand,
   Young girls went tripping down the sand;
And youths and maidens, sitting in the moon,
Dreamed o'er the old fond dream from which we
      wake too soon.

At times their fishing-lines they plied,
   With an old Triton at the oar,
Salt as the sea-wind, tough and dried
   As a lean cusk from Labrador.
Strange tales he told of wreck and storm, —
   Had seen the sea-snake's awful form,
And heard the ghosts on Haley's Isle complain,
Speak him off shore, and beg a passage to old
      Spain!

And there, on breezy morns, they saw
    The fishing-schooners outward run,
Their low-bent sails in tack and flaw
    Turned white or dark to shade and sun.
Sometimes, in calms of closing day,
    They watched the spectral mirage play,
Saw low, far islands looming tall and nigh,
And ships, with upturned keels, sail like a sea the
        sky.

Sometimes a cloud, with thunder black,
    Stooped low upon the darkening main,
Piercing the waves along its track
    With the slant javelins of rain.
And when west-wind and sunshine warm
    Chased out to sea its wrecks of storm,
They saw the prismy hues in thin spray showers
Where the green buds of waves burst into white
        froth flowers.

And when along the line of shore
    The mists crept upward chill and damp,
Stretched, careless, on their sandy floor
    Beneath the flaring lantern lamp,
They talked of all things old and new,
    Read, slept, and dreamed as idlers do ;
And in the unquestioned freedom of the tent,
Body and o'er-taxed mind to healthful ease unbent.

Once, when the sunset splendors died,
    And, trampling up the sloping sand,
In lines outreaching far and wide,
    The white-maned billows swept to land,

Dim seen across the gathering shade,
A vast and ghostly cavalcade,
They sat around their lighted kerosene,
Hearing the deep bass roar their every pause be-
  tween.

Then, urged thereto, the Editor
  Within his full portfolio dipped,
Feigning excuse while seaching for
  (With secret pride) his manuscript.
His pale face flushed from eye to beard,
  With nervous cough his throat he cleared,
And, in a voice so tremulous it betrayed
The anxious fondness of an author's heart, he read:
1867.

THE WRECK OF RIVERMOUTH.

The Goody Cole who figures in this poem and *The Changeling*
was Eunice Cole, who for a quarter of a century or more was
feared, persecuted, and hated as the witch of Hampton.   She lived
alone in a hovel a little distant from the spot where the Hampton
Academy now stands, and there she died, unattended.   When her
death was discovered, she was hastily covered up in the earth near
by, and a stake driven through her body, to exorcise the evil spirit.
Rev. Stephen Bachiler or Batchelder was one of the ablest of the
early New England preachers.   His marriage late in life to
a woman regarded by his church as disreputable induced him to
return to England, where he enjoyed the esteem and favor of
Oliver Cromwell during the Protectorate.

RIVERMOUTH Rocks are fair to see,
  By dawn or sunset shone across,
When the ebb of the sea has left them free,
  To dry their fringes of gold-green moss:
For there the river comes winding down,
From salt sea-meadows and uplands brown,

And waves on the outer rocks afoam
Shout to its waters, " Welcome home! "

And fair are the sunny isles in view
    East of the grisly Head of the Boar,
And Agamenticus lifts its blue
    Disk of a cloud the woodlands o'er ;
And southerly, when the tide is down,
'Twixt white sea-waves and sand-hills brown,
The beach-birds dance and the gray gulls wheel
Over a floor of burnished steel.

Once, in the old Colonial days,
    Two hundred years ago and more,
A boat sailed down through the winding ways
    Of Hampton River to that low shore,
Full of a goodly company
Sailing out on the summer sea,
Veering to catch the land-breeze light,
With the Boar to left and the Rocks to right.

In Hampton meadows, where mowers laid
    Their scythes to the swaths of salted grass,
" Ah, well-a-day! our hay must be made! "
    A young man sighed, who saw them pass.
Loud laughed his fellows to see him stand
Whetting his scythe with a listless hand,
Hearing a voice in a far-off song,
Watching a white hand beckoning long.

" Fie on the witch! " cried a merry girl,
    As they rounded the point where Goody **Cole**
Sat by her door with her wheel atwirl,[5]
    A bent and blear-eyed poor old soul.

" Oho ! " she muttered, " ye 're brave to-day !
  But I hear the little waves laugh and say,
' The broth will be cold that waits at home ;
  For it 's one to go, but another to come ! ' "

" She 's cursed," said the skipper ; " speak her fair :
    I 'm scary always to see her shake
  Her wicked head, with its wild gray hair,
    And nose like a hawk, and eyes like a snake."
  But merrily still, with laugh and shout,
  From Hampton River the boat sailed out,
  Till the huts and the flakes on Star seemed nigh,
  And they lost the scent of the pines of Rye.

  They dropped their lines in the lazy tide,
    Drawing up haddock and mottled cod ;
  They saw not the Shadow that walked beside,
    They heard not the feet with silence shod.
  But thicker and thicker a hot mist grew,
  Shot by the lightnings through and through ;
  And muffled growls, like the growl of a beast,
  Ran along the sky from west to east.

  Then the skipper looked from the darkening sea
    Up to the dimmed and wading sun ;
  But he spake like a brave man cheerily,
    " Yet there is time for our homeward run."
  Veering and tacking, they backward wore ;
  And just as a breath from the woods ashore
  Blew out to whisper of danger past,
  The wrath of the storm came down at last !

  The skipper hauled at the heavy sail :
    " God be our help ! " he only cried,

As the roaring gale, like the stroke of a flail,
   Smote the boat on its starboard side.
The Shoalsmen looked, but saw alone
Dark films of rain-cloud slantwise blown,
Wild rocks lit up by the lightning's glare,
The strife and torment of sea and air.

Goody Cole looked out from her door:
   The Isles of Shoals were drowned and gone,
Scarcely she saw the Head of the Boar
   Toss the foam from tusks of stone.
She clasped her hands with a grip of pain,
The tear on her cheek was not of rain:
"They are lost," she muttered, "boat and crew!
Lord, forgive me! my words were true!"

Suddenly seaward swept the squall;
   The low sun smote through cloudy rack;
The Shoals stood clear in the light, and all
   The trend of the coast lay hard and black.
But far and wide as eye could reach,
No life was seen upon wave or beach;
The boat that went out at morning never
Sailed back again into Hampton River.

O mower, lean on thy bended snath,
   Look from the meadows green and low:
The wind of the sea is a waft of death,
   The waves are singing a song of woe!
By silent river, by moaning sea,
Long and vain shall thy watching be:
Never again shall the sweet voice call,
Never the white hand rise and fall!

O Rivermouth Rocks, how sad a sight
   Ye saw in the light of breaking day!
Dead faces looking up cold and white
   From sand and seaweed where they lay.
The mad old witch-wife wailed and wept,
And cursed the tide as it backward crept:
" Crawl back, crawl back, blue water-snake!
Leave your dead for the hearts that break! "

Solemn it was in that old day
   In Hampton town and its log-built church,
Where side by side the coffins lay
   And the mourners stood in aisle and porch.
In the singing-seats young eyes were dim,
The voices faltered that raised the hymn,
And Father Dalton, grave and stern,
Sobbed through his prayer and wept in turn.

But his ancient colleague did not pray;
   Under the weight of his fourscore years
He stood apart with the iron-gray
   Of his strong brows knitted to hide his tears;
And a fair-faced woman of doubtful fame,
Linking her own with his honored name,
Subtle as sin, at his side withstood
The felt reproach of her neighborhood.

Apart with them, like them forbid,
   Old Goody Cole looked drearily round,
As, two by two, with their faces hid,
   The mourners walked to the burying-ground.
She let the staff from her clasped hands fall:
" Lord, forgive us! we 're sinners all! "

And the voice of the old man answered her:
" Amen ! " said Father Bachiler.

So, as I sat upon Appledore
   In the calm of a closing summer day,
And the broken lines of Hampton shore
   In purple mist of cloudland lay,
The Rivermouth Rocks their story told ;
And waves aglow with sunset gold,
Rising and breaking in steady chime,
Beat the rhythm and kept the time.

And the sunset paled, and warmed once more
   With a softer, tenderer after-glow ;
In the east was moon-rise, with boats off-shore
   And sails in the distance drifting slow.
The beacon glimmered from Portsmouth bar,
The White Isle kindled its great red star ;
And life and death in my old-time lay
Mingled in peace like the night and day !

" Well ! " said the Man of Books, " your story
   Is really not ill told in verse.
As the Celt said of purgatory,
   One might go farther and fare worse."
The Reader smiled ; and once again
With steadier voice took up his strain,
While the fair singer from the neighboring tent
Drew near, and at his side a graceful listener bent.
   1864.

THE GRAVE BY THE LAKE.

At the mouth of the Melvin River, which empties into Moulton-boro Bay in Lake Winnipesaukee, is a great mound. The Ossipee Indians had their home in the neighborhood of the bay, which is plentifully stocked with fish, and many relics of their occupation have been found.

WHERE the Great Lake's sunny smiles
Dimple round its hundred isles,
And the mountain's granite ledge
Cleaves the water like a wedge,
Ringed about with smooth, gray stones,
Rest the giant's mighty bones.

Close beside, in shade and gleam,
Laughs and ripples Melvin stream ;
Melvin water, mountain-born,
All fair flowers its banks adorn ;
All the woodland's voices meet,
Mingling with its murmurs sweet.

Over lowlands forest-grown,
Over waters island-strown,
Over silver-sanded beach,
Leaf-locked bay and misty reach,
Melvin stream and burial-heap,
Watch and ward the mountains keep.

Who that Titan cromlech fills ?
Forest-kaiser, lord o' the hills ?
Knight who on the birchen tree
Carved his savage heraldry ?
Priest o' the pine-wood temples dim,
Prophet, sage, or wizard grim ?

Rugged type of primal man,
Grim utilitarian,
Loving woods for hunt and prowl,
Lake and hill for fish and fowl,
As the brown bear blind and dull
To the grand and beautiful :

Not for him the lesson drawn
From the mountains smit with dawn.
Star-rise, moon-rise, flowers of May,
Sunset's purple bloom of day, —
Took his life no hue from thence,
Poor amid such affluence ?

Haply unto hill and tree
All too near akin was he :
Unto him who stands afar
Nature's marvels greatest are ;
Who the mountain purple seeks
Must not climb the higher peaks.

Yet who knows in winter tramp,
Or the midnight of the camp,
What revealings faint and far,
Stealing down from moon and star,
Kindled in that human clod
Thought of destiny and God ?

Stateliest forest patriarch,
Grand in robes of skin and bark,
What sepulchral mysteries,
What weird funeral-rites, were his ?
What sharp wail, what drear lament,
Back scared wolf and eagle sent ?

Now, whate'er he may have been,
Low he lies as other men ;
On his mound the partridge drums,
There the noisy blue-jay comes ;
Rank nor name nor pomp has he
In the grave's democracy.

Part thy blue lips, Northern lake !
Moss-grown rocks, your silence break !
Tell the tale, thou ancient tree !
Thou, too, slide-worn Ossipee !
Speak, and tell us how and when
Lived and died this king of men !

Wordless moans the ancient pine ;
Lake and mountain give no sign ;
Vain to trace this ring of stones ;
Vain the search of crumbling bones :
Deepest of all mysteries,
And the saddest, silence is.

Nameless, noteless, clay with clay
Mingles slowly day by day ;
But somewhere, for good or ill,
That dark soul is living still ;
Somewhere yet that atom's force
Moves the light-poised universe.

Strange that on his burial-sod
Harebells bloom, and golden-rod,
While the soul's dark horoscope
Holds no starry sign of hope !
Is the Unseen with sight at odds ?
Nature's pity more than God's ?

Thus I mused by Melvin's side,
While the summer eventide
Made the woods and inland sea
And the mountains mystery;
And the hush of earth and air
Seemed the pause before a prayer, —

Prayer for him, for all who rest,
Mother Earth, upon thy breast, —
Lapped on Christian turf, or hid
In rock-cave or pyramid:
All who sleep, as all who live,
Well may need the prayer, " Forgive! "

Desert-smothered caravan,
Knee-deep dust that once was man,
Battle-trenches ghastly piled,
Ocean-floors with white bones tiled,
Crowded tomb and mounded sod,
Dumbly crave that prayer to God.

Oh, the generations old
Over whom no church-bells tolled,
Christless, lifting up blind eyes
To the silence of the skies!
For the innumerable dead
Is my soul disquieted.

Where be now these silent hosts?
Where the camping-ground of ghosts?
Where the spectral conscripts led
To the white tents of the dead?
What strange shore or chartless sea
Holds the awful mystery?

Then the warm sky stooped to make
Double sunset in the lake ;
While above I saw with it,
Range on range, the mountains lit ;
And the calm and splendor stole
Like an answer to my soul.

Hear'st thou, O of little faith,
What to thee the mountain saith,
What is whispered by the trees? —
" Cast on God thy care for these ;
Trust Him, if thy sight be dim :
Doubt for them is doubt of Him.

" Blind must be their close-shut eyes
Where like night the sunshine lies,
Fiery-linked the self-forged chain
Binding ever sin to pain,
Strong their prison-house of will,
But without He waiteth still.

" Not with hatred's undertow
Doth the Love Eternal flow ;
Every chain that spirits wear
Crumbles in the breath of prayer ;
And the penitent's desire
Opens every gate of fire.

" Still Thy love, O Christ arisen,
Yearns to reach these souls in prison !
Through all depths of sin and loss
Drops the plummet of Thy cross !
Never yet abyss was found
Deeper than that cross could sound ! "

Therefore well may Nature keep
Equal faith with all who sleep,
Set her watch of hills around
Christian grave and heathen mound,
And to cairn and kirkyard send
Summer's flowery dividend.

Keep, O pleasant Melvin stream,
Thy sweet laugh in shade and gleam!
On the Indian's grassy tomb
Swing, O flowers, your bells of bloom!
Deep below, as high above,
Sweeps the circle of God's love.

1865.

———————

He paused and questioned with his eye
    The hearers' verdict on his song.
A low voice asked : Is 't well to pry
    Into the secrets which belong
Only to God? — The life to be
Is still the unguessed mystery :
Unsealed, unpierced the cloudy walls remain,
We beat with dream and wish the soundless doors
    in vain.

"But faith beyond our sight may go."
    He said : "The gracious Fatherhood
Can only know above, below,
    Eternal purposes of good.
From our free heritage of will,
The bitter springs of pain and ill
Flow only in all worlds.   The perfect day
Of God is shadowless, and love is love alway."

" I know," she said, " the letter kills ;
    That on our arid fields of strife
And heat of clashing texts distils
    The dew of spirit and of life.
But, searching still the written Word,
  I fain would find, Thus saith the Lord,
A voucher for the hope I also feel
That sin can give no wound beyond love's power to
    heal."

"Pray," said the Man of Books, " give o'er
    A theme too vast for time and place.
Go on, Sir Poet, ride once more
    Your hobby at his old free pace.
But let him keep, with step discreet,
    The solid earth beneath his feet.
In the great mystery which around us lies,
The wisest is a fool, the fool Heaven-helped is
    wise."

The Traveller said : " If songs have creeds,
    Their choice of them let singers make ;
But Art no other sanction needs
    Than beauty for its own fair sake.
It grinds not in the mill of use,
    Nor asks for leave, nor begs excuse ;
It makes the flexile laws it deigns to own,
And gives its atmosphere its color and its tone.

" Confess, old friend, your austere school
    Has left your fancy little chance ;
You square to reason's rigid rule
    The flowing outlines of romance.

With conscience keen from exercise,
And chronic fear of compromise,
You check the free play of your rhymes, to clap
A moral underneath, and spring it like a trap."

The sweet voice answered: " Better so
   Than bolder flights that know no check;
Better to use the bit, than throw
   The reins all loose on fancy's neck.
The liberal range of Art should be
The breadth of Christian liberty,
Restrained alone by challenge and alarm
Where its charmed footsteps tread the border land
    of harm.

" Beyond the poet's sweet dream lives
   The eternal epic of the man.
He wisest is who only gives,
   True to himself, the best he can;
Who, drifting in the winds of praise,
   The inward monitor obeys;
And, with the boldness that confesses fear,
Takes in the crowded sail, and lets his conscience
    steer.

" Thanks for the fitting word he speaks,
   Nor less for doubtful word unspoken;
For the false model that he breaks,
   As for the moulded grace unbroken;
For what is missed and what remains,
   For losses which are truest gains,
For reverence conscious of the Eternal eye,
And truth too fair to need the garnish of a lie."

Laughing, the Critic bowed. " I yield
  The point without another word ;
Who ever yet a case appealed
  Where beauty's judgment had been heard ?
And you, my good friend, owe to me
Your warmest thanks for such a plea,
As true withal as sweet.   For my offence
Of cavil, let her words be ample recompense."

Across the sea one lighthouse star,
  With crimson ray that came and went,
Revolving on its tower afar,
  Looked through the doorway of the tent.
While outward, over sand-slopes wet,
The lamp flashed down its yellow jet
On the long wash of waves, with red and green
Tangles of weltering weed through the white foam-
        wreaths seen.

" ' Sing while we may, — another day
  May bring enough of sorrow ; ' — thus
Our Traveller in his own sweet lay,
  His Crimean camp-song, hints to us," [6]
The lady said.   " So let it be ;
Sing us a song," exclaimed all three.
She smiled : " I can but marvel at your choice
To hear our poet's words through my poor bor-
        rowed voice."

        Her window opens to the bay,
        On glistening light or misty gray,
        And there at dawn and set of day
          In prayer she kneels .

" Dear Lord ! " she saith, " to many a home
From wind and wave the wanderers come ;
I only see the tossing foam
    Of stranger keels.

" Blown out and in by summer gales,
The stately ships, with crowded sails,
And sailors leaning o'er their rails,
    Before me glide ;
They come, they go, but nevermore,
Spice-laden from the Indian shore,
I see his swift-winged Isidore
    The waves divide.

" O Thou ! with whom the night is day
And one the near and far away,
Look out on yon gray waste, and say
    Where lingers he.
Alive, perchance, on some lone beach
Or thirsty isle beyond the reach
Of man, he hears the mocking speech
    Of wind and sea.

" O dread and cruel deep, reveal
The secret which thy waves conceal,
And, ye wild sea-birds, hither wheel
    And tell your tale.
Let winds that tossed his raven hair
A message from my lost one bear, —
Some thought of me, a last fond prayer
    Or dying wail !

" Come, with your dreariest truth shut out
The fears that haunt me round about ;

O God! I cannot bear this doubt
    That stifles breath.
The worst is better than the dread;
Give me but leave to mourn my dead
Asleep in trust and hope, instead
    Of life in death!"

It might have been the evening breeze
That whispered in the garden trees,
It might have been the sound of seas
    That rose and fell;
But, with her heart, if not her ear,
The old loved voice she seemed to hear:
" I wait to meet thee : be of cheer,
    For all is well!"

1865.

The sweet voice into silence went,
    A silence which was almost pain
As through it rolled the long lament,
    The cadence of the mournful main.
Glancing his written pages o'er,
    The Reader tried his part once more;
Leaving the land of hackmatack and pine
For Tuscan valleys glad with olive and with vine.

THE BROTHER OF MERCY.

PIERO LUCA, known of all the town
As the gray porter by the Pitti wall
    Where the noon shadows of the gardens fall,
Sick and in dolor, waited to lay down

His last sad burden, and beside his mat
The barefoot monk of La Certosa sat.

Unseen, in square and blossoming garden drifted,
Soft sunset lights through green Val d'Arno
    sifted ;
Unheard, below the living shuttles shifted
Backward and forth, and wove, in love or strife,
In mirth or pain, the mottled web of life:
But when at last came upward from the street
Tinkle of bell and tread of measured feet,
The sick man started, strove to rise in vain,
Sinking back heavily with a moan of pain.
And the monk said, " 'T is but the Brotherhood
Of Mercy going on some errand good :
Their black masks by the palace-wall I see."
Piero answered faintly, " Woe is me !
This day for the first time in forty years
In vain the bell hath sounded in my ears,
Calling me with my brethren of the mask,
Beggar and prince alike, to some new task
Of love or pity, — haply from the street
To bear a wretch plague-stricken, or, with feet
Hushed to the quickened ear and feverish brain,
To tread the crowded lazaretto's floors,
Down the long twilight of the corridors,
Midst tossing arms and faces full of pain.
I loved the work : it was its own reward.
I never counted on it to offset
My sins, which are many, or make less my debt
To the free grace and mercy of our Lord ;
But somehow, father, it has come to be
In these long years so much a part of me,

I should not know myself, if lacking it,
But with the work the worker too would die,
And in my place some other self would sit
Joyful or sad, — what matters, if not I ?
And now all 's over.   Woe is me ! " — " My son,"
The monk said soothingly, " thy work is done ;
And no more as a servant, but the guest
Of God thou enterest thy eternal rest.
No toil, no tears, no sorrow for the lost,
Shall mar thy perfect bliss.   Thou shalt sit
        down
Clad in white robes, and wear a golden crown
Forever and forever." — Piero tossed
On his sick-pillow : " Miserable me !
I am too poor for such grand company ;
The crown would be too heavy for this gray
Old head ; and God forgive me if I say
It would be hard to sit there night and day,
Like an image in the Tribune, doing naught
With these hard hands, that all my life have
        wrought,
Not for bread only, but for pity's sake.
I 'm dull at prayers : I could not keep awake,
Counting my beads.   Mine 's but a crazy head,
Scarce worth the saving, if all else be dead.
And if one goes to heaven without a heart,
God knows he leaves behind his better part.
I love my fellow-men : the worst I know
I would do good to.   Will death change me so
That I shall sit among the lazy saints,
Turning a deaf ear to the sore complaints
Of souls that suffer ?   Why, I never yet
Left a poor dog in the *strada* hard beset,

Or ass o'erladen!   Must I rate man less
Than dog or ass, in holy selfishness?
Methinks (Lord, pardon, if the thought be sin!)
The world of pain were better, if therein
One's heart might still be human, and desires
Of natural pity drop upon its fires
Some cooling tears."

     Thereat the pale monk crossed
His brow, and, muttering, "Madman! thou art
  lost!"
Took up his pyx and fled; and, left alone,
The sick man closed his eyes with a great groan
That sank into a prayer, "Thy will be done!"

 Then was he made aware, by soul or ear,
Of somewhat pure and holy bending o'er him,
And of a voice like that of her who bore him,
Tender and most compassionate: "Never fear!
For heaven is love, as God himself is love;
Thy work below shall be thy work above."
And when he looked, lo! in the stern monk's
  place
He saw the shining of an angel's face!
 1864.

————————

 The Traveller broke the pause. "I've seen
  The Brothers down the long street steal,
 Black, silent, masked, the crowd between,
  And felt to doff my hat and kneel
 With heart, if not with knee, in prayer,
 For blessings on their pious care."

The Reader wiped his glasses: " Friends of
    mine,
We'll try our home-brewed next, instead of foreign
    wine."

THE CHANGELING.

FOR the fairest maid in Hampton
    They needed not to search,
Who saw young Anna Favor
    Come walking into church, —

Or bringing from the meadows,
    At set of harvest-day,
The frolic of the blackbirds,
    The sweetness of the hay.

Now the weariest of all mothers,
    The saddest two-years bride,
She scowls in the face of her husband,
    And spurns her child aside.

" Rake out the red coals, goodman, —
    For there the child shall lie,
Till the black witch comes to fetch her
    And both up chimney fly.

" It's never my own little daughter,
    It's never my own," she said ;
" The witches have stolen my Anna,
    And left me an imp instead.

" Oh, fair and sweet was my baby,
    Blue eyes, and hair of gold ;
But this is ugly and wrinkled,
    Cross, and cunning, and old.

" I hate the touch of her fingers,
    I hate the feel of her skin ;
It 's not the milk from my bosom,
    But my blood, that she sucks in.

" My face grows sharp with the torment ;
    Look ! my arms are skin and bone !
Rake open the red coals, goodman,
    And the witch shall have her own.

" She 'll come when she hears it crying,
    In the shape of an owl or bat,
And she 'll bring us our darling Anna
    In place of her screeching brat."

Then the goodman, Ezra Dalton,
    Laid his hand upon her head :
" Thy sorrow is great, O woman !
    I sorrow with thee," he said.

" The paths to trouble are many,
    And never but one sure way
Leads out to the light beyond it :
    My poor wife, let us pray."

Then he said to the great All-Father,
    " Thy daughter is weak and blind ;
Let her sight come back, and clothe her
    Once more in her right mind.

" Lead her out of this evil shadow,
  Out of these fancies wild ;
Let the holy love of the mother
  Turn again to her child.

" Make her lips like the lips of Mary
  Kissing her blessed Son ;
Let her hands, like the hands of Jesus,
  Rest on her little one.

" Comfort the soul of thy handmaid,
  Open her prison-door,
And thine shall be all the glory
  And praise forevermore."

Then into the face of its mother
  The baby looked up and smiled ;
And the cloud of her soul was lifted,
  And she knew her little child.

A beam of the slant west sunshine
  Made the wan face almost fair,
Lit the blue eyes' patient wonder,
  And the rings of pale gold hair.

She kissed it on lip and forehead,
  She kissed it on cheek and chin,
And she bared her snow-white bosom
  To the lips so pale and thin.

Oh, fair on her bridal morning
  Was the maid who blushed and smiled,
But fairer to Ezra Dalton
  Looked the mother of his child.

With more than a lover's fondness
  He stooped to her worn young face.
And the nursing child and the mother
  He folded in one embrace.

" Blessed be God ! " he murmured.
  " Blessed be God ! " she said ;
" For I see, who once was blinded, —
  I live, who once was dead.

" Now mount and ride, my goodman,
  As thou lovest thy own soul !
Woe 's me, if my wicked fancies
  Be the death of Goody Cole ! "

His horse he saddled and bridled,
  And into the night rode he,
Now through the great black woodland,
  Now by the white-beached sea.

He rode through the silent clearings,
  He came to the ferry wide,
And thrice he called to the boatman
  Asleep on the other side.

He set his horse to the river,
  He swam to Newbury town,
And he called up Justice Sewall
  In his nightcap and his gown.

And the grave and worshipful justice
  (Upon whose soul be peace !)
Set his name to the jailer's warrant
  For Goodwife Cole's release.

Then through the night the hoof-beats
   Went sounding like a flail ;
And Goody Cole at cockcrow
   Came forth from Ipswich jail.

1865.

———————

" Here is a rhyme : I hardly dare
   To venture on its theme worn out ;
What seems so sweet by Doon and Ayr
   Sounds simply silly hereabout ;
And pipes by lips Arcadian blown
Are only tin horns at our own.
Yet still the muse of pastoral walks with us,
While Hosea Biglow sings, our new Theocritus."

THE MAIDS OF ATTITASH.

Attitash, an Indian word signifying " huckleberry," is the
name of a large and beautiful lake in the northern part of Amesbury.

In sky and wave the white clouds swam,
And the blue hills of Nottingham
   Through gaps of leafy green
   Across the lake were seen,

When, in the shadow of the ash
That dreams its dream in Attitash,
   In the warm summer weather,
   Two maidens sat together.

They sat and watched in idle mood
The gleam and shade of lake and wood;
   The beach the keen light smote,
   The white sail of a boat;

Swan flocks of lilies shoreward lying,
In sweetness, not in music, dying;
   Hardhack, and virgin's-bower,
   And white-spiked clethra-flower.

With careless ears they heard the plash
And breezy wash of Attitash,
   The wood-bird's plaintive cry,
   The locust's sharp reply.

And teased the while, with playful hand,
The shaggy dog of Newfoundland,
   Whose uncouth frolic spilled
   Their baskets berry-filled.

Then one, the beauty of whose eyes
Was evermore a great surprise,
   Tossed back her queenly head,
   And, lightly laughing, said:

"No bridegroom's hand be mine to hold
That is not lined with yellow gold;
   I tread no cottage-floor;
   I own no lover poor.

"My love must come on silken wings,
With bridal lights of diamond rings,
   Not foul with kitchen smirch,
   With tallow-dip for torch."

The other, on whose modest head
Was lesser dower of beauty shed,
  With look for home-hearths meet,
  And voice exceeding sweet,

Answered, " We will not rivals be ;
Take thou the gold, leave love to me ;
  Mine be the cottage small,
  And thine the rich man's hall.

" I know, indeed, that wealth is good ;
But lowly roof and simple food,
  With love that hath no doubt,
  Are more than gold without."

Hard by a farmer hale and young
His cradle in the rye-field swung,
  Tracking the yellow plain
  With windrows of ripe grain.

And still, whene'er he paused to whet
His scythe, the sidelong glance he met
  Of large dark eyes, where strove
  False pride and secret love.

Be strong, young mower of the grain ;
That love shall overmatch disdain,
  Its instincts soon or late
  The heart shall vindicate.

In blouse of gray, with fishing-rod,
Half screened by leaves, a stranger trod
  The margin of the pond,
  Watching the group beyond.

The supreme hours unnoted come ;
Unfelt the turning tides of doom ;
 And so the maids laughed on,
 Nor dreamed what Fate had done, —

Nor knew the step was Destiny's
That rustled in the birchen trees,
 As, with their lives forecast,
 Fisher and mower passed.

Erelong by lake and rivulet side
The summer roses paled and died,
 And Autumn's fingers shed
 The maple's leaves of red.

Through the long gold-hazed afternoon,
Alone, but for the diving loon,
 The partridge in the brake,
 The black duck on the lake,

Beneath the shadow of the ash
Sat man and maid by Attitash ;
 And earth and air made room
 For human hearts to bloom.

Soft spread the carpets of the sod,
And scarlet-oak and golden-rod
 With blushes and with smiles
 Lit up the forest aisles.

The mellow light the lake aslant,
The pebbled margin's ripple-chant
 Attempered and low-toned,
 The tender mystery owned.

And through the dream the lovers dreamed
Sweet sounds stole in and soft lights streamed;
   The sunshine seemed to bless,
   The air was a caress.

Not she who lightly laughed is there,
With scornful toss of midnight hair,
   Her dark, disdainful eyes,
   And proud lip worldly-wise.

Her haughty vow is still unsaid,
But all she dreamed and coveted
   Wears, half to her surprise,
   The youthful farmer's guise!

With more than all her old-time pride
She walks the rye-field at his side,
   Careless of cot or hall,
   Since love transfigures all.

Rich beyond dreams, the vantage-ground
Of life is gained; her hands have found
   The talisman of old
   That changes all to gold.

While she who could for love dispense
With all its glittering accidents,
   And trust her heart alone,
   Finds love and gold her own.

What wealth can buy or art can build
Awaits her; but her cup is filled

 Even now unto the brim;
 Her world is love and him!

1866.

The while he heard, the Book-man drew
 A length of make-believing face,
With smothered mischief laughing through:
 " Why, you shall sit in Ramsay's place,
And, with his Gentle Shepherd, keep
On Yankee hills immortal sheep,
While love-lorn swains and maids the seas beyond
Hold dreamy tryst around your huckleberry-pond."

The Traveller laughed: " Sir Galahad
 Singing of love the Trouvere's lay!
How should he know the blindfold lad
 From one of Vulcan's forge-boys?" — " Nay,
He better sees who stands outside
Than they who in procession ride,"
The Reader answered: " selectmen and squire
Miss, while they make, the show that wayside folks
  admire.

" Here is a wild tale of the North,
 Our travelled friend will own as one
Fit for a Norland Christmas hearth
 And lips of Christian Andersen.
They tell it in the valleys green
Of the fair island he has seen,
Low lying off the pleasant Swedish shore,
Washed by the Baltic Sea, and watched by Elsi-
  nore."

KALLUNDBORG CHURCH.

" Tie stille, barn min !
Imorgen kommer Fin,
Fa'er din,
Og gi'er dig Esbern Snares öine og hjerte at lege med ! "
Zealand Rhyme.

" BUILD at Kallundborg by the sea
  A church as stately as church may be,
  And there shalt thou wed my daughter fair,"
Said the Lord of Nesvek to Esbern Snare.

And the Baron laughed.   But Esbern said,
" Though I lose my soul, I will Helva wed ! "
  And off he strode, in his pride of will,
  To the Troll who dwelt in Ulshoi hill.

" Build, O Troll, a church for me
  At Kallundborg by the mighty sea ;
  Build it stately, and build it fair,
  Build it quickly," said Esbern Snare.

But the sly Dwarf said, " No work is wrought
By Trolls of the Hills, O man, for naught.
  What wilt thou give for thy church so fair ? "
" Set thy own price," quoth Esbern Snare.

" When Kallundborg church is builded well,
  Thou must the name of its builder tell,
  Or thy heart and thy eyes must be my boon."
" Build," said Esbern, " and build it soon."

By night and by day the Troll wrought on ;
He hewed the timbers, he piled the stone ;

But day by day, as the walls rose fair,
Darker and sadder grew Esbern Snare.

He listened by night, he watched by day,
He sought and thought, but he dared not pray;
In vain he called on the Elle-maids shy,
And the Neck and the Nis gave no reply.

Of his evil bargain far and wide
A rumor ran through the country-side;
And Helva of Nesvek, young and fair,
Prayed for the soul of Esbern Snare.

And now the church was wellnigh done;
One pillar it lacked, and one alone;
And the grim Troll muttered, " Fool thou art!
To-morrow gives me thy eyes and heart! "

By Kallundborg in black despair,
Through wood and meadow, walked Esbern
        Snare,
Till, worn and weary, the strong man sank
Under the birches on Ulshoi bank.

At his last day's work he heard the Troll
Hammer and delve in the quarry's hole;
Before him the church stood large and fair:
" I have builded my tomb," said Esbern Snare.

And he closed his eyes the sight to hide,
When he heard a light step at his side:
" O Esbern Snare! " a sweet voice said,
" Would I might die now in thy stead! "

With a grasp by love and by fear made strong,
He held her fast, and he held her long ;
With the beating heart of a bird afeard,
She hid her face in his flame-red beard.

" O love ! " he cried, " let me look to-day
In thine eyes ere mine are plucked away ;
Let me hold thee close, let me feel thy heart
Ere mine by the Troll is torn apart !

" I sinned, O Helva, for love of thee !
Pray that the Lord Christ pardon me ! "
But fast as she prayed, and faster still,
Hammered the Troll in Ulshoi hill.

He knew, as he wrought, that a loving heart
Was somehow baffling his evil art ;
For more than spell of Elf or Troll
Is a maiden's prayer for her lover's soul.

And Esbern listened, and caught the sound
Of a Troll-wife singing underground :
" To-morrow comes Fine, father thine :
Lie still and hush thee, baby mine !

" Lie still, my darling ! next sunrise
Thou 'lt play with Esbern Snare's heart and
eyes ! "
" Ho ! ho ! " quoth Esbern, " is that your game ?
Thanks to the Troll-wife, I know his name ! "

The Troll he heard him, and hurried on
To Kallundborg church with the lacking stone.

" Too late, Gaffer Fine ! " cried Esbern Snare ;
And Troll and pillar vanished in air !

That night the harvesters heard the sound
Of a woman sobbing underground,
And the voice of the Hill-Troll loud with blame
Of the careless singer who told his name.

Of the Troll of the Church they sing the rune
By the Northern Sea in the harvest moon ;
And the fishers of Zealand hear him still
Scolding his wife in Ulshoi hill.

And seaward over its groves of birch
Still looks the tower of Kallundborg church,
Where, first at its altar, a wedded pair,
Stood Helva of Nesvek and Esbern Snare !
        1865.

" What," asked the Traveller, " would our sires,
        The old Norse story-tellers, say
Of sun-graved pictures, ocean wires,
        And smoking steamboats of to-day ?
And this, O lady, by your leave,
Recalls your song of yester eve :
Pray, let us have that Cable-hymn once more."
" Hear, hear ! " the Book-man cried, " the lady
        has the floor.

" These noisy waves below perhaps
        To such a strain will lend their ear,
With softer voice and lighter lapse
        Come stealing up the sands to hear,

And what they once refused to do
For old King Knut accord to you.
Nay, even the fishes shall your listeners be,
As once, the legend runs, they heard St. Anthony."

THE CABLE HYMN.

O LONELY bay of Trinity,
    O dreary shores, give ear!
Lean down unto the white-lipped sea
    The voice of God to hear!

From world to world His couriers fly,
    Thought-winged and shod with fire;
The angel of His stormy sky
    Rides down the sunken wire.

What saith the herald of the Lord?
    " The world's long strife is done;
Close wedded by that mystic cord,
    Its continents are one.

" And one in heart, as one in blood,
    Shall all her peoples be;
The hands of human brotherhood
    Are clasped beneath the sea.

" Through Orient seas, o'er Afric's plain
    And Asian mountains borne,
The vigor of the Northern brain
    Shall nerve the world outworn.

" From clime to clime, from shore to shore,
    Shall thrill the magic thread;

The new Prometheus steals once more
    The fire that wakes the dead."

Throb on, strong pulse of thunder! beat
    From answering beach to beach;
Fuse nations in thy kindly heat,
    And melt the chains of each!

Wild terror of the sky above,
    Glide tamed and dumb below!
Bear gently, Ocean's carrier-dove,
    Thy errands to and fro.

Weave on, swift shuttle of the Lord,
    Beneath the deep so far,
The bridal robe of earth's accord,
    The funeral shroud of war!

For lo! the fall of Ocean's wall
    Space mocked and time outrun;
And round the world the thought of all
    Is as the thought of one!

The poles unite, the zones agree,
    The tongues of striving cease;
As on the Sea of Galilee
    The Christ is whispering, Peace!

1858.

" Glad prophecy! to this at last,"
    The Reader said, " shall all things come.
Forgotten be the bugle's blast,
    And battle-music of the drum.

A little while the world may run
Its old mad way, with needle-gun
And iron-clad, but truth, at last, shall reign :
The cradle-song of Christ was never sung in vain!"

Shifting his scattered papers, " Here,"
    He said, as died the faint applause,
" Is something that I found last year
    Down on the island known as Orr's.
I had it from a fair-haired girl
Who, oddly, bore the name of Pearl,
(As if by some droll freak of circumstance,)
Classic, or wellnigh so, in Harriet Stowe's ro-
    mance."

THE DEAD SHIP OF HARPSWELL.

WHAT flecks the outer gray beyond
    The sundown's golden trail ?
The white flash of a sea-bird's wing,
    Or gleam of slanting sail ?
Let young eyes watch from Neck and Point,
    And sea-worn elders pray, —
The ghost of what was once a ship
    Is sailing up the bay !

From gray sea-fog, from icy drift,
    From peril and from pain,
The home-bound fisher greets thy lights,
    O hundred-harbored Maine !
But many a keel shall seaward turn,
    And many a sail outstand,

When, tall and white, the Dead Ship looms
    Against the dusk of land.

She rounds the headland's bristling pines;
    She threads the isle-set bay;
No spur of breeze can speed her on,
    Nor ebb of tide delay.
Old men still walk the Isle of Orr
    Who tell her date and name,
Old shipwrights sit in Freeport yards
    Who hewed her oaken frame.

What weary doom of baffled quest,
    Thou sad sea-ghost, is thine?
What makes thee in the haunts of home
    A wonder and a sign?
No foot is on thy silent deck,
    Upon thy helm no hand;
No ripple hath the soundless wind
    That smites thee from the land!

For never comes the ship to port,
    Howe'er the breeze may be;
Just when she nears the waiting shore
    She drifts again to sea.
No tack of sail, nor turn of helm,
    Nor sheer of veering side;
Stern-fore she drives to sea and night,
    Against the wind and tide.

In vain o'er Harpswell Neck the star
    Of evening guides her in;
In vain for her the lamps are lit
    Within thy tower, Seguin!

In vain the harbor-boat shall hail,
　　In vain the pilot call ;
No hand shall reef her spectral sail,
　　Or let her anchor fall.

Shake, brown old wives, with dreary joy,
　　Your gray-head hints of ill ;
And, over sick-beds whispering low,
　　Your prophecies fulfil.
Some home amid yon birchen trees
　　Shall drape its door with woe ;
And slowly where the Dead Ship sails,
　　The burial boat shall row !

From Wolf Neck and from Flying Point,
　　From island and from main,
From sheltered cove and tided creek,
　　Shall glide the funeral train.
The dead-boat with the bearers four,
　　The mourners at her stern, —
And one shall go the silent way
　　Who shall no more return !

And men shall sigh, and women weep,
　　Whose dear ones pale and pine,
And sadly over sunset seas
　　Await the ghostly sign.
They know not that its sails are filled
　　By pity's tender breath,
Nor see the Angel at the helm
　　Who steers the Ship of Death !

1866.

———————

" Chill as a down-east breeze should be,"
 The Book-man said.   " A ghostly touch
The legend has.   I 'm glad to see
 Your flying Yankee beat the Dutch."
" Well, here is something of the sort
 Which one midsummer day I caught
In Narragansett Bay, for lack of fish."
" We wait," the Traveller said ; " serve hot or cold
  your dish."

THE PALATINE.

 Block Island in Long Island Sound, called by the Indians Manisees, the isle of the little god, was the scene of a tragic incident a
hundred years or more ago, when *The Palatine*, an emigrant ship
bound for Philadelphia, driven off its course, came upon the coast
at this point. A mutiny on board, followed by an inhuman de-
sertion on the part of the crew, had brought the unhappy passen-
gers to the verge of starvation and madness. Tradition says
that wreckers on shore, after rescuing all but one of the sur-
vivors, set fire to the vessel, which was driven out to sea before
a gale which had sprung up. Every twelvemonth, according to
the same tradition, the spectacle of a ship on fire is visible to the
inhabitants of the island.

  LEAGUES north, as fly the gull and auk,
  Point Judith watches with eye of hawk ;
  Leagues south, thy beacon flames, Montauk !

  Lonely and wind-shorn, wood-forsaken,
  With never a tree for Spring to waken,
  For tryst of lovers or farewells taken,

  Circled by waters that never freeze,
  Beaten by billow and swept by breeze,
  Lieth the island of Manisees,

Set at the mouth of the Sound to hold
The coast lights up on its turret old,
Yellow with moss and sea-fog mould.

Dreary the land when gust and sleet
At its doors and windows howl and beat,
And Winter laughs at its fires of peat!

But in summer time, when pool and pond,
Held in the laps of valleys fond,
Are blue as the glimpses of sea beyond;

When the hills are sweet with the brier-rose,
And, hid in the warm, soft dells, unclose
Flowers the mainland rarely knows;

When boats to their morning fishing go,
And, held to the wind and slanting low,
Whitening and darkening the small sails show, —

Then is that lonely island fair;
And the pale health-seeker findeth there
The wine of life in its pleasant air.

No greener valleys the sun invite,
On smoother beaches no sea-birds light,
No blue waves shatter to foam more white!

There, circling ever their narrow range,
Quaint tradition and legend strange
Live on unchallenged, and know no change.

Old wives spinning their webs of tow,
Or rocking weirdly to and fro
In and out of the peat's dull glow,

And old men mending their nets of twine,
Talk together of dream and sign,
Talk of the lost ship Palatine, —

The ship that, a hundred years before,
Freighted deep with its goodly store,
In the gales of the equinox went ashore.

The eager islanders one by one
Counted the shots of her signal gun,
And heard the crash when she drove right on!

Into the teeth of death she sped:
(May God forgive the hands that fed
The false lights over the rocky Head!)

O men and brothers! what sights were there!
White upturned faces, hands stretched in prayer!
Where waves had pity, could ye not spare?

Down swooped the wreckers, like birds of prey
Tearing the heart of the ship away,
And the dead had never a word to say.

And then, with ghastly shimmer and shine
Over the rocks and the seething brine,
They burned the wreck of the Palatine.

In their cruel hearts, as they homeward sped,
" The sea and the rocks are dumb," they said :
" There 'll be no reckoning with the dead."

But the year went round, and when once more
Along their foam-white curves of shore
They heard the line-storm rave and roar,

Behold! again, with shimmer and shine,
Over the rocks and the seething brine,
The flaming wreck of the Palatine!

So, haply in fitter words than these,
Mending their nets on their patient knees
They tell the legend of Manisees.

Nor looks nor tones a doubt betray;
" It is known to us all," they quietly say ;
" We too have seen it in our day."

Is there, then, no death for a word once spoken ?
Was never a deed but left its token
Written on tables never broken ?

Do the elements subtle reflections give ?
Do pictures of all the ages live
On Nature's infinite negative,

Which, half in sport, in malice half,
She shows at times, with shudder or laugh,
Phantom and shadow in photograph ?

For still, on many a moonless night,
From Kingston Head and from Montauk light
The spectre kindles and burns in sight.

Now low and dim, now clear and higher,
Leaps up the terrible Ghost of Fire,
Then, slowly sinking, the flames expire.

And the wise Sound skippers, though skies be
      fine,
Reef their sails when they see the sign
Of the blazing wreck of the Palatine !
      1867.

————

" A fitter tale to scream than sing,"
    The Book-man said.   " Well, fancy, then,"
The Reader answered, " on the wing
    The sea-birds shriek it, not for men,
But in the ear of wave and breeze ! "
The Traveller mused : " Your Manisees
Is fairy-land : off Narragansett shore
Who ever saw the isle or heard its name before ?

" 'T is some strange land of Flyaway,
    Whose dreamy shore the ship beguiles,
St. Brandan's in its sea-mist gray,
    Or sunset loom of Fortunate Isles ! "
" No ghost, but solid turf and rock
Is the good island known as Block,"
The Reader said.   " For beauty and for ease
I chose its Indian name, soft-flowing Manisees !

"But let it pass ; here is a bit
  Of unrhymed story, with a hint
Of the old preaching mood in it,
  The sort of sidelong moral squint
Our friend objects to, which has grown,
  I fear, a habit of my own.
'T was written when the Asian plague drew near,
And the land held its breath and paled with sud-
      den fear."

ABRAHAM DAVENPORT.

The famous Dark Day of New England, May 19, 1780, was a
physical puzzle for many years to our ancestors, but its occurrence
brought something more than philosophical speculation into the
minds of those who passed through it. The incident of Colonel
Abraham Davenport's sturdy protest is a matter of history.

IN the old days (a custom laid aside
With breeches and cocked hats) the people sent
Their wisest men to make the public laws.
And so, from a brown homestead, where the Sound
Drinks the small tribute of the Mianas,
Waved over by the woods of Rippowams,
And hallowed by pure lives and tranquil deaths,
Stamford sent up to the councils of the State
Wisdom and grace in Abraham Davenport.

  'T was on a May-day of the far old year
Seventeen hundred eighty, that there fell
Over the bloom and sweet life of the Spring,
Over the fresh earth and the heaven of noon,
A horror of great darkness, like the night
In day of which the Norland sagas tell, —

The Twilight of the Gods.   The low-hung sky
Was black with ominous clouds, save where its rim
Was fringed with a dull glow, like that which
    climbs
The crater's sides from the red hell below.
Birds ceased to sing, and all the barn-yard fowls
Roosted ; the cattle at the pasture bars
Lowed, and looked homeward ; bats on leathern
    wings
Flitted abroad ; the sounds of labor died ;
Men prayed, and women wept ; all ears grew sharp
To hear the doom-blast of the trumpet shatter
The black sky, that the dreadful face of Christ
Might look from the rent clouds, not as he looked
A loving guest at Bethany, but stern
As Justice and inexorable Law.

Meanwhile in the old State House, dim as ghosts,
Sat the lawgivers of Connecticut,
Trembling beneath their legislative robes.
"It is the Lord's Great Day !   Let us adjourn,"
Some said ; and then, as if with one accord,
All eyes were turned to Abraham Davenport.
He rose, slow cleaving with his steady voice
The intolerable hush.   " This well may be
The Day of Judgment which the world awaits ;
But be it so or not, I only know
My present duty, and my Lord's command
To occupy till He come.   So at the post
Where He hath set me in His providence,
I choose, for one, to meet Him face to face, —
No faithless servant frightened from my task,
But ready when the Lord of the harvest calls ;

And therefore, with all reverence, I would say,
Let God do His work, we will see to ours.
Bring in the candles." And they brought them in.

Then by the flaring lights the Speaker read,
Albeit with husky voice and shaking hands,
An act to amend an act to regulate
The shad and alewive fisheries. Whereupon
Wisely and well spake Abraham Davenport,
Straight to the question, with no figures of speech
Save the ten Arab signs, yet not without
The shrewd dry humor natural to the man :
His awe-struck colleagues listening all the while,
Between the pauses of his argument,
To hear the thunder of the wrath of God
Break from the hollow trumpet of the cloud.

And there he stands in memory to this day,
Erect, self-poised, a rugged face, half seen
Against the background of unnatural dark,
A witness to the ages as they pass,
That simple duty hath no place for fear.
    1866.

————————

He ceased : just then the ocean seemed
    To lift a half-faced moon in sight;
And, shore-ward, o'er the waters gleamed,
    From crest to crest, a line of light,
Such as of old, with solemn awe,
    The fishers by Gennesaret saw,
When dry-shod o'er it walked the Son of God,
Tracking the waves with light where'er his sandals
        trod.

Silently for a space each eye
    Upon that sudden glory turned :
Cool from the land the breeze blew by,
    The tent-ropes flapped, the long beach churned
Its waves to foam ; on either hand
Stretched, far as sight, the hills of sand ;
With bays of marsh, and capes of bush and tree,
The wood's black shore-line loomed beyond the
        meadowy sea.

The lady rose to leave.   " One song,
    Or hymn," they urged, " before we part."
And she, with lips to which belong
    Sweet intuitions of all art,
Gave to the winds of night a strain
Which they who heard would hear again ;
And to her voice the solemn ocean lent,
Touching its harp of sand, a deep accompaniment.

THE WORSHIP OF NATURE.

THE harp at Nature's advent strung
    Has never ceased to play ;
The song the stars of morning sung
    Has never died away.

And prayer is made, and praise is given,
    By all things near and far ;
The ocean looketh up to heaven,
    And mirrors every star.

Its waves are kneeling on the strand,
    As kneels the human knee,

Their white locks bowing to the sand,
  The priesthood of the sea!

They pour their glittering treasures forth,
  Their gifts of pearl they bring,
And all the listening hills of earth
  Take up the song they sing.

The green earth sends her incense up
  From many a mountain shrine;
From folded leaf and dewy cup
  She pours her sacred wine.

The mists above the morning rills
  Rise white as wings of prayer;
The altar-curtains of the hills
  Are sunset's purple air.

The winds with hymns of praise are loud,
  Or low with sobs of pain, —
The thunder-organ of the cloud,
  The dropping tears of rain.

With drooping head and branches crossed
  The twilight forest grieves,
Or speaks with tongues of Pentecost
  From all its sunlit leaves.

The blue sky is the temple's arch,
  Its transept earth and air,
The music of its starry march
  The chorus of a prayer.

So Nature keeps the reverent frame
    With which her years began,
And all her signs and voices shame
    The prayerless heart of man.

The singer ceased. The moon's white rays
    Fell on the rapt, still face of her.
" *Allah il Allah !* He hath praise
    From all things," said the Traveller.
" Oft from the desert's silent nights,
And mountain hymns of sunset lights,
My heart has felt rebuke, as in his tent
The Moslem's prayer has shamed my Christian
        knee unbent."

He paused, and lo ! far, faint, and slow
    The bells in Newbury's steeples tolled
The twelve dead hours ; the lamp burned low ;
    The singer sought her canvas fold.
One sadly said, " At break of day
We strike our tent and go our way."
But one made answer cheerily, " Never fear,
We 'll pitch this tent of ours in type another
        year."

AT SUNDOWN

To E. C. S.

Poet and friend of poets, if thy glass
Detects no flower in winter's tuft of grass,
Let this slight token of the debt I owe
 Outlive for thee December's frozen day,
And, like the arbutus budding under snow,
 Take bloom and fragrance from some morn of May
When he who gives it shall have gone the way
Where faith shall see and reverent trust shall know.

THE CHRISTMAS OF 1888.

Low in the east, against a white, cold dawn,
The black-lined silhouette of the woods was drawn,
  And on a wintry waste
Of frosted streams and hillsides bare and brown,
Through thin cloud-films a pallid ghost looked
  down,
  The waning moon half-faced!

In that pale sky and sere, snow-waiting earth,
What sign was there of the immortal birth?
  What herald of the One?
Lo! swift as thought the heavenly radiance came,
A rose-red splendor swept the sky like flame,
  Up rolled the round, bright sun!

And all was changed.   From a transfigured world
The moon's ghost fled, the smoke of home-hearths
      curled
      Up the still air unblown.
In Orient warmth and brightness, did that morn
O'er Nain and Nazareth, when the Christ was
      born,
      Break fairer than our own?

The morning's promise noon and eve fulfilled
In warm, soft sky and landscape hazy-hilled
      And sunset fair as they;
A sweet reminder of His holiest time,
A summer-miracle in our winter clime,
      God gave a perfect day.

The near was blended with the old and far,
And Bethlehem's hillside and the Magi's star
      Seemed here, as there and then, —
Our homestead pine-tree was the Syrian palm,
Our heart's desire the angels' midnight psalm,
      Peace, and good-will to men!

THE VOW OF WASHINGTON.

Read in New York, April 30, 1889, at the Centennial Celebration of the Inauguration of George Washington as the first President of the United States.

THE sword was sheathed: in April's sun
   Lay green the fields by Freedom won;
And severed sections, weary of debates,
Joined hands at last and were United States.

O City sitting by the Sea!
How proud the day that dawned on thee,
When the new era, long desired, began,
And, in its need, the hour had found the man!

One thought the cannon salvos spoke,
The resonant bell-tower's vibrant stroke,
The voiceful streets, the plaudit-echoing halls,
And prayer and hymn borne heavenward from St.
      Paul's!

How felt the land in every part
The strong throb of a nation's heart,
As its great leader gave, with reverent awe,
His pledge to Union, Liberty, and Law!

That pledge the heavens above him heard,
That vow the sleep of centuries stirred;
In world-wide wonder listening peoples bent
Their gaze on Freedom's great experiment.

Could it succeed?   Of honor sold
And hopes deceived all history told.
Above the wrecks that strewed the mournful past,
Was the long dream of ages true at last?

Thank God! the people's choice was just,
The one man equal to his trust,
Wise beyond lore, and without weakness good,
Calm in the strength of flawless rectitude!

His rule of justice, order, peace,
Made possible the world's release;

Taught prince and serf that power is but a trust,
And rule, alone, which serves the ruled, is just;

That Freedom generous is, but strong
  In hate of fraud and selfish wrong,
Pretence that turns her holy truths to lies,
And lawless license masking in her guise.

Land of his love! with one glad voice
  Let thy great sisterhood rejoice ;
A century's suns o'er thee have risen and set,
And, God be praised, we are one nation yet.

And still we trust the years to be
  Shall prove his hope was destiny,
Leaving our flag, with all its added stars,
Unrent by faction and unstained by wars.

Lo! where with patient toil he nursed
  And trained the new-set plant at first,
The widening branches of a stately tree
Stretch from the sunrise to the sunset sea.

And in its broad and sheltering shade,
  Sitting with none to make afraid,
Were we now silent, through each mighty limb,
The winds of heaven would sing the praise of
        him.

Our first and best ! — his ashes lie
  Beneath his own Virginian sky.
Forgive, forget, O true and just and brave,
The storm that swept above thy sacred grave !

For, ever in the awful strife
And dark hours of the nation's life,
Through the fierce tumult pierced his warning
       word,
Their father's voice his erring children heard!

The change for which he prayed and sought
In that sharp agony was wrought;
No partial interest draws its alien line
'Twixt North and South, the cypress and the pine!

One people now, all doubt beyond,
His name shall be our Union-bond;
We lift our hands to Heaven, and here and now.
Take on our lips the old Centennial vow.

For rule and trust must needs be ours;
Chooser and chosen both are powers
Equal in service as in rights; the claim
Of Duty rests on each and all the same.

Then let the sovereign millions, where
Our banner floats in sun and air,
From the warm palm-lands to Alaska's cold,
Repeat with us the pledge a century old!

THE CAPTAIN'S WELL.

The story of the shipwreck of Captain Valentine Bagley, on
the coast of Arabia, and his sufferings in the desert, has been
familiar from my childhood. It has been partially told in the
singularly beautiful lines of my friend, Harriet Prescott Spofford,
on the occasion of a public celebration at the Newburyport Library.

To the charm and felicity of her verse, as far as it goes, nothing can be added; but in the following ballad I have endeavored to give a fuller detail of the touching incident upon which it is founded.

FROM pain and peril, by land and main,
The shipwrecked sailor came back again;

And like one from the dead, the threshold cross'd
Of his wondering home, that had mourned him lost.

Where he sat once more with his kith and kin,
And welcomed his neighbors thronging in.

But when morning came he called for his spade.
"I must pay my debt to the Lord," he said.

"Why dig you here?" asked the passer-by;
"Is there gold or silver the road so nigh?"

"No, friend," he answered: "but under this sod
Is the blessed water, the wine of God."

"Water! the Powow is at your back,
And right before you the Merrimac,

"And look you up, or look you down,
There's a well-sweep at every door in town."

"True," he said, "we have wells of our own;
But this I dig for the Lord alone."

Said the other: "This soil is dry, you know.
I doubt if a spring can be found below;

" You had better consult, before you dig,
Some water-witch, with a hazel twig."

" No, wet or dry, I will dig it here,
Shallow or deep, if it takes a year.

" In the Arab desert, where shade is none,
The waterless land of sand and sun,

" Under the pitiless, brazen sky
My burning throat as the sand was dry;

" My crazed brain listened in fever dreams
For plash of buckets and ripple of streams;

" And opening my eyes to the blinding glare,
And my lips to the breath of the blistering air,

" Tortured alike by the heavens and earth,
I cursed, like Job, the day of my birth.

" Then something tender, and sad, and mild
As a mother's voice to her wandering child,

" Rebuked my frenzy; and bowing my head,
I prayed as I never before had prayed :

" *Pity me, God ! for I die of thirst;*
Take me out of this land accurst;

" *And if ever I reach my home again,*
Where earth has springs, and the sky has rain,

" *I will dig a well for the passers-by,*
And none shall suffer from thirst as I.

" I saw, as I prayed, my home once more,
The house, the barn, the elms by the door,

" The grass-lined road, that riverward wound,
The tall slate stones of the burying-ground,

" The belfry and steeple on meeting-house hill,
The brook with its dam, and gray grist mill,

" And I knew in that vision beyond the sea,
The very place where my well must be.

"God heard my prayer in that evil day;
He led my feet in their homeward way,

" From false mirage and dried-up well,
And the hot sand storms of a land of hell,

" Till I saw at last through the coast-hill's gap,
A city held in its stony lap,

" The mosques and the domes of scorched Muscat,
And my heart leaped up with joy thereat;

" For there was a ship at anchor lying,
A Christian flag at its mast-head flying,

" And sweetest of sounds to my homesick ear
Was my native tongue in the sailor's cheer.

" Now the Lord be thanked, I am back again,
Where earth has springs, and the skies have rain,

"And the well I promised by Oman's Sea,
I am digging for him in Amesbury."

His kindred wept, and his neighbors said:
" The poor old captain is out of his head."

But from morn to noon, and from noon to night,
He toiled at his task with main and might;

And when at last, from the loosened earth,
Under his spade the stream gushed forth,

And fast as he climbed to his deep well's brim,
The water he dug for followed him,

He shouted for joy: "I have kept my word,
And here is the well I promised the Lord!"

The long years came and the long years went,
And he sat by his roadside well content;

He watched the travellers, heat-oppressed,
Pause by the way to drink and rest,

And the sweltering horses dip, as they drank,
Their nostrils deep in the cool, sweet tank,

And grateful at heart, his memory went
Back to that waterless Orient,

And the blessed answer of prayer, which came
To the earth of iron and sky of flame.

And when a wayfarer weary and hot,
Kept to the mid road, pausing not

For the well's refreshing, he shook his head;
" He don't know the value of water," he said;

" Had he prayed for a drop, as I have done,
In the desert circle of sand and sun,

" He would drink and rest, and go home to tell
That God's best gift is the wayside well! "

AN OUTDOOR RECEPTION.

The substance of these lines, hastily pencilled several years ago,
I find among such of my unprinted scraps as have escaped the
waste-basket and the fire. In transcribing it I have made some
changes, additions, and omissions.

On these green banks, where falls too soon
The shade of Autumn's afternoon,
The south wind blowing soft and sweet,
The water gliding at my feet,
The distant northern range uplit
By the slant sunshine over it,
With changes of the mountain mist
From tender blush to amethyst,
The valley's stretch of shade and gleam
Fair as in Mirza's Bagdad dream,
With glad young faces smiling near

And merry voices in my ear,
I sit, methinks, as Hafiz might
In Iran's Garden of Delight.
For Persian roses blushing red,
Aster and gentian bloom instead ;
For Shiraz wine, this mountain air ;
For feast, the blueberries which I share
With one who proffers with stained hands
Her gleanings from yon pasture lands,
Wild fruit that art and culture spoil,
The harvest of an untilled soil ;
And with her one whose tender eyes
Reflect the change of April skies,
Midway 'twixt child and maiden yet,
Fresh as Spring's earliest violet ;
And one whose look and voice and ways
Make where she goes idyllic days ;
And one whose sweet, still countenance
Seems dreamful of a child's romance ;
And others, welcome as are these,
Like and unlike, varieties
Of pearls on nature's chaplet strung,
And all are fair, for all are young.
Gathered from seaside cities old,
From midland prairie, lake, and wold,
From the great wheat-fields, which might feed
The hunger of a world at need,
In healthful change of rest and play
Their school-vacations glide away.

No critics these : they only see
An old and kindly friend in me,
In whose amused, indulgent look

Their innocent mirth has no rebuke.
They scarce can know my rugged rhymes,
The harsher songs of evil times,
Nor graver themes in minor keys
Of life's and death's solemnities;
But haply, as they bear in mind
Some verse of lighter, happier kind, —
Hints of the boyhood of the man,
Youth viewed from life's meridian,
Half seriously and half in play
My pleasant interviewers pay
Their visit, with no fell intent
Of taking notes and punishment.

As yonder solitary pine
Is ringed below with flower and vine,
More favored than that lonely tree,
The bloom of girlhood circles me.
In such an atmosphere of youth
I half forget my age's truth;
The shadow of my life's long date
Runs backward on the dial-plate,
Until it seems a step might span
The gulf between the boy and man.

My young friends smile, as if some jay
On bleak December's leafless spray
Essayed to sing the songs of May.
Well, let them smile, and live to know,
When their brown locks are flecked with snow,
'T is tedious to be always sage
And pose the dignity of age,
While so much of our early lives

On memory's playground still survives,
And owns, as at the present hour,
The spell of youth's magnetic power.

But though I feel, with Solomon,
'T is pleasant to behold the sun,
I would not if I could repeat
A life which still is good and sweet;
I keep in age, as in my prime,
A not uncheerful step with time,
And, grateful for all blessings sent,
I go the common way, content
To make no new experiment.
On easy terms with law and fate,
For what must be I calmly wait,
And trust the path I cannot see, —
That God is good sufficeth me.
And when at last on life's strange play
The curtain falls, I only pray
That hope may lose itself in truth,
And age in Heaven's immortal youth,
And all our loves and longing prove
The foretaste of diviner love!

The day is done. Its afterglow
Along the west is burning low.
My visitors, like birds, have flown;
I hear their voices, fainter grown,
And dimly through the dusk I see
Their 'kerchiefs wave good-night to me, —
Light hearts of girlhood, knowing nought
Of all the cheer their coming brought;
And, in their going, unaware

Of silent-following feet of prayer :
Heaven make their budding promise good
With flowers of gracious womanhood!

R. S. S., AT DEER ISLAND ON THE MERRI-MAC.

MAKE, for he loved thee well, our Merrimac,
    From wave and shore a low and long lament
    For him, whose last look sought thee, as he
        went
The unknown way from which no step comes
    back.
And ye, O ancient pine-trees, at whose feet
    He watched in life the sunset's reddening glow,
    Let the soft south wind through your needles
        blow
A fitting requiem tenderly and sweet !
No fonder lover of all lovely things
    Shall walk where once he walked, no smile
        more glad
    Greet friends than his who friends in all men
        had,
Whose pleasant memory to that Island clings,
Where a dear mourner in the home he left
Of love's sweet solace cannot be bereft.

BURNING DRIFT-WOOD.

BEFORE my drift-wood fire I sit,
    And see, with every waif I burn,
Old dreams and fancies coloring it,
    And folly's unlaid ghosts return.

O ships of mine, whose swift keels cleft
  The enchanted sea on which they sailed,
Are these poor fragments only left
  Of vain desires and hopes that failed?

Did I not watch from them the light
  Of sunset on my towers in Spain,
And see, far off, uploom in sight
  The Fortunate Isles I might not gain?

Did sudden lift of fog reveal
  Arcadia's vales of song and spring,
And did I pass, with grazing keel,
  The rocks whereon the sirens sing?

Have I not drifted hard upon
  The unmapped regions lost to man,
The cloud-pitched tents of Prester John,
  The palace domes of Kubla Khan?

Did land winds blow from jasmine flowers,
  Where Youth the ageless Fountain fills?
Did Love make sign from rose blown bowers,
  And gold from Eldorado's hills?

Alas! the gallant ships, that sailed
  On blind Adventure's errand sent,
Howe'er they laid their courses, failed
  To reach the haven of Content.

And of my ventures, those alone
  Which Love had freighted, safely sped,
Seeking a good beyond my own,
  By clear-eyed Duty piloted.

O mariners, hoping still to meet
　　The luck Arabian voyagers met,
And find in Bagdad's moonlit street,
　　Haroun al Raschid walking yet,

Take with you, on your Sea of Dreams,
　　The fair, fond fancies dear to youth.
I turn from all that only seems,
　　And seek the sober grounds of truth.

What matter that it is not May,
　　That birds have flown, and trees are bare,
That darker grows the shortening day,
　　And colder blows the wintry air!

The wrecks of passion and desire,
　　The castles I no more rebuild,
May fitly feed my drift-wood fire,
　　And warm the hands that age has chilled.

Whatever perished with my ships,
　　I only know the best remains;
A song of praise is on my lips
　　For losses which are now my gains.

Heap high my hearth!　No worth is lost;
　　No wisdom with the folly dies.
Burn on, poor shreds, your holocaust
　　Shall be my evening sacrifice!

Far more than all I dared to dream,
　　Unsought before my door I see;
On wings of fire and steeds of steam
　　The world's great wonders come to me,

And holier signs, unmarked before,
   Of Love to seek and Power to save, —
The righting of the wronged and poor,
   The man evolving from the slave ;

And life, no longer chance or fate,
   Safe in the gracious Fatherhood.
I fold o'er-wearied hands and wait,
   In full assurance of the good.

And well the waiting time must be,
   Though brief or long its granted days,
If Faith and Hope and Charity
   Sit by my evening hearth-fire's blaze.

And with them, friends whom Heaven has spared,
   Whose love my heart has comforted,
And, sharing all my joys, has shared
   My tender memories of the dead, —

Dear souls who left us lonely here,
   Bound on their last, long voyage, to whom
We, day by day, are drawing near,
   Where every bark has sailing room

I know the solemn monotone
   Of waters calling unto me :
I know from whence the airs have blown
   That whisper of the Eternal Sea.

As low my fires of drift-wood burn,
   I hear that sea's deep sounds increase,
And, fair in sunset light, discern
   Its mirage-lifted Isles of Peace.

O. W. HOLMES ON HIS EIGHTIETH BIRTH-
DAY.

CLIMBING a path which leads back never more
    We heard behind his footsteps and his cheer ;
Now, face to face, we greet him standing here
Upon the lonely summit of Fourscore !
Welcome to us, o'er whom the lengthened day
    Is closing and the shadows colder grow,
    His genial presence, like an afterglow,
Following the one just vanishing away.
Long be it ere the table shall be set
    For the last breakfast of the Autocrat,
    And love repeat with smiles and tears thereat
His own sweet songs that time shall not forget.
Waiting with us the call to come up higher,
Life is not less, the heavens are only nigher !

JAMES RUSSELL LOWELL.

FROM purest wells of English undefiled
None deeper drank than he, the New World's
        child,
Who in the language of their farm-fields spoke
The wit and wisdom of New England folk,
Shaming a monstrous wrong. The world-wide
        laugh
Provoked thereby might well have shaken half
The walls of Slavery down, ere yet the ball
And mine of battle overthrew them all.

HAVERHILL.

1640–1890.

Read at the Celebration of the Two Hundred and Fiftieth Anniversary of the City, July 2, 1890.

O RIVER winding to the sea !
We call the old time back to thee ;
From forest paths and water-ways
The century-woven veil we raise.

The voices of to-day are dumb,
Unheard its sounds that go and come ;
We listen, through long-lapsing years,
To footsteps of the pioneers.

Gone steepled town and cultured plain,
The wilderness returns again,
The drear, untrodden solitude,
The gloom and mystery of the wood !

Once more the bear and panther prowl,
The wolf repeats his hungry howl,
And, peering through his leafy screen,
The Indian's copper face is seen.

We see, their rude-built huts beside,
Grave men and women anxious-eyed,
And wistful youth remembering still
Dear homes in England's Haverhill.

We summon forth to mortal view
Dark Passaquo and Saggahew, —
Wild chiefs, who owned the mighty sway
Of wizard Passaconaway.

Weird memories of the border town,
By old tradition handed down,
In chance and change before us pass
Like pictures in a magic glass, —

The terrors of the midnight raid,
The death-concealing ambuscade,
The winter march, through deserts wild,
Of captive mother, wife, and child.

Ah! bleeding hands alone subdued
And tamed the savage habitude
Of forests hiding beasts of prey,
And human shapes as fierce as they.

Slow from the plough the woods withdrew,
Slowly each year the corn-lands grew;
Nor fire, nor frost, nor foe could kill
The Saxon energy of will.

And never in the hamlet's bound
Was lack of sturdy manhood found,
And never failed the kindred good
Of brave and helpful womanhood.

That hamlet now a city is,
Its log-built huts are palaces;
The wood-path of the settler's cow
Is Traffic's crowded highway now.

And far and wide it stretches still,
Along its southward sloping hill,
And overlooks on either hand
A rich and many-watered land.

And, gladdening all the landscape, fair
As Pison was to Eden's pair,
Our river to its valley brings
The blessing of its mountain springs.

And Nature holds with narrowing space,
From mart and crowd, her old-time grace,
And guards with fondly jealous arms
The wild growths of outlying farms.

Her sunsets on Kenoza fall,
Her autumn leaves by Saltonstall;
No lavished gold can richer make
Her opulence of hill and lake.

Wise was the choice which led out sires
To kindle here their household fires,
And share the large content of all
Whose lines in pleasant places fall.

More dear, as years on years advance,
We prize the old inheritance,
And feel, as far and wide we roam,
That all we seek we leave at home.

Our palms are pines, our oranges
Are apples on our orchard trees;
Our thrushes are our nightingales,
Our larks the blackbirds of our vales.

No incense which the Orient burns
Is sweeter than our hillside ferns;
What tropic splendor can outvie
Our autumn woods, our sunset sky?

If, where the slow years came and went,
And left not affluence, but content,
Now flashes in our dazzled eyes
The electric light of enterprise;

And if the old idyllic ease
Seems lost in keen activities,
And crowded workshops now replace
The hearth's and farm-field's rustic grace;

No dull, mechanic round of toil
Life's morning charm can quite despoil;
And youth and beauty, hand in hand,
Will always find enchanted land.

No task is ill where hand and brain
And skill and strength have equal gain,
And each shall each in honor hold,
And simple manhood outweigh gold.

Earth shall be near to Heaven when all
That severs man from man shall fall,
For, here or there, salvation's plan
Alone is love of God and man.

O dwellers by the Merrimac,
The heirs of centuries at your back,
Still reaping where you have not sown,
A broader field is now your own.

Hold fast your Puritan heritage,
But let the free thought of the age
Its light and hope and sweetness add
To the stern faith the fathers had.

Adrift on Time's returnless tide,
As waves that follow waves, we glide.
God grant we leave upon the shore
Some waif of good it lacked before;

Some seed, or flower, or plant of worth,
Some added beauty to the earth;
Some larger hope, some thought to make
The sad world happier for its sake.

As tenants of uncertain stay,
So may we live our little day
That only grateful hearts shall fill
The homes we leave in Haverhill.

The singer of a farewell rhyme,
Upon whose outmost verge of time
The shades of night are falling down,
I pray, God bless the good old town!

TO G. G.

AN AUTOGRAPH.

The daughter of Daniel Gurteen, Esq., delegate from Haverhill, England, to the two hundred and fiftieth anniversary celebration of Haverhill, Massachusetts. The Rev. John Ward of the former place and many of his old parishioners were the pioneer settlers of the new town on the Merrimac.

GRACEFUL in name and in thyself, our river
  None fairer saw in John Ward's pilgrim flock,
  Proof that upon their century-rooted stock
The English roses bloom as fresh as ever.

Take the warm welcome of new friends with thee,
  And listening to thy home's familiar chime
  Dream that thou hearest, with it keeping time,
The bells on Merrimac sound across the sea.

Think of our thrushes, when the lark sings clear,
  Of our sweet Mayflowers when the daisies
    bloom ;
  And bear to our and thy ancestral home
The kindly greeting of its children here.

Say that our love survives the severing strain ;
  That the New England, with the Old, holds fast
  The proud, fond memories of a common past ;
Unbroken still the ties of blood remain !

INSCRIPTION.

For the bass-relief by Preston Powers, carved upon the huge boulder in Denver Park, Col., and representing the Last Indian and the Last Bison.

THE eagle, stooping from yon snow-blown peaks,
For the wild hunter and the bison seeks,
In the changed world below; and finds alone
Their graven semblance in the eternal stone.

LYDIA H. SIGOURNEY.

Inscription on her Memorial Tablet in Christ Church at Hartford, Conn.

SHE sang alone, ere womanhood had known
    The gift of song which fills the air to-day:
Tender and sweet, a music all her own
    May fitly linger where she knelt to pray.

MILTON.

Inscription on the Memorial Window in St. Margaret's Church, Westminster, the gift of George W. Childs, of America.

THE new world honors him whose lofty plea
    For England's freedom made her own more
        sure,
Whose song, immortal as its theme, shall be
    Their common freehold while both worlds
        endure.

THE BIRTHDAY WREATH.

December 17, 1891.

BLOSSOM and greenness, making all
The winter birthday tropical,
    And the plain Quaker parlors gay,
Have gone from bracket, stand, and wall;
We saw them fade, and droop, and fall,
    And laid them tenderly away.

White virgin lilies, mignonette,
Blown rose, and pink, and violet,
    A breath of fragrance passing by;
Visions of beauty and decay,
Colors and shapes that could not stay,
    The fairest, sweetest, first to die.

But still this rustic wreath of mine,
Of acorned oak and needled pine,
    And lighter growths of forest lands,
Woven and wound with careful pains,
And tender thoughts, and prayers, remains,
    As when it dropped from love's dear hands.

And not unfitly garlanded,
Is he, who, country-born and bred,
    Welcomes the sylvan ring which gives
A feeling of old summer days,
The wild delight of woodland ways,
    The glory of the autumn leaves.

And, if the flowery meed of song
To other bards may well belong,
  Be his, who from the farm-field spoke
A word for Freedom when her need
Was not of dulcimer and reed,
  This Isthmian wreath of pine and oak.

THE WIND OF MARCH.

Up from the sea, the wild north wind is blowing
    Under the sky's gray arch;
Smiling, I watch the shaken elm-boughs, knowing
    It is the wind of March.

Between the passing and the coming season,
    This stormy interlude
Gives to our winter-wearied hearts a reason
    For trustful gratitude.

Welcome to waiting ears its harsh forewarning
    Of light and warmth to come,
The longed-for joy of Nature's Easter morning,
    The earth arisen in bloom!

In the loud tumult winter's strength is breaking;
    I listen to the sound,
As to a voice of resurrection, waking
    To life the dead, cold ground.

Between these gusts, to the soft lapse I hearken
    Of rivulets on their way;
I see these tossed and naked tree-tops darken
    With the fresh leaves of May.

This roar of storm, this sky so gray and lowering
    Invite the airs of Spring,
A warmer sunshine over fields of flowering,
    The bluebird's song and wing.

Closely behind, the Gulf's warm breezes follow
    This northern hurricane,
And, borne thereon, the bobolink and swallow
    Shall visit us again.

And, in green wood-paths, in the kine-fed pasture
    And by the whispering rills,
Shall flowers repeat the lesson of the Master,
    Taught on his Syrian hills.

Blow, then, wild wind! thy roar shall end in
        singing,
    Thy chill in blossoming;
Come, like Bethesda's troubling angel, bringing
    The healing of the Spring.

BETWEEN THE GATES.

BETWEEN the gates of birth and death
    An old and saintly pilgrim passed,
With look of one who witnesseth
    The long-sought goal at last.

" O thou whose reverent feet have found
    The Master's footprints in thy way,
And walked thereon as holy ground,
    A boon of thee I pray.

" My lack would borrow thy excess,
　　My feeble faith the strength of thine ;
　I need thy soul's white saintliness
　　To hide the stains of mine.

" The grace and favor else denied
　　May well be granted for thy sake."
So, tempted, doubting, sorely tried,
　　A younger pilgrim spake.

" Thy prayer, my son, transcends my gift ;
　　No power is mine," the sage replied,
" The burden of a soul to lift
　　Or stain of sin to hide.

" Howe'er the outward life may seem,
　　For pardoning grace we all must pray ;
No man his brother can redeem
　　Or a soul's ransom pay.

" Not always age is growth of good ;
　　Its years have losses with their gain ;
Against some evil youth withstood
　　Weak hands may strive in vain.

" With deeper voice than any speech
　　Of mortal lips from man to man,
What earth's unwisdom may not teach
　　The Spirit only can.

" Make thou that holy guide thine own,
　　And following where it leads the way,
The known shall lapse in the unknown
　　As twilight into day.

" The best of earth shall still remain,
  And heaven's eternal years shall prove
That life and death, and joy and pain,
  Are ministers of Love."

THE LAST EVE OF SUMMER.

SUMMER'S last sun nigh unto setting shines
    Through yon columnar pines,
And on the deepening shadows of the lawn
    Its golden lines are drawn.

Dreaming of long gone summer days like this,
    Feeling the wind's soft kiss,
Grateful and glad that failing ear and sight
    Have still their old delight,

I sit alone, and watch the warm, sweet day
    Lapse tenderly away ;
And, wistful, with a feeling of forecast,
    I ask, " Is this the last ?

" Will nevermore for me the seasons run
    Their round, and will the sun
Of ardent summers yet to come forget
    For me to rise and set ? "

Thou shouldst be here, or I should be with thee
    Wherever thou mayst be,
Lips mute, hands clasped, in silences of speech
    Each answering unto each.

For this still hour, this sense of mystery far
    Beyond the evening star,
No words outworn suffice on lip or scroll :
    The soul would fain with soul

Wait, while these few swift-passing days fulfil
    The wise-disposing Will,
And, in the evening as at morning, trust
    The All-Merciful and Just.

The solemn joy that soul-communion feels
    Immortal life reveals ;
And human love, its prophecy and sign,
    Interprets love divine.

Come then, in thought, if that alone may be,
    O friend ! and bring with thee
Thy calm assurance of transcendent Spheres
    And the Eternal Years !

    August 31, 1890.

TO OLIVER WENDELL HOLMES.
8TH MO. 29TH, 1892.

This, the last of Mr. Whittier's poems, was written but a few
weeks before his death.

AMONG the thousands who with hail and cheer
    Will welcome thy new year,
How few of all have passed, as thou and I,
    So many milestones by !

We have grown old together; we have seen,
   Our youth and age between,
Two generations leave us, and to-day
   We with the third hold way,

Loving and loved.   If thought must backward run
   To those who, one by one,
In the great silence and the dark beyond
   Vanished with farewells fond,

Unseen, not lost; our grateful memories still
   Their vacant places fill,
And with the full-voiced greeting of new friends
   A tenderer whisper blends.

Linked close in a pathetic brotherhood
   Of mingled ill and good,
Of joy and grief, of grandeur and of shame,
   For pity more than blame, —

The gift is thine the weary world to make
   More cheerful for thy sake,
Soothing the ears its Miserere pains,
   With the old Hellenic strains,

Lighting the sullen face of discontent
   With smiles for blessings sent.
Enough of selfish wailing has been had,
   Thank God! for notes more glad.

Life is indeed no holiday; therein
   Are want, and woe, and sin,
Death and its nameless fears, and over all
   Our pitying tears must fall.

Sorrow is real; but the counterfeit
    Which folly brings to it,
We need thy wit and wisdom to resist,
    O rarest Optimist !

Thy hand, old friend ! the service of our days,
    In differing moods and ways,
May prove to those who follow in our train
    Not valueless nor vain.

Far off, and faint as echoes of a dream,
    The songs of boyhood seem,
Yet on our autumn boughs, unflown with spring,
    The evening thrushes sing.

The hour draws near, howe'er delayed and late,
    When at the Eternal Gate
We leave the words and works we call our own,
    And lift void hands alone

For love to fill.   Our nakedness of soul
    Brings to that Gate no toll;
Giftless we come to Him, who all things gives,
    And live because He lives.

POEMS BY ELIZABETH H. WHITTIER

———◆———

Originally published in the volume entitled *Hazel Blossoms*, and accompanied by the following prefatory note : —

I have ventured, in compliance with the desire of dear friends of my beloved sister, ELIZABETH H. WHITTIER, to add to this little volume the few poetical pieces which she left behind her. As she was very distrustful of her own powers, and altogether without ambition for literary distinction, she shunned everything like publicity, and found far greater happiness in generous appreciation of the gifts of her friends than in the cultivation of her own. Yet it has always seemed to me, that had her health, sense of duty and fitness, and her extreme self-distrust permitted, she might have taken a high place among lyrical singers. These poems, with perhaps two or three exceptions, afford but slight indications of the inward life of the writer, who had an almost morbid dread of spiritual and intellectual egotism, or of her tenderness of sympathy, chastened mirthfulness, and pleasant play of thought and fancy, when her shy, beautiful soul opened like a flower in the warmth of social communion. In the lines on Dr. Kane her friends will see something of her fine individuality, — the rare mingling of delicacy and intensity of feeling which made her dear to them. This little poem reached Cuba while the great explorer lay on his death-bed, and we are told that he listened with grateful tears while it was read to him by his mother.

I am tempted to say more, but I write as under the eye of her who, while with us, shrank with painful deprecation from the praise or mention of performances which seemed so far below her ideal of excellence. To those who best knew her, the beloved circle of her intimate friends, I dedicate this slight memorial.

J. G. W.

AMESBURY, *9th mo.*, 1874.

THE DREAM OF ARGYLE.

EARTHLY arms no more uphold him
  On his prison's stony floor;
Waiting death in his last slumber,
  Lies the doomed MacCallum More.

And he dreams a dream of boyhood;
  Rise again his heathery hills,
Sound again the hound's long baying,
  Cry of moor-fowl, laugh of rills.

Now he stands amidst his clansmen
  In the low, long banquet-hall,
Over grim, ancestral armor
  Sees the ruddy firelight fall.

Once again, with pulses beating,
  Hears the wandering minstrel tell
How Montrose on Inverary
  Thief-like from his mountains fell.

Down the glen, beyond the castle,
  Where the linn's swift waters shine,
Round the youthful heir of Argyle
  Shy feet glide and white arms twine.

Fairest of the rustic dancers,
  Blue-eyed Effie smiles once more,
Bends to him her snooded tresses,
  Treads with him the grassy floor.

Now he hears the pipes lamenting,
  Harpers for his mother mourn,
Slow, with sable plume and pennon,
  To her cairn of burial borne.

Then anon his dreams are darker,
  Sounds of battle fill his ears,
And the pibroch's mournful wailing
  For his father's fall he hears.

Wild Lochaber's mountain echoes
  Wail in concert for the dead,
And Loch Awe's deep waters murmur
  For the Campbell's glory fled!

Fierce and strong the godless tyrants
  Trample the apostate land,
While her poor and faithful remnant
  Wait for the Avenger's hand.

Once again at Inverary,
  Years of weary exile o'er,
Armed to lead his scattered clansmen,
  Stands the bold MacCallum More.

Once again to battle calling
  Sound the war-pipes through the glen;
And the court-yard of Dunstaffnage
  Rings with tread of armèd men.

All is lost! The godless triumph,
  And the faithful ones and true
From the scaffold and the prison
  Covenant with God anew.

On the darkness of his dreaming
    Great and sudden glory shone;
Over bonds and death victorious
    Stands he by the Father's throne!

From the radiant ranks of martyrs
    Notes of joy and praise he hears,
Songs of his poor land's deliverance
    Sounding from the future years.

Lo, he wakes! but airs celestial
    Bathe him in immortal rest,
And he sees with unsealed vision
    Scotland's cause with victory blest.

Shining hosts attend and guard him
    As he leaves his prison door;
And to death as to a triumph
    Walks the great MacCallum More!

LINES

Written on the departure of Joseph Sturge, after his visit to
the abolitionists of the United States.

FAIR islands of the sunny sea! midst all rejoicing
    things,
No more the wailing of the slave a wild discordance
    brings;
On the lifted brows of freemen the tropic breezes
    blow,
The mildew of the bondman's toil the land no more
    shall know.

How swells from those green islands, where bird
    and leaf and flower
Are praising in their own sweet way the dawn of
    freedom's hour,
The glorious resurrection song from hearts re-
    joicing poured,
Thanksgiving for the priceless gift, — man's regal
    crown restored !

How beautiful through all the green and tranquil
    summer land,
Uplifted, as by miracle, the solemn churches stand !
The grass is trodden from the paths where waiting
    freemen throng,
Athirst and fainting for the cup of life denied so
    long.

Oh, blessed were the feet of him whose generous
    errand here
Was to unloose the captive's chain and dry the
    mourner's tear ;
To lift again the fallen ones a brother's robber hand
Had left in pain and wretchedness by the waysides
    of the land.

The islands of the sea rejoice ; the harvest anthems
    rise ;
The sower of the seed must own 't is marvellous in
    his eyes ;
The old waste places are rebuilt, — the broken
    walls restored, —
And the wilderness is blooming like the garden of
    the Lord !

Thanksgiving for the holy fruit! should not the
    laborer rest,
His earnest faith and works of love have been so
    richly blest?
The pride of all fair England shall her ocean
    islands be,
And their peasantry with joyful hearts keep cease-
    less jubilee.

Rest, never! while his countrymen have trampled
    hearts to bleed,
The stifled murmur of their wrongs his listening
    ear shall heed,
Where England's far dependencies her *might*, not
    mercy, know,
To all the crushed and suffering there his pitying
    love shall flow.

The friend of freedom everywhere, how mourns he
    for our land,
The brand of whose hypocrisy burns on her guilty
    hand!
Her thrift a theft, the robber's greed and cunning
    in her eye,
Her glory shame, her flaunting flag on all the winds
    a lie!

For us with steady strength of heart and zeal for-
    ever true,
The champion of the island slave the conflict doth
    renew,
His labor here hath been to point the Pharisaic eye
Away from empty creed and form to where the
    wounded lie.

How beautiful to us should seem the coming feet
    of such!
Their garments of self-sacrifice have healing in
    their touch;
Their gospel mission none may doubt, for they heed
    the Master's call,
Who here walked with the multitude, and sat at
    meat with all!

JOHN QUINCY ADAMS.

HE rests with the immortals; his journey has been
    long:
For him no wail of sorrow, but a pæan full and
    strong!
So well and bravely has he done the work he found
    to do,
To justice, freedom, duty, God, and man forever
    true.

Strong to the end, a man of men, from out the
    strife he passed;
The grandest hour of all his life was that of earth
    the last.
Now midst his snowy hills of home to the grave
    they bear him down,
The glory of his fourscore years resting on him like
    a crown.

The mourning of the many bells, the drooping flags,
    all seem
Like some dim, unreal pageant passing onward in
    a dream;

And following with the living to his last and narrow bed,
Methinks I see a shadowy band, a train of noble
dead.

'T is a strange and weird procession that is slowly
moving on,
The phantom patriots gathered to the funeral of
their son!
In shadowy guise they move along, brave Otis with
hushed tread,
And Warren walking reverently by the father of
the dead.

Gliding foremost in the misty band a gentle form
is there,
In the white robes of the angels and their glory
round her hair.
She hovers near and bends above her world-wide
honored child,
And the joy that heaven alone can know beams on
her features mild.

And so they bear him to his grave in the fulness
of his years,
True sage and prophet, leaving us in a time of
many fears.
Nevermore amid the darkness of our wild and evil
day
Shall his voice be heard to cheer us, shall his
finger point the way.

DR. KANE IN CUBA.

A NOBLE life is in thy care,
    A sacred trust to thee is given;
Bright Island! let thy healing air
    Be to him as the breath of Heaven.

The marvel of his daring life —
    The self-forgetting leader bold —
Stirs, like the trumpet's call to strife,
    A million hearts of meaner mould.

Eyes that shall never meet his own
    Look dim with tears across the sea,
Where from the dark and icy zone,
    Sweet Isle of Flowers! he comes to thee.

Fold him in rest, O pitying clime!
    Give back his wasted strength again;
Soothe, with thy endless summer time,
    His winter-wearied heart and brain.

Sing soft and low, thou tropic bird,
    From out the fragrant, flowery tree, —
The ear that hears thee now has heard
    The ice-break of the winter sea.

Through his long watch of awful night,
    He saw the Bear in Northern skies;
Now, to the Southern Cross of light
    He lifts in hope his weary eyes.

Prayers from the hearts that watched in fear,
   When the dark North no answer gave,
Rise, trembling, to the Father's ear,
   That still His love may help and save.

LADY FRANKLIN.

FOLD thy hands, thy work is over;
   Cool thy watching eyes with tears;
Let thy poor heart, over-wearied,
   Rest alike from hopes and fears, —

Hopes, that saw with sleepless vision
   One sad picture fading slow;
Fears, that followed, vague and nameless,
   Lifting back the veils of snow.

For thy brave one, for thy lost one,
   Truest heart of woman, weep!
Owning still the love that granted
   Unto thy beloved sleep.

Not for him that hour of terror
   When, the long ice-battle o'er,
In the sunless day his comrades
   Deathward trod the Polar shore.

Spared the cruel cold and famine,
   Spared the fainting heart's despair,
What but that could mercy grant him?
   What but that has been thy prayer?

Dear to thee that last memorial
  From the cairn beside the sea;
Evermore the month of roses
  Shall be sacred time to thee.

Sad it is the mournful yew-tree
  O'er his slumbers may not wave;
Sad it is the English daisy
  May not blossom on his grave.

But his tomb shall storm and winter
  Shape and fashion year by year,
Pile his mighty mausoleum,
  Block by block, and tier on tier.

Guardian of its gleaming portal
  Shall his stainless honor be,
While thy love, a sweet immortal,
  Hovers o'er the winter sea.

NIGHT AND DEATH.

THE storm-wind is howling
  Through old pines afar;
The drear night is falling
  Without moon or star.

The roused sea is lashing
  The bold shore behind,
And the moan of its ebbing
  Keeps time with the wind.

On, on through the darkness,
   A spectre, I pass
Where, like moaning of broken hearts,
   Surges the grass!

I see her lone head-stone, —
   'T is white as a shroud;
Like a pall, hangs above it
   The low drooping cloud.

Who speaks through the dark night
   And lull of the wind?
'T is the sound of the pine-leaves
   And sea-waves behind.

The dead girl is silent, —
   I stand by her now;
And her pulse beats no quicker,
   Nor crimsons her brow.

The small hand that trembled,
   When last in my own,
Lies patient and folded,
   And colder than stone.

Like the white blossoms falling
   To-night in the gale,
So she in her beauty
   Sank mournful and pale.

Yet I loved her! I utter
   Such words by her grave,
As I would not have spoken
   Her last breath to save.

Of her love the angels
　　In heaven might tell,
While mine would be whispered
　　With shudders in hell!

'T was well that the white ones
　　Who bore her to bliss
Shut out from her new life
　　The vision of this;

Else, sure as I stand here,
　　And speak of my love,
She would leave for my darkness
　　Her glory above.

THE MEETING WATERS.

CLOSE beside the meeting waters,
　　Long I stood as in a dream,
Watching how the little river
　　Fell into the broader stream.

Calm and still the mingled current
　　Glided to the waiting sea;
On its breast serenely pictured
　　Floating cloud and skirting tree.

And I thought, " O human spirit!
　　Strong and deep and pure and blest,
Let the stream of my existence
　　Blend with thine, and find its rest!"

I could die as dies the river,
  In that current deep and wide;
I would live as live its waters,
  Flashing from a stronger tide!

THE WEDDING VEIL.

DEAR Anna, when I brought her veil,
  Her white veil, on her wedding night,
Threw o'er my thin brown hair its folds,
  And, laughing, turned me to the light.

"See, Bessie, see! you wear at last
  The bridal veil, forsworn for years!"
She saw my face, — her laugh was hushed,
  Her happy eyes were filled with tears.

With kindly haste and trembling hand
  She drew away the gauzy mist;
"Forgive, dear heart!" her sweet voice said:
  Her loving lips my forehead kissed.

We passed from out the searching light;
  The summer night was calm and fair:
I did not see her pitying eyes,
  I felt her soft hand smooth my hair.

Her tender love unlocked my heart;
  Mid falling tears, at last I said,
"Forsworn indeed to me that veil
  Because I only love the dead!"

She stood one moment statue-still,
   And, musing, spake, in undertone,
" The living love may colder grow ;
   The dead is safe with God alone ! "

CHARITY.

THE pilgrim and stranger who through the day
Holds over the desert his trackless way,
Where the terrible sands no shade have known,
No sound of life save his camel's moan,
Hears, at last, through the mercy of Allah to all,
From his tent-door at evening the Bedouin's call :
" *Whoever thou art whose need is great,*
In the name of God, the Compassionate
And Merciful One, for thee I wait ! "

For gifts in His name of food and rest
The tents of Islam of God are blest,
Thou who hast faith in the Christ above,
Shall the Koran teach thee the Law of Love ? —
O Christian ! — open thy heart and door,
Cry east and west to the wandering poor :
" *Whoever thou art whose need is great,*
In the name of Christ, the Compassionate
And Merciful One, for thee I wait ! "

APPENDIX

I. EARLY AND UNCOLLECTED VERSES.

I AM yielding to what seems, under the circumstances, almost a necessity, in adding to the pieces assigned for one reason or another to the limbo of an appendix, some of my very earliest attempts at verse, which have been kept alive in the newspapers for the last half century. A few of them have even been printed in book form without my consent, and greatly to my annoyance, with all their accumulated errors of the press added to their original defects and crudity. I suppose they should have died a natural death long ago, but their feline tenacity of life seems to contradict the theory of the "survival of the fittest." I have consented, at my publishers' request, to take the poor vagrants home and give them a more presentable appearance, in the hope that they may at least be of some interest to those who are curious enough to note the weak beginnings of the graduate of a small country district school, sixty years ago. That they met with some degree of favor at that time may be accounted for by the fact that the makers of verse were then few in number, with little competition in their unprofitable vocation, and that the standard of criticism was not discouragingly high.

The earliest of the author's verses that found their way into print were published in the Newburyport *Free Press,* edited by William Lloyd Garrison, in 1826.

THE EXILE'S DEPARTURE.

Fond scenes, which delighted my youthful existence,
  With feelings of sorrow I bid ye adieu —
A lasting adieu ! for now, dim in the distance,
  The shores of Hibernia recede from my view.

Farewell to the cliffs, tempest-beaten and gray,
   Which guard the lov'd shores of my own native land ;
Farewell to the village and sail-shadow'd bay,
   The forest-crown'd hill and the water-wash'd strand.

I 've fought for my country — I 've brav'd all the dangers
   That throng round the path of the warrior in strife ;
I now must depart to a nation of strangers,
   And pass in seclusion the remnant of life ;
Far, far from the friends to my bosom most dear,
   With none to support me in peril and pain,
And none but the stranger to drop the sad tear
   On the grave where the heart-broken Exile is lain.

Friends of my youth ! I must leave you forever,
   And hasten to dwell in a region unknown : —
Yet time cannot change, nor the broad ocean sever,
   Hearts firmly united and tried as our own.
Ah, no ! though I wander, all sad and forlorn,
   In a far distant land, yet shall memory trace,
When far o'er the ocean's white surges I 'm borne,
   The scene of past pleasures, — my own native place.

Farewell shores of Erin, green land of my fathers : —
   Once more, and forever, a mournful adieu !
For round thy dim headlands the ocean-mist gathers,
   And shrouds the fair isle I no longer can view.
I go — but wherever my footsteps I bend,
   For freedom and peace to my own native isle,
And contentment and joy to each warm-hearted friend
   Shall be the heart's prayer of the lonely Exile ! ·

HAVERHILL, 1825.

THE DEITY.

            The Prophet stood
On the high mount, and saw the tempest cloud
Pour the fierce whirlwind from its reservoir
Of congregated gloom. The mountain oak,
Torn from the earth, heaved high its roots where once
Its branches waved. The fir-tree's shapely form,
Smote by the tempest, lashed the mountain's side.
Yet, calm in conscious purity, the Seer
Beheld the awful desolation, for
The Eternal Spirit moved not in the storm.

The tempest ceased. The caverned earthquake burst
Forth from its prison, and the mountain rocked
Even to its base. The topmost crags were thrown,
With fearful crashing, down its shuddering sides.
Unawed, the Prophet saw and heard ; he felt

Not in the earthquake moved the God of Heaven.
The murmur died away; and from the height,
Torn by the storm and shattered by the shock,
Rose far and clear, a pyramid of flame
Mighty and vast; the startled mountain deer
Shrank from its glare, and cowered within the shade;
The wild fowl shrieked — but even then the Seer
Untrembling stood and marked the fearful glow,
For Israel's God came not within the flame!

The fiery beacon sank.   A still, small voice,
Unlike to human sound, at once conveyed
Deep awe and reverence to his pious heart.
Then bowed the holy man; his face he veiled
Within his mantle — and in meekness owned
The presence of his God, discerned not in
The storm, the earthquake, or the mighty flame.

1825.

THE VALE OF THE MERRIMAC.

There are streams which are famous in history's story,
  Whose names are familiar to pen and to tongue,
Renowned in the records of love and of glory,
  Where knighthood has ridden and minstrels have sung : —
Fair streams thro' more populous regions are gliding,
  Tower, temple, and palace their borders adorning,
With tall-masted ships on their broad bosoms riding,
  Their banners stretch'd out in the breezes of morning ;
And their vales may be lovely and pleasant — but never
  Was skiff ever wafted, or wav'd a white sail
O'er a lovelier wave than my dear native river,
  Or brighter tides roll'd than in Merrimac's vale !

And fair streams may glide where the climate is milder,
  Where winter ne'er gathers and spring ever blooms,
And others may roll where the region is wilder,
  Their dark waters hid in some forest's deep gloom,
Where the thunder-scath'd peaks of Helvetia are frowning,
  And the Rhine's rapid waters encircle their bases,
Where the snows of long years are the hoary Alps crowning,
  And the tempest-charg'd vapor their tall tops embraces : —
There sure might be fix'd, amid scenery so frightful,
  The region of romance and wild fairy-tale, —
But such scenes could not be to my heart so delightful
  As the home of my fathers, — fair Merrimac's vale !

There are streams where the bounty of Providence musters
  The fairest of fruits by their warm sunny sides,
The vine bending low with the grape's heavy clusters,
  And the orange-tree waving its fruit o'er their tides : —

But I envy not him whose lot has been cast there,
    For oppression is there — and the hand of the spoiler,
Regardless of justice or mercy, has past there,
    And made him a wretched and indigent toiler.
No — dearer to me are the scenes of my childhood,
    The moss-cover'd bank and the breeze-wafted sail,
The age-stinted oak and the green groves of wild-wood
    That wave round the borders of Merrimac's vale !

Oh, lovely the scene, when the gray misty vapor
    Of morning is lifted from Merrimac's shore ;
When the fire-fly, lighting his wild gleaming taper,
    Thy dimly seen lowlands comes glimmering o'er ;
When on thy calm surface the moonbeam falls brightly,
    And the dull bird of night is his covert forsaking,
When the whippoorwill's notes from thy margin sound lightly,
    And break on the sound which thy small waves are making,
O brightest of visions ! my heart shall forever,
    Till memory shall perish and reason shall fail,
Still preference give to my own native river,
    The name of my fathers, and Merrimac's vale !

1825.

BENEVOLENCE.

Hail, heavenly gift ! within the human breast,
    Germ of unnumber'd virtues — by thy aid
The fainting heart, with riving grief opprest,
    Survives the ruin adverse scenes have made :
Woes that have wrung the bosom, cares that preyed
    Long on the spirit, are dissolv'd by thee —
Misfortune's frown, despair's disastrous shade,
    Ghastly disease, and pining poverty,
Thy influence dread, and at thy approach they flee.

Thy spirit led th' immortal Howard on ;
    Nurtur'd by thee, on many a foreign shore
Imperishable fame, by virtue won,
    Adorns his memory, tho' his course is o'er ;
Thy animating smile his aspect wore,
    To cheer the sorrow-desolated soul,
Compassion's balm in grief-worn hearts to pour,
    And snatch the prisoner from despair's control,
Steal half his woes away and lighter make the whole.

Green be the sod on Cherson's honor'd field,
    Where wraps the turf around his mouldering clay;
There let the earth her choicest beauties yield,
    And there the breeze in gentlest murmurs play ;
There let the widow and the orphan stray,
    To wet with tears their benefactor's tomb ;

There let the rescued prisoner bend his way,
  And mourn o'er him, who in the dungeon's gloom
Had sought him and averted misery's fearful doom.

His grave perfum'd with heartfelt sighs of grief,
  And moistened by the tear of gratitude, —
Oh, how unlike the spot where war's grim chief
  Sinks on the field, in sanguine waves imbrued !
Who mourns for him, whose footsteps can be viewed
  With reverential awe imprinted near
The monument rear'd o'er the man of blood ?
  Or who waste on it sorrow's balmy tear ?
None ! shame and misery rest alone upon his bier.

Offspring of heaven ! Benevolence, thy pow'r
  Bade Wilberforce its mighty champion be,
And taught a Clarkson's ardent mind to soar
  O'er every obstacle, when serving thee : —
Theirs was the task to set the sufferer free,
  To break the bonds which bound th' unwilling slave,
To shed abroad the light of liberty,
  And leave to all the rights their Maker gave,
To bid the world rejoice o'er hated slavery's grave.

Diffuse thy charms, Benevolence ! let thy light
  Pierce the dark clouds which ages past have thrown
Before the beams of truth — and nature's right,
  Inborn, let every hardened tyrant own ;
On our fair shore, be thy mild presence known ;
  And every portion of Columbia's land
Be as God's garden with thy blessings sown ;
  Yea, o'er Earth's regions let thy love expand
Till all united are in friendship's sacred band !

Then in that hour of joy will be fulfilled
  The prophet's heart-consoling prophecy ;
Then war's commotion shall on earth be stilled,
  And men their swords to other use apply ;
Then Afric's injured sons no more shall try
  The bitterness of slavery's toil and pain,
Nor pride nor love of gain direct the eye
  Of stern oppression to their homes again ;
But peace, a lasting peace, throughout the world shall reign.

9th mo., 1825.

OCEAN.

Unfathomed deep, unfetter'd waste
  Of never-silent waves,
Each by its rushing follower chas'd,
  Through unillumin'd caves,

And o'er the rocks whose turrets rude,
   E'en since the birth of time,
Have heard amid thy solitude
   The billow's ceaseless chime.

O'er what recesses, depths unknown,
   Dost thou thy waves impel,
Where never yet a sunbeam shone,
   Or gleam of moonlight fell ?
For never yet did mortal eyes
   Thy gloom-wrapt deeps behold,
And naught of thy dread mysteries
   The tongue of man hath told.

What, though proud man presume to hold
   His course upon thy tide,
O'er thy dark billows uncontroll'd
   His fragile bark to guide —
Yet who, upon thy mountain waves,
   Can feel himself secure
While sweeping o'er thy yawning caves,
   Deep, awful and obscure ?

But thou art mild and tranquil now —
   Thy wrathful spirits sleep,
And gentle billows, calm and slow,
   Across thy bosom sweep.
Yet where the dim horizon's bound
   Rests on thy sparkling bed,
The tempest-cloud, in gloom profound,
   Prepares its wrath to shed.

Thus, mild and calm in youth's bright hour
   The tide of life appears,
When fancy paints, with magic spell,
   The bliss of coming years ;
But clouds will rise, and darkness bring
   O'er life's deceitful way,
And cruel disappointment fling
   Its shade on hope's dim ray.

1*st mo.*, 1827.

THE SICILIAN VESPERS.

Silence o'er sea and earth
   With the veil of evening fell,
Till the convent-tower sent deeply forth
   The chime of its vesper bell.
One moment — and that solemn sound
   Fell heavy on the ear ;

But a sterner echo passed around,
  And the boldest shook to hear.

The startled monks thronged up,
  In the torchlight cold and dim ;
And the priest let fall his incense-cup,
  And the virgin hushed her hymn,
For a boding clash, and a clanging tramp,
  And a summoning voice were heard,
And fretted wall, and dungeon damp,
  To the fearful echo stirred.

The peasant heard the sound,
  As he sat beside his hearth ;
And the song and the dance were hushed around,
  With the fire-side tale of mirth.
The chieftain shook in his banner'd hall,
  As the sound of fear drew nigh,
And the warder shrank from the castle wall,
  As the gleam of spears went by.

Woe ! woe ! to the stranger, then,
  At the feast and flow of wine,
In the red array of mailëd men,
  Or bowed at the holy shrine ;
For the wakened pride of an injured land
  Had burst its iron thrall,
From the plumëd chief to the pilgrim band ;
  Woe ! woe ! to the sons of Gaul !

Proud beings fell that hour,
  With the young and passing fair,
And the flame went up from dome and tower,
  The avenger's arm was there !
The stranger priest at the altar stood,
  And clasped his beads in prayer,
But the holy shrine grew dim with blood,
  The avenger found him there !

Woe ! woe ! to the sons of Gaul,
  To the serf and mailed lord ;
They were gathered darkly, one and all,
  To the harvest of the sword :
And the morning sun, with a quiet smile,
  Shone out o'er hill and glen,
On ruined temple and smouldering pile,
  And the ghastly forms of men.

Ay, the sunshine sweetly smiled,
  As its early glance came forth,
It had no sympathy with the wild
  And terrible things of earth.

And the man of blood that day might read,
 In a language freely given,
How ill his dark and midnight deed
 Became the calm of Heaven.

20th of 11th mo., 1828.

THE SPIRIT OF THE NORTH.

Spirit of the frozen North,
 Where the wave is chained and still,
And the savage bear looks forth
 Nightly from his caverned hill !
Down from thy eternal throne,
 From thy land of cloud and storm,
Where the meeting icebergs groan,
 Sweepeth on thy wrathful form.

Spirit of the frozen wing !
 Dweller of a voiceless clime,
Where no coming on of spring,
 Gilds the weary course of time !
Monarch of a realm untrod,
 By the restless feet of men,
Where alone the hand of God,
 'Mid his mighty works hath been !

Throned amid the ancient hills,
 Piled with undecaying snow,
Flashing with the path of rills,
 Frozen in their first glad flow ;
Thou hast seen the gloomy north,
 Gleaming with unearthly light,
Spreading its pale banners forth,
 Checkered with the stars of night.

Thou hast gazed untrembling, where
 Giant forms of flame were driven,
Like the spirits of the air,
 Striding up the vault of heaven !
Thou hast seen that midnight glow,
 Hiding moon and star and sky,
And the icy hills below,
 Reddening to the fearful dye.

Dark and desolate and lone,
 Curtained with the tempest-cloud,
Drawn around thy ancient throne
 Like oblivion's moveless shroud,
Dim and distantly the sun
 Glances on thy palace walls,
But a shadow cold and dun
 Broods along its pillared halls.

Lord of sunless depths and cold !
  Chainer of the northern sea !
At whose feet the storm is rolled,
  Who hath power to humble thee ?
Spirit of the stormy north !
  Bow thee to thy Maker's nod ;
Bend to him who sent thee forth,
  Servant of the living God.

1st month, 1829.

THE EARTHQUAKE.

Calmly the night came down
  O'er Scylla's shatter'd walls ;
How desolate that silent town !
  How tenantless the halls,
Where yesterday her thousands trod,
And princes graced their proud abode !

Low, on the wet sea sand,
  Humbled in anguish now,
The despot, midst his menial band,
  Bent down his kingly brow ;
And prince and peasant knelt in prayer,
For grief had made them equal there.

Again as at the morn,
  The earthquake roll'd its car :
Lowly the castle-towers were borne,
  That mock'd the storms of war ;
The mountain reeled, its shiver'd brow
Went down among the waves below.

Up rose the kneelers then,
  As the wave's rush was heard :
The horror of those fated men
  Was uttered by no word.
But closer still the mother prest
The infant to her faithful breast.

One long, wild shriek went up,
  Full mighty in despair ;
As bow'd to drink death's bitter cup,
  The thousands gathered there ;
And man's strong wail, and woman's cry
Blent as the waters hurried by.

On swept the whelming sea ;
  The mountains felt its shock,
As the long cry of agony
  Thrills thro' their towers of rock ;

An echo round that fatal shore,
The death wail of the sufferers bore.

The morning sun shed forth
  Its light upon the scene,
Where tower and palace strew'd the earth
  With wrecks of what had been.
But of the thousands who were gone,
No trace was left, no vestige shown.

1828.

JUDITH AT THE TENT OF HOLOFERNES.

Night was down among the mountains,
  In her dim and quiet manner,
Where Bethulia's silver fountains
  Gushed beneath the Assyrian banner.
Moonlight, o'er her meek dominion,
  As a mighty flag unfurled,
Like an angel's snowy pinion
  Resting on a darkened world !

Faintly rose the city's murmur,
  But the crowded camp was calm ;
Girded in their battle armor,
  Each a falchion at his arm,
Lordly chief and weary vassal
  In the arms of slumber fell ;
It had been a day of wassail,
  And the wine had circled well.

Underneath his proud pavilion
  Lay Assyria's champion,
Where the ruby's rich vermilion
  Shone beside the beryl-stone.
With imperial purple laden,
  Breathing in the perfumed air,
Dreams he of the Jewish maiden,
  With her dark and jewelled hair.

Who is she, the pale-browed stranger,
  Bending o'er that son of slaughter ?
God be with thee in thy danger,
  Israel's lone and peerless daughter !
She hath bared her queenly beauty
  To the dark Assyrian's glance ;
Now, a high and sterner duty
  Bids her to his couch advance.

Beautiful and pale she bendeth
  In her earnest prayer to Heaven ;

Look again, that maiden standeth
  In the strength her God has given !
Strangely is her dark eye kindled,
  Hot blood through her cheek is poured;
Lo, her every fear hath dwindled,
  And her hand is on the sword !

Upward to the flashing curtain,
  See, that mighty blade is driven,
And its fall ! — 't is swift and certain
  As the cloud-fire's track in heaven !
Down, as with a power supernal,
  Twice the lifted weapon fell ;
Twice, his slumber is eternal —
  Who shall wake the infidel ?

Sunlight on the mountains streameth
  Like an air-borne wave of gold ;
And Bethulia's armor gleameth
  Round Judea's banner-fold.
Down they go, the mailèd warriors,
  As the upper torrents sally
Headlong from their mountain-barriers
  Down upon the sleeping valley.

Rouse thee from thy couch, Assyrian !
  Dream no more of woman's smile ;
Fiercer than the leaguered Tyrian,
  Or the dark-browed sons of Nile,
Foes are on thy slumber breaking,
  Chieftain to thy battle rise !
Vain the call — he will not waken —
  Headless on his couch he lies.

Who hath dimmed your boasted glory ?
  What hath woman's weakness done ?
Whose dark brow is up before ye,
  Blackening in the fierce-haired sun ?
Lo ! an eye that never slumbers
  Looketh in its vengeance down ;
And the thronged and mailèd numbers
  Wither at Jehovah's frown !

1829.

METACOM.

Metacom, or Philip, the chief of the Wampanoags, was
the most powerful and sagacious Sachem who ever made
war upon the English.

Red as the banner which enshrouds
  The warrior-dead, when strife is done,

A broken mass of crimson clouds
  Hung over the departed sun.
The shadow of the western hill
Crept swiftly down, and darkly still,
As if a sullen wave of night
Were rushing on the pale twilight ;
The forest-openings grew more dim,
  As glimpses of the arching blue
  And waking stars came softly through
The rifts of many a giant limb.
Above the wet and tangled swamp
White vapors gathered thick and damp,
And through their cloudy curtaining
Flapped many a brown and dusky wing —
Pinions that fan the moonless dun,
But fold them at the rising sun !

Beneath the closing veil of night,
  And leafy bough and curling fog,
With his few warriors ranged in sight —
Scarred relics of his latest fight —
  Rested the fiery Wampanoag.
He leaned upon his loaded gun,
Warm with its recent work of death,
And, save the struggling of his breath,
That, slow and hard and long-repressed,
Shook the damp folds around his breast,]
An eye that was unused to scan
The sterner moods of that dark man]
Had deemed his tall and silent form
With hidden passion fierce and warm,
With that fixed eye, as still and dark
As clouds which veil their lightning spark,
That of some forest-champion,
Whom sudden death had passed upon —
A giant frozen into stone !
Son of the thronëd Sachem ! — Thou,
The sternest of the forest kings, —
Shall the scorned pale-one trample now,
Unambushed on thy mountain's brow,
Yea, drive his vile and hated plough
  Among thy nation's holy things,
Crushing the warrior-skeleton
In scorn beneath his armëd heel,
And not a hand be left to deal
A kindred vengeance fiercely back,
And cross in blood the Spoiler's track ?

He turned him to his trustiest one,
The old and war-tried Annawon —
"Brother ! " — The favored warrior stood
In hushed and listening attitude —

"This night the Vision-Spirit hath
  Unrolled the scroll of fate before me ;
And ere the sunrise cometh, Death
  Will wave his dusky pinion o'er me !
Nay, start not — well I know thy faith —
Thy weapon now may keep its sheath ;
But, when the bodeful morning breaks,
And the green forest widely wakes
  Unto the roar of English thunder,
Then trusted brother, be it thine
To burst upon the foeman's line,
And rend his serried strength asunder.
Perchance thyself and yet a few
Of faithful ones may struggle through,
And, rallying on the wooded plain,
Strike deep for vengeance once again,
And offer up in pale-face blood
An offering to the Indian's God."

A musket shot — a sharp, quick yell —
  And then the stifled groan of pain,
Told that another red man fell, —
  And blazed a sudden light again
Across that kingly brow and eye,
Like lightning on a clouded sky, —
And a low growl, like that which thrills
The hunter of the Eastern hills,
  Burst through clenched teeth and rigid lip —
And, when the great chief spoke again
His deep voice shook beneath its rein,
  As wrath and grief held fellowship.

"Brother ! methought when as but now
  I pondered on my nation's wrong,
With sadness on his shadowy brow
  My father's spirit passed along !
He pointed to the far south-west,
  Where sunset's gold was growing dim,
  And seemed to beckon me to him,
And to the forests of the blest ! —
My father loved the white men, when
They were but children, shelterless,
For his great spirit at distress
Melted to woman's tenderness —
Nor was it given him to know
  That children whom he cherished then
  Would rise at length, like arm\u00ebd men,
To work his people's overthrow.
Yet thus it is ; — the God before
  Whose awful shrine the pale ones bow
Hath frowned upon, and given o'er
  The red man to the stranger now !

A few more moons, and there will be
No gathering to the council tree ;
The scorchëd earth — the blackened log —
    The naked bones of warriors slain,
    Be the sole relics which remain
Of the once mighty Wampanoag !
The forests of our hunting-land,
    With all their old and solemn green,
Will bow before the Spoiler's axe —
The plough displace the hunter's tracks,
And the tall prayer-house steeple stand
    Where the Great Spirit's shrine hath been !

" Yet, brother, from this awful hour
    The dying curse of Metacom
Shall linger with abiding power
    Upon the spoilers of my home.
    The fearful veil of things to come,
By Kitchtan's hand is lifted from
The shadows of the embryo years ;
    And I can see more clearly through
Than ever visioned Powwah did,
For all the future comes unbid
    Yet welcome to my trancëd view,
As battle-yell to warrior-ears !
From stream and lake and hunting-hill
    Our tribes may vanish like a dream,
    And even my dark curse may seem
Like idle winds when Heaven is still,
    No bodeful harbinger of ill ;
But, fiercer than the downright thunder,
When yawns the mountain-rock asunder,
And riven pine and knotted oak
Are reeling to the fearful stroke,
    That curse shall work its master's will !
The bed of yon blue mountain stream
Shall pour a darker tide than rain —
The sea shall catch its blood-red stain,
And broadly on its banks shall gleam
    The steel of those who should be brothers ;
Yea, those whom one fond parent nursed
Shall meet in strife, like fiends accursed,
And trample down the once loved form,
While yet with breathing passion warm,
    As fiercely as they would another's ! "

The morning star sat dimly on
The lighted eastern horizon —
The deadly glare of levelled gun
    Came streaking through the twilight haze
    And naked to its reddest blaze,
A hundred warriors sprang in view ;
    One dark red arm was tossed on high,

One giant shout came hoarsely through
    The clangor and the charging cry,
Just as across the scattering gloom,
Red as the naked hand of Doom,
    The English volley hurtled by —
The arm — the voice of Metacom ! —
    One piercing shriek — one vengeful yell,
Sent like an arrow to the sky,
    Told when the hunter-monarch fell !

1829.

MOUNT AGIOCHOOK.

The Indians supposed the White Mountains were the residence of powerful spirits, and in consequence rarely ascended them.

Gray searcher of the upper air,
    There 's sunshine on thy ancient walls,
A crown upon thy forehead bare,
    A flash upon thy waterfalls.
A rainbow glory in the cloud
    Upon thine awful summit bowed,
The radiant ghost of a dead storm !
    And music from the leafy shroud
Which swathes in green thy giant form,
    Mellowed and softened from above
Steals downward to the lowland ear,
    Sweet as the first, fond dream of love
That melts upon the maiden's ear.

The time has been, white giant, when
    Thy shadows veiled the red man's home,
And over crag and serpent den,
And wild gorge where the steps of men
    In chase or battle might not come,
The mountain eagle bore on high
    The emblem of the free of soul,
And, midway in the fearful sky,
Sent back the Indian battle cry,
    And answered to the thunder's roll.

The wigwam fires have all burned out,
    The moccasin has left no track ;
Nor wolf nor panther roam about
    The Saco and the Merrimac.
And thou, that liftest up on high
Thy mighty barriers to the sky,
    Art not the haunted mount of old,
Where on each crag of blasted stone
Some dreadful spirit found his throne,
    And hid within the thick cloud fold,

Heard only in the thunder's crash,
Seen only in the lightning's flash,
When crumbled rock and riven branch
Went down before the avalanche !

No more that spirit moveth there ;
    The dwellers of the vale are dead ;
No hunter's arrow cleaves the air ;
    No dry leaf rustles to his tread.
The pale-face climbs thy tallest rock,
His hands thy crystal gates unlock ;
From steep to steep his maidens call,
Light laughing, like the streams that fall
In music down thy rocky wall,
And only when their careless tread
Lays bare an Indian arrow-head,
Spent and forgetful of the deer,
Think of the race that perished here.

Oh, sacred to the Indian seer,
    Gray altar of the men of old !
Not vainly to the listening ear
    The legends of thy past are told, —
Tales of the downward sweeping flood,
When bowed like reeds thy ancient wood ;
Of armèd hands, and spectral forms ;
Of giants in their leafy shroud,
And voices calling long and loud
In the dread pauses of thy storms.
For still within their caverned home
Dwell the strange gods of heathendom !

1829.

THE DRUNKARD TO HIS BOTTLE.

I was thinking of the temperance lyrics the great poet of
Scotland might have written had he put his name to a pledge
of abstinence, a thing unhappily unknown in his day. The
result of my cogitation was this poor imitation of his dia-
lect.

Hoot ! — daur ye shaw ye're face again,
Ye auld black thief o' purse an' brain?
For foul disgrace, for dool an' pain
    An' shame I ban ye :
Wae 's me, that e'er my lips have ta'en
    Your kiss uncanny !

Nae mair, auld knave, without a shillin'
To keep a starvin' wight frae stealin'

Ye 'll sen' me hameward, blin' and reelin',
    Frae nightly swagger,
By wall an' post my pathway feelin',
    Wi' mony a stagger.

Nae mair o' fights that bruise an' mangle,
Nae mair o' nets my feet to tangle,
Nae mair o' senseless brawl an' wrangle,
    Wi' frien' an' wife too,
Nae mair o' deavin' din an' jangle
    My feckless life through.

Ye thievin', cheatin', auld Cheap Jack,
Peddlin' your poison brose, I crack
Your banes against my ingle-back
    Wi' meikle pleasure.
Deil mend ye i' his workshop black,
    E'en at his leisure !

I 'll brak ye're neck, ye foul auld sinner,
I 'll spill ye're bluid, ye vile beginner
O' a' the ills an' aches that winna
    Quat saul an' body !
Gie me hale breeks an' weel-spread dinner —
    Deil tak' ye're toddy !

Nae mair wi' witches' broo gane gyte,
Gie me ance mair the auld delight
O' sittin' wi' my bairns in sight,
    The gude wife near,
The weel-spent day, the peacefu' night,
    The mornin' cheer !

Cock a' ye're heids, my bairns fu' gleg,
My winsome Robin, Jean, an' Meg,
For food and claes ye shall na beg
    A doited daddie.
Dance, auld wife, on your girl-day leg,
    Ye 've foun' your laddie !

1829.

THE FAIR QUAKERESS.

She was a fair young girl, yet on her brow
No pale pearl shone, a blemish on the pure
And snowy lustre of its living light,
No radiant gem shone beautifully through
The shadowing of her tresses, as a star
Through the dark sky of midnight ; and no wreath
Of coral circled on her queenly neck,
In mockery of the glowing cheek and lip,
Whose hue the fairy guardian of the flowers

Might never rival when her delicate touch
Tinges the rose of springtime.

                          Unadorned,
Save by her youthful charms, and with a garb
Simple as Nature's self, why turn to her
The proud and gifted, and the versed in all
The pageantry of fashion ?

                         She hath not
Moved down the dance to music, when the hall
Is lighted up like sunshine, and the thrill
Of the light viol and the mellow flute,
And the deep tones of manhood, softened down
To very music melt upon the ear. —
She has not mingled with the hollow world
Nor tampered with its mockeries, until all
The delicate perceptions of the heart,
The innate modesty, the watchful sense
Of maiden dignity, are lost within
The maze of fashion and the din of crowds.

Yet Beauty hath its homage.   Kings have bowed
From the tall majesty of ancient thrones
With a prostrated knee, yea, cast aside
The awfulness of time-created power
For the regardful glances of a child.
Yea, the high ones and powerful of Earth,
The helmëd sons of victory, the grave
And schooled philosophers, the giant men
Of overmastering intellect, have turned
Each from the separate idol of his high
And vehement ambition for the low
Idolatry of human loveliness ;
And bartered the sublimity of mind,
The godlike and commanding intellect
Which nations knelt to, for a woman's tear,
A soft-toned answer, or a wanton's smile.

And in the chastened beauty of that eye,
And in the beautiful play of that red lip,
And in the quiet smile, and in the voice
Sweet as the tuneful greeting of a bird
To the first flowers of springtime, there is more
Than the perfection of the painter's skill
Or statuary's moulding.   *Mind* is there,
The pure and holy attributes of soul,
The seal of virtue, the exceeding grace
Of meekness blended with a maiden pride ;
Nor deem ye that beneath the gentle smile,
And the calm temper of a chastened mind
No warmth of passion kindles, and no tide

Of quick and earnest feeling courses on
From the warm heart's pulsations.   There are springs
Of deep and pure affection, hidden now,
Within that quiet bosom, which but wait
The thrilling of some kindly touch, to flow
Like waters from the Desert-rock of old.

1830.

BOLIVAR.

A dirge is wailing from the Gulf of storm-vexed Mexico,
To where through Pampas' solitudes the mighty rivers flow ;
The dark Sierras hear the sound, and from each mountain rift,
Where Andes and Cordilleras their awful summits lift,
Where Cotopaxi's fiery eye glares redly upon heaven,
And Chimborazo's shattered peak the upper sky has riven ;
From mount to mount, from wave to wave, a wild and long lament,
A sob that shakes like her earthquakes the startled continent !

A light dies out, a life is sped — the hero's at whose word
The nations started as from sleep, and girded on the sword ;
The victor of a hundred fields where blood was poured like rain,
And Freedom's loosened avalanche hurled down the hosts of Spain,
The eagle soul on Junin's slope who showed his shouting men
A grander sight than Balboa saw from wave-washed Darien,
As from the snows with battle red died out the sinking sun,
And broad and vast beneath him lay a world for freedom won.

How died that victor ?   In the field with banners o'er him thrown,
With trumpets in his failing ear, by charging squadrons blown,
With scattered foemen flying fast and fearfully before him,
With shouts of triumph swelling round and brave men bending o'er him ?
Not on his fields of victory, nor in his council hall,
The worn and sorrowing leader heard the inevitable call.
Alone he perished in the land he saved from slavery's ban,
Maligned and doubted and denied, a broken-hearted man !

Now let the New World's banners droop above the fallen chief,
And let the mountaineer's dark eyes be wet with tears of grief !
For slander's sting, for envy's hiss, for friendship hatred grown,
Can funeral pomp, and tolling bell, and priestly mass atone ?
Better to leave unmourned the dead than wrong men while they live ;
What if the strong man failed or erred, could not his own forgive ?
O people freed by him, repent above your hero's bier :
The sole resource of late remorse is now his tomb to rear !
1830.

ISABELLA OF AUSTRIA.

Isabella, Infanta of Parma, and consort of Joseph of Austria, predicted her own death, immediately after her mar-

riage with the Emperor. Amidst the gayety and splendor
of Vienna and Presburg, she was reserved and melancholy;
she believed that Heaven had given her a view of the future,
and that her child, the namesake of the great Maria The-
resa, would perish with her. Her prediction was fulfilled.

'Midst the palace bowers of Hungary, imperial Presburg's pride,
With the noble born and beautiful assembled at her side,
She stood beneath the summer heavens, the soft wind sighing on,
Stirring the green and arching boughs like dancers in the sun.
The beautiful pomegranate flower, the snowy orange bloom,
The lotus and the trailing vine, the rose's meek perfume,
The willow crossing with its green some statue's marble hair,
All that might charm the fresh young sense, or light the soul, was there!

But she, a monarch's treasured one, leaned gloomily apart,
With her dark eyes tearfully cast down, and a shadow on her heart.
Young, beautiful, and dearly loved, what sorrow hath she known?
Are not the hearts and swords of all held sacred as her own?
Is not her lord the kingliest in battle-field or tower?
The wisest in the council-hall, the gayest in the bower?
Is not his love as full and deep as his own Danube's tide?
And wherefore in her princely home weeps Isabel his bride?

She raised her jewelled hand, and flung her veiling tresses back,
Bathing its snowy tapering within their glossy black.
A tear fell on the orange leaves, rich gem and mimic blossom,
And fringëd robe shook fearfully upon her sighing bosom.
"Smile on, smile on," she murmured low, "for all is joy around,
Shadow and sunshine, stainless sky, soft airs, and blossomed ground.
'T is meet the light of heart should smile, when nature's smile is fair,
And melody and fragrance meet, twin sisters of the air.

"But ask me not to share with you the beauty of the scene,
The fountain-fall, mosaic walk, and breadths of tender green;
And point not to the mild blue sky, or glorious summer sun,
I know how very fair is all the hand of God has done.
The hills, the sky, the sunlit cloud, the waters leaping forth,
The swaying trees, the scented flowers, the dark green robes of earth,—
I love them well, but I have learned to turn aside from all,
And nevermore my heart must own their sweet but fatal thrall.

"And I could love the noble one whose mighty name I bear,
And closer to my breaking heart his princely image wear,
And I could love our sweet young flower, unfolding day by day,
And taste of that unearthly joy which mothers only may, —
But what am I to cling to these? — A voice is in my ear,
A shadow lingers at my side, the death-wail and the bier!
The cold and starless night of Death where day may never beam,
The silence and forgetfulness, the sleep that hath no dream!

"O God, to leave this fair bright world, and more than all to know
The moment when the Spectral One shall strike his fearful blow;
To know the day, the very hour, to feel the tide roll on,
To shudder at the gloom before and weep the sunshine gone;
To count the days, the few short days, of light and love and breath
Between me and the noisome grave, the voiceless home of death!
Alas ! — if feeling, knowing this, I murmur at my doom,
Let not thy frowning, O my God! lend darkness to the tomb.

"Oh, I have borne my spirit up, and smiled amidst the chill
Remembrance of my certain doom which lingers with me still;
I would not cloud my fair child's brow, nor let a tear-drop dim
The eye that met my wedded lord's, lest it should sadden him;
But there are moments when the strength of feeling must have way;
That hidden tide of unnamed woe nor fear nor love can stay.
Smile on, smile on, light-hearted ones! Your sun of joy is high:
Smile on, and leave the doomed of Heaven alone to weep and die!"

A funeral chant was wailing through Vienna's holy pile,
A coffin with its gorgeous pall was borne along the aisle;
The drooping flags of many lands waved slow above the dead,
A mighty band of mourners came, a king was at its head, —
A youthful king, with mournful tread, and dim and tearful eye;
He scarce had dreamed that one so pure as his fair bride could die.
And sad and long above the throng the funeral anthem rung:
"Mourn for the hope of Austria! Mourn for the loved and young!"

The wail went up from other lands, the valleys of the Hun,
Fair Parma with its orange bowers, and hills of vine and sun;
The lilies of imperial France drooped as the sound went by,
The long lament of cloistered Spain was mingled with the cry.
The dwellers in Colorno's halls, the Slowak at his cave,
The bowed at the Escurial, the Magyar stoutly brave,
All wept the early stricken flower ; and still the anthem rung:
"Mourn for the pride of Austria! Mourn for the loved and young!"

1831.

THE FRATRICIDE.

He stood on the brow of the well-known hill,
Its few gray oaks moan'd over him still;
The last of that forest which cast the gloom
Of its shadow at eve o'er his childhood's home;
And the beautiful valley beneath him lay
With its quivering leaves, and its streams at play,
And the sunshine over it all the while
Like the golden shower of the Eastern isle.

He knew the rock with its fingering vine,
And its gray top touch'd by the slant sunshine,
And the delicate stream which crept beneath
Soft as the flow of an infant's breath;

And the flowers which lean'd to the West wind's sigh,
Kissing each ripple which glided by;
And he knew every valley and wooded swell,
For the visions of childhood are treasured well.

Why shook the old man as his eye glanced down
That narrow ravine where the rude cliffs frown,
With their shaggy brows and their teeth of stone,
And their grim shade back from the sunlight thrown?
What saw he there save the dreary glen,
Where the shy fox crept from the eye of men,
And the great owl sat on the leafy limb
That the hateful sun might not look on him?

Fix'd, glassy, and strange was that old man's eye,
As if a spectre were stealing by,
And glared it still on that narrow dell
Where thicker and browner the twilight fell;
Yet at every sigh of the fitful wind,
Or stirring of leaves in the wood behind,
His wild glance wander'd the landscape o'er,
Then fix'd on that desolate dell once more.

Oh, who shall tell of the thoughts which ran
Through the dizzied brain of that gray old man?
His childhood's home, and his father's toil,
And his sister's kiss, and his mother's smile,
And his brother's laughter and gamesome mirth,
At the village school and the winter hearth;
The beautiful thoughts of his early time,
Ere his heart grew dark with its later crime.

And darker and wilder his visions came
Of the deadly feud and the midnight flame,
Of the Indian's knife with its slaughter red,
Of the ghastly forms of the scalpless dead,
Of his own fierce deeds in that fearful hour
When the terrible Brandt was forth in power,
And he clasp'd his hands o'er his burning eye
To shadow the vision which glided by.

It came with the rush of the battle-storm —
With a brother's shaken and kneeling form,
And his prayer for life when a brother's arm
Was lifted above him for mortal harm,
And the fiendish curse, and the groan of death,
And the welling of blood, and the gurgling breath,
And the scalp torn off while each nerve could feel
The wrenching hand and the jagged steel!

And the old man groan'd — for he saw, again,
The mangled corse of his kinsman slain,

As it lay where his hand had hurl'd it then,
At the shadow'd foot of that fearful glen!
And it rose erect, with the death-pang grim,
And pointed its bloodied finger at him!
And his heart grew cold — and the curse of Cain
Burn'd like a fire in the old man's brain.

Oh, had he not seen that spectre rise
On the blue of the cold Canadian skies?
From the lakes which sleep in the ancient wood,
It had risen to whisper its tale of blood,
And follow'd his bark to the sombre shore,
And glared by night through the wigwam door;
And here, on his own familiar hill,
It rose on his haunted vision still!

Whose corse was that which the morrow's sun,
Through the opening boughs, look'd calmly on?
There were those who bent o'er that rigid face
Who well in its darken'd lines might trace
The features of him who, a traitor, fled
From a brother whose blood himself had shed,
And there, on the spot where he strangely died,
They made the grave of the Fratricide!

1831.

ISABEL.

I do not love thee, Isabel, and yet thou art most fair!
I know the tempting of thy lips, the witchcraft of thy hair,
The winsome smile that might beguile the shy bird from his tree;
But from their spell I know so well, I shake my manhood free.

I might have loved thee, Isabel; I know I should if aught
Of all thy words and ways had told of one unselfish thought;
If through the cloud of fashion, the pictured veil of art,
One casual flash had broken warm, earnest from the heart.

But words are idle, Isabel, and if I praise or blame,
Or cheer or warn, it matters not; thy life will be the same;
Still free to use, and still abuse, unmindful of the harm,
The fatal gift of beauty, the power to choose and charm.

Then go thy way, fair Isabel, nor heed that from thy train
A doubtful follower falls away, enough will still remain.
But what the long-rebuking years may bring to them or thee
No prophet and no prophet's son am I to guess or see.

I do not love thee, Isabel; I would as soon put on
A crown of slender frost-work beneath the heated sun,

Or chase the winds of summer, or trust the sleeping sea,
Or lean upon a shadow as think of loving thee.

1832.

STANZAS.

Bind up thy tresses, thou beautiful one,
Of brown in the shadow and gold in the sun !
Free should their delicate lustre be thrown
O'er a forehead more pure than the Parian stone ;
Shaming the light of those Orient pearls
Which bind o'er its whiteness thy soft wreathing curls.

Smile, for thy glance on the mirror is thrown,
And the face of an angel is meeting thine own !
Beautiful creature, I marvel not
That thy cheek a lovelier tint hath caught ;
And the kindling light of thine eye hath told
Of a dearer wealth than the miser's gold.

Away, away, there is danger here !
A terrible phantom is bending near :
Ghastly and sunken, his rayless eye
Scowls on thy loveliness scornfully,
With no human look, with no human breath,
He stands beside thee, the haunter, Death !

Fly ! but, alas ! he will follow still,
Like a moonlight shadow, beyond thy will ;
In thy noonday walk, in thy midnight sleep,
Close at thy hand will that phantom keep ;
Still in thine ear shall his whispers be ;
Woe, that such phantom should follow thee !

In the lighted hall where the dancers go,
Like beautiful spirits, to and fro ;
When thy fair arms glance in their stainless white,
Like ivory bathed in still moonlight ;
And not one star in the holy sky
Hath a clearer light than thine own blue eye !

Oh, then, even then, he will follow thee,
As the ripple follows the bark at sea ;
In the soften'd light, in the turning dance,
He will fix on thine his dead, cold glance ;
The chill of his breath on thy cheek shall linger,
And thy warm blood shrink from his icy finger !

And yet there is hope. Embrace it now,
While thy soul is open as thy brow ;
While thy heart is fresh, while its feelings still
Gush clear as the unsoil'd mountain-rill ;

And thy smiles are free as the airs of spring,
Greeting and blessing each breathing thing.

When the after cares of thy life shall come,
When the bud shall wither before its bloom ;
When thy soul is sick of the emptiness
And changeful fashion of human bliss ;
When the weary torpor of blighted feeling
Over thy heart as ice is stealing ;

Then, when thy spirit is turn'd above,
By the mild rebuke of the Chastener's love ;
When the hope of that joy in thy heart is stirr'd,
Which eye hath not seen, nor ear hath heard,
Then will that phantom of darkness be
Gladness, and promise, and bliss to thee.

1832.

MOGG MEGONE.

This poem was commenced in 1830, but did not assume its present shape until four years after. It deals with the border strife of the early settlers of eastern New England and their savage neighbors ; but its personages and incidents are mainly fictitious. Looking at it, at the present time, it suggests the idea of a big Indian in his war-paint strutting about in Sir Walter Scott's plaid.

PART I.

Who stands on that cliff, like a figure of stone,
    Unmoving and tall in the light of the sky,
    Where the spray of the cataract sparkles on high,
Lonely and sternly, save Mogg Megone ? [7]
Close to the verge of the rock is he,
    While beneath him the Saco its work is doing,
    Hurrying down to its grave, the sea,
    And slow through the rock its pathway hewing !
Far down, through the mist of the falling river,
Which rises up like an incense ever,
The splintered points of the crags are seen,
With water howling and vexed between,
While the scooping whirl of the pool beneath
Seems an open throat, with its granite teeth !

But Mogg Megone never trembled yet
Wherever his eye or his foot was set.
He is watchful : each form in the moonlight dim,
Of rock or of tree, is seen of him :

He listens ; each sound from afar is caught,
The faintest shiver of leaf and limb :
But he sees not the waters, which foam and fret,
Whose moonlit spray has his moccasin wet, —
And the roar of their rushing, he hears it not.

The moonlight, through the open bough
  Of the gnarl'd beech, whose naked root
  Coils like a serpent at his foot,
Falls, checkered, on the Indian's brow.
His head is bare, save only where
Waves in the wind one lock of hair,
  Reserved for him, whoe'er he be,
More mighty than Megone in strife,
  When breast to breast and knee to knee,
Above the fallen warrior's life
Gleams, quick and keen, the scalping-knife.

Megone hath his knife and hatchet and gun,
  And his gaudy and tasselled blanket on :
His knife hath a handle with gold inlaid,
And magic words on its polished blade, —
'T was the gift of Castine [8] to Mogg Megone,
For a scalp or twain from the Yengees torn :
His gun was the gift of the Tarrantine,
  And Modocawando's wives had strung
The brass and the beads, which tinkle and shine
On the polished breach, and broad bright line
  Of beaded wampum around it hung.

What seeks Megone ? His foes are near, —
  Grey Jocelyn's [9] eye is never sleeping,
And the garrison lights are burning clear,
  Where Phillips' [10] men their watch are keeping.
Let him hie him away through the dank river fog,
  Never rustling the boughs nor displacing the rocks,
For the eyes and the ears which are watching for Mogg
  Are keener than those of the wolf or the fox.

He starts, — there 's a rustle among the leaves :
  Another, — the click of his gun is heard !
A footstep, — is it the step of Cleaves,
  With Indian blood on his English sword ?
Steals Harmon [11] down from the sands of York,
With hand of iron and foot of cork ?
Has Scamman, versed in Indian wile,
For vengeance left his vine-hung isle ? [12]
Hark ! at that whistle, soft and low,
  How lights the eye of Mogg Megone !
A smile gleams o'er his dusky brow, —
  "Boon welcome, Johnny Boniton ! "

Out steps, with cautious foot and slow,
And quick, keen glances to and fro,
    The hunted outlaw, Boniton ! [13]
A low, lean, swarthy man is he,
With blanket-garb and buskined knee,
    And naught of English fashion on ;
For he hates the race from whence he sprung,
And he couches his words in the Indian tongue.

" Hush, — let the Sachem's voice be weak ;
The water-rat shall hear him speak, —
The owl shall whoop in the white man's ear,
That Mogg Megone, with his scalps, is here ! "
He pauses, — dark, over cheek and brow,
A flush, as of shame, is stealing now :
" Sachem ! " he says, " let me have the land,
Which stretches away upon either hand,
As far about as my feet can stray
In the half of a gentle summer's day,
    From the leaping brook [14] to the Saco river, —
And the fair-haired girl, thou hast sought of me,
Shall sit in the Sachem's wigwam, and be
    The wife of Mogg Megone forever."

There 's a sudden light in the Indian's glance,
    A moment's trace of powerful feeling,
Of love or triumph, or both perchance,
    Over his proud, calm features stealing.
" The words of my father are very good ;
He shall have the land, and water, and wood ;
And he who harms the Sagamore John,
Shall feel the knife of Mogg Megone ;
But the fawn of the Yengees shall sleep on my breast,
And the bird of the clearing shall sing in my nest."

" But, father ! " — and the Indian's hand
    Falls gently on the white man's arm,
And with a smile as shrewdly bland
    As the deep voice is slow and calm, —
" Where is my father's singing-bird, —
    The sunny eye, and sunset hair ?
I know I have my father's word,
    And that his word is good and fair ;
    But will my father tell me where
Megone shall go and look for his bride ? —
For he sees her not by her father's side."

The dark, stern eye of Boniton
    Flashes over the features of Mogg Megone,
    In one of those glances which search within ;
But the stolid calm of the Indian alone
    Remains where the trace of emotion has been.

"Does the Sachem doubt? Let him go with me,
And the eyes of the Sachem his bride shall see."

Cautious and slow, with pauses oft,
And watchful eyes and whispers soft,
The twain are stealing through the wood,
Leaving the downward-rushing flood,
Whose deep and solemn roar behind
Grows fainter on the evening wind.

Hark! — is that the angry howl
　　Of the wolf, the hills among? —
Or the hooting of the owl,
　　On his leafy cradle swung? —
Quickly glancing, to and fro,
Listening to each sound they go
Round the columns of the pine,
　　Indistinct, in shadow, seeming
Like some old and pillared shrine;
　　With the soft and white moonshine,
Round the foliage-tracery shed
Of each column's branching head,
For its lamps of worship gleaming!
And the sounds awakened there,
　　In the pine-leaves fine and small,
　　　Soft and sweetly musical,
By the fingers of the air,
For the anthem's dying fall
Lingering round some temple's wall!
Niche and cornice round and round
Wailing like the ghost of sound!
Is not Nature's worship thus,
　　Ceaseless ever, going on?
Hath it not a voice for us
　　In the thunder, or the tone
Of the leaf-harp faint and small,
　　Speaking to the unsealed ear
　　Words of blended love and fear,
Of the mighty Soul of all?

Naught had the twain of thoughts like these
As they wound along through the crowded trees,
Where never had rung the axeman's stroke
On the gnarlëd trunk of the rough-barked oak; —
Climbing the dead tree's mossy log,
　　Breaking the mesh of the bramble fine,
　　Turning aside the wild grapevine,
And lightly crossing the quaking bog
Whose surface shakes at the leap of the frog,
And out of whose pools the ghostly fog
　　Creeps into the chill moonshine!

Yet, even that Indian's ear had heard
The preaching of the Holy Word:

Sanchekantacket's isle of sand
Was once his father's hunting land,
Where zealous Hiacoomes [15] stood, —
The wild apostle of the wood,
Shook from his soul the fear of harm,
And trampled on the Powwaw's charm;
Until the wizard's curses hung
Suspended on his palsying tongue,
And the fierce warrior, grim and tall,
Trembled before the forest Paul!

A cottage hidden in the wood, —
  Red through its seams a light is glowing,
On rock and bough and tree-trunk rude,
  A narrow lustre throwing.
" Who 's there ? " a clear, firm voice demands;
  " Hold, Ruth, — 't is I, the Sagamore ! "
Quick, at the summons, hasty hands
  Unclose the bolted door;
And on the outlaw's daughter shine
The flashes of the kindled pine.

Tall and erect the maiden stands,
  Like some young priestess of the wood,
  The freeborn child of Solitude,
  And bearing still the wild and rude,
Yet noble trace of Nature's hands.
Her dark brown cheek has caught its stain
More from the sunshine than the rain ;
Yet, where her long fair hair is parting,
A pure white brow into light is starting;
And, where the folds of her blanket sever,
Are neck and a bosom as white as ever
The foam-wreaths rise on the leaping river.
But in the convulsive quiver and grip
Of the muscles around her bloodless lip,
  There is something painful and sad to see;
And her eye has a glance more sternly wild
Than even that of a forest child
  In its fearless and untamed freedom should be.
Yet, seldom in hall or court are seen
So queenly a form and so noble a mien,
  As freely and smiling she welcomes them there, —
Her outlawed sire and Mogg Megone :
  " Pray, father, how does thy hunting fare ?
And, Sachem, say, — does Scamman wear,
In spite of thy promise, a scalp of his own ? "
Hurried and light is the maiden's tone ;
  But a fearful meaning lurks within
Her glance, as it questions the eye of Megone, —
  An awful meaning of guilt and sin ! —
The Indian hath opened his blanket, and there
Hangs a human scalp by its long damp hair !

With hand upraised, with quick-drawn breath,
She meets that ghastly sign of death.
In one long, glassy, spectral stare
The enlarging eye is fastened there,
As if that mesh of pale brown hair
  Had power to change at sight alone,
Even as the fearful locks which wound
Medusa's fatal forehead round,
  The gazer into stone.
With such a look Herodias read
The features of the bleeding head,
So looked the mad Moor on his dead,
Or the young Cenci as she stood,
O'er-dabbled with a father's blood!

Look! — feeling melts that frozen glance,
It moves that marble countenance,
As if at once within her strove
Pity with shame, and hate with love.
The Past recalls its joy and pain,
Old memories rise before her brain, —
The lips which love's embraces met,
The hand her tears of parting wet,
The voice whose pleading tones beguiled
The pleased ear of the forest-child, —
And tears she may no more repress
Reveal her lingering tenderness.

Oh, woman wronged can cherish hate
  More deep and dark than manhood may;
But when the mockery of Fate
  Hath left Revenge its chosen way,
And the fell curse, which years have nursed,
Full on the spoiler's head hath burst, —
When all her wrong, and shame, and pain,
Burns fiercely on his heart and brain, —
Still lingers something of the spell
  Which bound her to the traitor's bosom, —
Still, midst the vengeful fires of hell,
  Some flowers of old affection blossom.

John Boniton's eyebrows together are drawn
With a fierce expression of wrath and scorn, —
He hoarsely whispers, "Ruth, beware!
  Is this the time to be playing the fool, —
Crying over a paltry lock of hair,
  Like a love-sick girl at school? —
Curse on it! — an Indian can see and hear:
Away, — and prepare our evening cheer!"

How keenly the Indian is watching now
Her tearful eye and her varying brow, —

With a serpent eye, which kindles and burns,
  Like a fiery star in the upper air :
On sire and daughter his fierce glance turns : —
  " Has my old white father a scalp to spare ?
  For his young one loves the pale brown hair
Of the scalp of an English dog far more
Than Mogg Megone, or his wigwam floor ;
  Go, — Mogg is wise : he will keep his land, —
  And Sagamore John, when he feels with his hand,
Shall miss his scalp where it grew before."

The moment's gust of grief is gone, —
  The lip is clenched, — the tears are still, —
God pity thee, Ruth Boniton !
  With what a strength of will
Are nature's feelings in thy breast,
As with an iron hand, repressed !
And how, upon that nameless woe,
Quick as the pulse can come and go,
While shakes the unsteadfast knee, and yet
The bosom heaves, — the eye is wet, —
Has thy dark spirit power to stay
The heart's wild current on its way ?
  And whence that baleful strength of guile,
Which over that still working brow
And tearful eye and cheek can throw
  The mockery of a smile ?
Warned by her father's blackening frown,
With one strong effort crushing down
Grief, hate, remorse, she meets again
  The savage murderer's sullen gaze,
  And scarcely look or tone betrays
How the heart strives beneath its chain.

" Is the Sachem angry, — angry with Ruth,
Because she cries with an ache in her tooth,[16]
Which would make a Sagamore jump and cry,
And look about with a woman's eye ?
No, — Ruth will sit in the Sachem's door
And braid the mats for his wigwam floor,
And broil his fish and tender fawn,
And weave his wampum, and grind his corn, —
For she loves the brave and the wise, and none
Are braver and wiser than Mogg Megone ! "

The Indian's brow is clear once more :
  With grave, calm face, and half-shut eye,
He sits upon the wigwam floor,
  And watches Ruth go by,
Intent upon her household care ;
  And ever and anon, the while,
Or on the maiden, or her fare,

Which smokes in grateful promise there,
 Bestows his quiet smile.

Ah, Mogg Megone ! — what dreams are thine,
 But those which love's own fancies dress, —
 The sum of Indian happiness ! —
A wigwam, where the warm sunshine
Looks in among the groves of pine, —
A stream, where, round thy light canoe,
The trout and salmon dart in view,
And the fair girl, before thee now,
Spreading thy mat with hand of snow,
Or plying, in the dews of morn,
Her hoe amidst thy patch of corn,
Or offering up, at eve, to thee,
Thy birchen dish of hominy !

From the rude board of Boniton,
Venison and succotash have gone, —
For long these dwellers of the wood
Have felt the gnawing want of food.
But untasted of Ruth is the frugal cheer, —
With head averted, yet ready ear,
She stands by the side of her austere sire,
Feeding, at times, the unequal fire
With the yellow knots of the pitch-pine tree,
Whose flaring light, as they kindle, falls
On the cottage-roof, and its black log walls,
And over its inmates three.

From Sagamore Boniton's hunting flask
 The fire-water burns at the lip of Megone :
" Will the Sachem hear what his father shall ask ?
 Will he make his mark, that it may be known,
On the speaking-leaf, that he gives the land,
From the Sachem's own, to his father's hand ? "
The fire-water shines in the Indian's eyes,
 As he rises, the white man's bidding to do :
' Wuttamuttata — weekan ! [17] Mogg is wise, —
 For the water he drinks is strong and new, —
Mogg's heart is great ! — will he shut his hand,
When his father asks for a little land ? " —
With unsteady fingers, the Indian has drawn
 On the parchment the shape of a hunter's bow,
' Boon water, — boon water, — Sagamore John !
 Wuttamuttata, — weekan ! our hearts will grow ! "
He drinks yet deeper, — he mutters low, —
He reels on his bear-skin to and fro, —
His head falls down on his naked breast, —
He struggles, and sinks to a drunken rest.

" Humph — drunk as a beast ! " — and Boniton's brow
 Is darker than ever with evil thought —

"The fool has signed his warrant; but how
    And when shall the deed be wrought?
Speak, Ruth! why, what the devil is there,
To fix thy gaze in that empty air? —
Speak, Ruth! by my soul, if I thought that tear,
Which shames thyself and our purpose here,
Were shed for that cursed and pale-faced dog,
Whose green scalp hangs from the belt of Mogg,
    And whose beastly soul is in Satan's keeping, —
This — this!'" — he dashes his hand upon
The rattling stock of his loaded gun, —
    "Should send thee with him to do thy weeping!"

"Father!" — the eye of Boniton
Sinks at that low, sepulchral tone,
Hollow and deep, as it were spoken
    By the unmoving tongue of death, —
Or from some statue's lips had broken, —
    A sound without a breath!
"Father! — my life I value less
Than yonder fool his gaudy dress;
And how it ends it matters not,
By heart-break or by rifle-shot;
But spare awhile the scoff and threat, —
Our business is not finished yet."

"True, true, my girl, — I only meant
To draw up again the bow unbent.
Harm thee, my Ruth! I only sought
To frighten off thy gloomy thought;
Come, — let's be friends!" He seeks to clasp
His daughter's cold, damp hand in his.
Ruth startles from her father's grasp,
As if each nerve and muscle felt,
Instinctively, the touch of guilt,
Through all their subtle sympathies.

He points her to the sleeping Mogg:
"What shall be done with yonder dog?
Scamman is dead, and revenge is thine, —
The deed is signed and the land is mine;
And this drunken fool is of use no more,
Save as thy hopeful bridegroom, and sooth,
'T were Christian mercy to finish him, Ruth,
Now, while he lies like a beast on our floor, —
If not for thine, at least for his sake,
Rather than let the poor dog awake
To drain my flask, and claim as his bride
Such a forest devil to run by his side, —
Such a Wetuomanit [18] as thou wouldst make!"

He laughs at his jest. Hush — what is there? —
    The sleeping Indian is striving to rise,

With his knife in his hand, and glaring eyes ! —
"Wagh ! — Mogg will have the pale-face's hair,
   For his knife is sharp, and his fingers can help
The hair to pull and the skin to peel, —
Let him cry like a woman and twist like an eel,
   The great Captain Scamman must lose his scalp !
And Ruth, when she sees it, shall dance with Mogg."
His eyes are fixed, — but his lips draw in, —
With a low, hoarse chuckle, and fiendish grin, —
   And he sinks again, like a senseless log.

Ruth does not speak, — she does not stir ;
But she gazes down on the murderer,
Whose broken and dreamful slumbers tell
Too much for her ear of that deed of hell.
She sees the knife, with its slaughter red,
And the dark fingers clenching the bearskin bed !
What thoughts of horror and madness whirl
Through the burning brain of that fallen girl !

John Boniton lifts his gun to his eye,
   Its muzzle is close to the Indian's ear, —
But he drops it again.   "Some one may be nigh,
   And I would not that even the wolves should hear."
He draws his knife from its deer-skin belt, —
Its edge with his fingers is slowly felt ; —
Kneeling down on one knee, by the Indian's side,
From his throat he opens the blanket wide ;
And twice or thrice he feebly essays
A trembling hand with the knife to raise.

"I cannot," — he mutters, — "did he not save
My life from a cold and wintry grave,
When the storm came down from Agioochook,
And the north-wind howled, and the tree-tops shook, —
And I strove, in the drifts of the rushing snow,
Till my knees grew weak and I could not go,
And I felt the cold to my vitals creep,
And my heart's blood stiffen, and pulses sleep !
I cannot strike him — Ruth Boniton !
In the Devil's name, tell me — what 's to be done ? "

Oh, when the soul, once pure and high,
Is stricken down from Virtue's sky,
As, with the downcast star of morn,
Some gems of light are with it drawn,
And, through its night of darkness, play
Some tokens of its primal day,
Some lofty feelings linger still, —
   The strength to dare, the nerve to meet
   Whatever threatens with defeat
Its all-indomitable will ! —

But lacks the mean of mind and heart,
Though eager for the gains of crime,
Or, at his chosen place and time,
The strength to bear his evil part ;
And, shielded by his very Vice,
Escapes from Crime by Cowardice.

Ruth starts erect, — with bloodshot eye,
    And lips drawn tight across her teeth,
Showing their locked embrace beneath,
In the red firelight : " Mogg must die !
Give me the knife ! " The outlaw turns,
    Shuddering in heart and limb away, —
But, fitfully there, the hearth-fire burns,
    And he sees on the wall strange shadows play.
A lifted arm, a tremulous blade,
Are dimly pictured in light and shade,
    Plunging down in the darkness.   Hark, that cry
Again — and again — he sees it fall,
That shadowy arm down the lighted wall !
    He hears quick footsteps — a shape flits by —
    The door on its rusted hinges creaks : —
" Ruth — daughter Ruth ! " the outlaw shrieks.
    But no sound comes back, — he is standing alone
    By the mangled corse of Mogg Megone !

PART II.

'T is morning over Norridgewock, —
On tree and wigwam, wave and rock.
Bathed in the autumnal sunshine, stirred
At intervals by breeze and bird,
And wearing all the hues which glow
In heaven's own pure and perfect bow,
    That glorious picture of the air,
Which summer's light-robed angel forms
On the dark ground of fading storms,
    With pencil dipped in sunbeams there, —
And, stretching out, on either hand,
O'er all that wide and unshorn land,
Till, weary of its gorgeousness,
The aching and the dazzled eye
Rests, gladdened, on the calm blue sky, —
    Slumbers the mighty wilderness !
The oak, upon the windy hill,
    Its dark green burthen upward heaves—
The hemlock broods above its rill,
Its cone-like foliage darker still,
    Against the birch's graceful stem,
And the rough walnut-bough receives
The sun upon its crowded leaves,

Each colored like a topaz gem ;
And the tall maple wears with them
The coronal, which autumn gives,
The brief, bright sign of ruin near,
The hectic of a dying year !

The hermit priest, who lingers now
On the Bald Mountain's shrubless brow,
The gray and thunder-smitten pile
Which marks afar the Desert Isle,[19]
While gazing on the scene below,
May half forget the dreams of home,
That nightly with his slumbers come, —
The tranquil skies of sunny France,
The peasant's harvest song and dance,
The vines around the hillsides wreathing,
The soft airs midst their clusters breathing,
The wings which dipped, the stars which shone
Within thy bosom, blue Garonne !
And round the Abbey's shadowed wall,
At morning spring and even-fall,
Sweet voices in the still air singing, —
The chant of many a holy hymn, —
The solemn bell of vespers ringing, —
And hallowed torchlight falling dim
On pictured saint and seraphim !
For here beneath him lies unrolled,
Bathed deep in morning's flood of gold,
A vision gorgeous as the dream
Of the beatified may seem,
When, as his Church's legends say,
Borne upward in ecstatic bliss,
The rapt enthusiast soars away
Unto a brighter world than this :
A mortal's glimpse beyond the pale, —
A moment's lifting of the veil !

Far eastward o'er the lovely bay,
Penobscot's clustered wigwams lay ;
And gently from that Indian town
The verdant hillside slopes adown,
To where the sparkling waters play
Upon the yellow sands below ;
And shooting round the winding shores
Of narrow capes, and isles which lie
Slumbering to ocean's lullaby, —
With birchen boat and glancing oars,
The red men to their fishing go ;
While from their planting ground is borne
The treasure of the golden corn,
By laughing girls, whose dark eyes glow
Wild through the locks which o'er them flow.

The wrinkled squaw, whose toil is done,
Sits on her bear-skin in the sun,
Watching the huskers, with a smile
For each full ear which swells the pile;
And the old chief, who nevermore
May bend the bow or pull the oar,
Smokes gravely in his wigwam door,
Or slowly shapes, with axe of stone,
The arrow-head from flint and bone.

Beneath the westward turning eye
A thousand wooded islands lie,
Gems of the waters! with each hue
Of brightness set in ocean's blue.
Each bears aloft its tuft of trees
    Touched by the pencil of the frost,
And, with the motion of each breeze,
    A moment seen, a moment lost,
    Changing and blent, confused and tossed,
        The brighter with the darker crossed,
Their thousand tints of beauty glow
Down in the restless waves below,
    And tremble in the sunny skies,
As if, from waving bough to bough,
    Flitted the birds of paradise.
There sleep Placentia's group, and there
Père Breteaux marks the hour of prayer;
And there, beneath the sea-worn cliff,
    On which the Father's hut is seen,
The Indian stays his rocking skiff,
    And peers the hemlock-boughs between,
Half trembling, as he seeks to look
Upon the Jesuit's Cross and Book.[20]
There, gloomily against the sky
The Dark Isles rear their summits high;
And Desert Rock, abrupt and bare,
Lifts its gray turrets in the air,
Seen from afar, like some stronghold
Built by the ocean kings of old;
And, faint as smoke-wreath white and thin,
Swells in the north vast Katahdin:
And, wandering from its marshy feet,
The broad Penobscot comes to meet
    And mingle with his own bright bay.
Slow sweep his dark and gathering floods,
Arched over by the ancient woods,
Which Time, in those dim solitudes,
    Wielding the dull axe of Decay,
    Alone hath ever shorn away.

Not thus, within the woods which hide
The beauty of thy azure tide,

And with their falling timbers block
Thy broken currents, Kennebec !
Gazes the white man on the wreck
Of the down-trodden Norridgewock ;
In one lone village hemmed at length,
In battle shorn of half their strength,
Turned, like the panther in his lair,
  With his fast-flowing life-blood wet,
For one last struggle of despair,
  Wounded and faint, but tameless yet !
Unreaped, upon the planting lands,
The scant, neglected harvest stands :
  No shout is there, no dance, no song :
The aspect of the very child
Scowls with a meaning sad and wild
  Of bitterness and wrong.
The almost infant Norridgewock
Essays to lift the tomahawk ;
And plucks his father's knife away,
To mimic, in his frightful play,
  The scalping of an English foe :
Wreathes on his lip a horrid smile,
Burns, like a snake's, his small eye, while
  Some bough or sapling meets his blow.
The fisher, as he drops his line,
Starts, when he sees the hazels quiver
Alorg the margin of the river,
Looks up and down the rippling tide,
And grasps the firelock at his side.
For Bomazeen [21] from Tacconock
Has sent his runners to Norridgewock,
With tidings that Moulton and Harmon of York
  Far up the river have come :
They have left their boats, they have entered the wood,
And filled the depths of the solitude
  With the sound of the ranger's drum.

On the brow of a hill, which slopes to meet
The flowing river, and bathe its feet ;
The bare-washed rock, and the drooping grass,
And the creeping vine, as the waters pass,
A rude and unshapely chapel stands,
Built up in that wild by unskilled hands,
Yet the traveller knows it a place of prayer,
For the holy sign of the cross is there :
And should he chance at that place to be,
  Of a Sabbath morn, or some hallowed day,
When prayers are made and masses are said,
Some for the living and some for the dead,
Well might that traveller start to see
  The tall dark forms, that take their way
From the birch canoe, on the river-shore,
And the forest paths, to that chapel door ;

And marvel to mark the naked knees
  And the dusky foreheads bending there,
While, in coarse white vesture, over these
  In blessing or in prayer,
Stretching abroad his thin pale hands,
Like a shrouded ghost, the Jesuit [22] stands.

Two forms are now in that chapel dim,
  The Jesuit, silent and sad and pale,
  Anxiously heeding some fearful tale,
Which a stranger is telling him.
That stranger's garb is soiled and torn,
And wet with dew and loosely worn ;
Her fair neglected hair falls down
O'er cheeks with wind and sunshine brown ;
Yet still, in that disordered face,
The Jesuit's cautious eye can trace
Those elements of former grace
Which, half effaced, seem scarcely less,
Even now, than perfect loveliness.

With drooping head, and voice so low
  That scarce it meets the Jesuit's ears,
While through her clasped fingers flow,
From the heart's fountain, hot and slow,
  Her penitential tears, —
She tells the story of the woe
  And evil of her years.

" O father, bear with me ; my heart
  Is sick and death-like, and my brain
  Seems girdled with a fiery chain,
Whose scorching links will never part,
  And never cool again.
Bear with me while I speak, but turn
  Away that gentle eye, the while ;
The fires of guilt more fiercely burn
  Beneath its holy smile ;
For half I fancy I can see
My mother's sainted look in thee.

" My dear lost mother ! sad and pale,
  Mournfully sinking day by day,
And with a hold on life as frail
  As frosted leaves, that, thin and gray,
  Hang feebly on their parent spray,
And tremble in the gale ;
Yet watching o'er my childishness
With patient fondness, not the less
For all the agony which kept
Her blue eye wakeful, while I slept ;
And checking every tear and groan

That haply might have waked my own,
And bearing still, without offence,
My idle words, and petulance ;
  Reproving with a tear, and, while
The tooth of pain was keenly preying
Upon her very heart, repaying
  My brief repentance with a smile.

" Oh, in her meek, forgiving eye
  There was a brightness not of mirth,
A light whose clear intensity
  Was borrowed not of earth.
Along her cheek a deepening red
Told where the feverish hectic fed ;
  And yet, each fatal token gave
To the mild beauty of her face
A newer and a dearer grace,
  Unwarning of the grave.
'T was like the hue which Autumn gives
To yonder changed and dying leaves,
  Breathed over by his frosty breath ;
Scarce can the gazer feel that this
Is but the spoiler's treacherous kiss,
  The mocking-smile of Death !

" Sweet were the tales she used to tell
  When summer's eve was dear to us,
And, fading from the darkening dell,
The glory of the sunset fell
  On wooded Agamenticus, —
When, sitting by our cottage wall,
The murmur of the Saco's fall,
  And the south-wind's expiring sighs,
Came, softly blending, on my ear,
With the low tones I loved to hear :
  Tales of the pure, the good, the wise,
The holy men and maids of old,
In the all-sacred pages told ;
Of Rachel, stooped at Haran's fountains,
  Amid her father's thirsty flock,
Beautiful to her kinsman seeming
As the bright angels of his dreaming,
  On Padan-aran's holy rock ;
Of gentle Ruth, and her who kept
  Her awful vigil on the mountains,
By Israel's virgin daughters wept ;
Of Miriam, with her maidens, singing
  The song for grateful Israel meet,
While every crimson wave was bringing
  The spoils of Egypt at her feet ;
Of her, Samaria's humble daughter,
  Who paused to hear, beside her well,
  Lessons of love and truth, which fell

Softly as Shiloh's flowing water ;
  And saw, beneath his pilgrim guise,
The Promised One, so long foretold
By holy seer and bard of old,
  Revealed before her wondering eyes!

  " Slowly she faded.   Day by day
Her step grew weaker in our hall,
And fainter, at each even-fall,
  Her sad voice died away.
Yet on her thin, pale lip, the while,
Sat Resignation's holy smile :
And even my father checked his tread,
And hushed his voice, beside her bed :
Beneath the calm and sad rebuke
Of her meek eye's imploring look,
The scowl of hate his brow forsook,
  And in his stern and gloomy eye,
At times, a few unwonted tears
Wet the dark lashes, which for years
  Hatred and pride had kept so dry.

" Calm as a child to slumber soothed,
As if an angel's hand had smoothed
  The still, white features into rest,
Silent and cold, without a breath
  To stir the drapery on her breast,
Pain, with its keen and poisoned fang,
The horror of the mortal pang,
The suffering look her brow had worn,
The fear, the strife, the anguish gone, —
  She slept at last in death !

" Oh, tell me, father, *can* the dead
  Walk on the earth, and look on us,
And lay upon the living's head
  Their blessing or their curse ?
For, oh, last night she stood by me,
As I lay beneath the woodland tree ! "

The Jesuit crosses himself in awe, —
" Jesu ! what was it my daughter saw ? "

" *She* came to me last night.
  The dried leaves did not feel her tread;
She stood by me in the wan moonlight,
  In the white robes of the dead !
Pale, and very mournfully
She bent her light form over me.
I heard no sound, I felt no breath
Breathe o'er me from that face of death :
Its blue eyes rested on my own,
  Rayless and cold as eyes of stone ;

Yet, in their fixed, unchanging gaze,
Something, which spoke of early days, —
A sadness in their quiet glare,
As if love's smile were frozen there, —
Came o'er me with an icy thrill ;
O God ! I feel its presence still ! "

The Jesuit makes the holy sign, —
" How passed the vision, daughter mine ? "

" All dimly in the wan moonshine,
  As a wreath of mist will twist and twine,
And scatter, and melt into the light ;
So scattering, melting on my sight,
  The pale, cold vision passed ;
But those sad eyes were fixed on mine
  Mournfully to the last."

" God help thee, daughter, tell me why
That spirit passed before thine eye ! "

" Father, I know not, save it be
    That deeds of mine have summoned her
    From the unbreathing sepulchre,
To leave her last rebuke with me.
Ah, woe for me ! my mother died
Just at the moment when I stood
Close on the verge of womanhood,
A child in everything beside ;
And when my wild heart needed most
Her gentle counsels, they were lost.

" My father lived a stormy life,
Of frequent change and daily strife ;
And — God forgive him ! left his child
To feel, like him, a freedom wild ;
To love the red man's dwelling-place,
  The birch boat on his shaded floods,
The wild excitement of the chase
  Sweeping the ancient woods,
The camp-fire, blazing on the shore
  Of the still lakes, the clear stream where
  The idle fisher sets his weir,
Or angles in the shade, far more
  Than that restraining awe I felt
Beneath my gentle mother's care,
  When nightly at her knee I knelt,
With childhood's simple prayer.

" There came a change. The wild, glad mood
  Of unchecked freedom passed.
Amid the ancient solitude
Of unshorn grass and waving wood

And waters glancing bright and fast,
A softened voice was in my ear,
Sweet as those lulling sounds and fine
The hunter lifts his head to hear,
Now far and faint, now full and near —
  The murmur of the wind-swept pine.
A manly form was ever nigh,
A bold, free hunter, with an eye
  Whose dark, keen glance had power to wake
Both fear and love, to awe and charm;
  'T was as the wizard rattlesnake,
Whose evil glances lure to harm —
Whose cold and small and glittering eye,
And brilliant coil, and changing dye,
Draw, step by step, the gazer near,
With drooping wing and cry of fear,
Yet powerless all to turn away,
A conscious, but a willing prey!

"Fear, doubt, thought, life itself, erelong
Merged in one feeling deep and strong.
Faded the world which I had known,
  A poor vain shadow, cold and waste;
In the warm present bliss alone
  Seemed I of actual life to taste.
Fond longings dimly understood,
The glow of passion's quickening blood,
And cherished fantasies which press
The young lip with a dream's caress;
The heart's forecast and prophecy
Took form and life before my eye,
Seen in the glance which met my own,
Heard in the soft and pleading tone,
Felt in the arms around me cast,
And warm heart-pulses beating fast.
Ah! scarcely yet to God above
With deeper trust, with stronger love,
Has prayerful saint his meek heart lent,
Or cloistered nun at twilight bent,
Than I, before a human shrine,
As mortal and as frail as mine,
With heart, and soul, and mind, and form,
Knelt madly to a fellow-worm.

"Full soon, upon that dream of sin,
An awful light came bursting in.
The shrine was cold at which I knelt,
  The idol of that shrine was gone;
A humbled thing of shame and guilt,
  Outcast, and spurned and lone,
Wrapt in the shadows of my crime,
  With withering heart and burning brain,

And tears that fell like fiery rain,
I passed a fearful time.

"There came a voice — it checked the tear,
    In heart and soul it wrought a change ;
My father's voice was in my ear ;
    It whispered of revenge !
A new and fiercer feeling swept
    All lingering tenderness away ;
And tiger passions, which had slept
    In childhood's better day,
Unknown, unfelt, arose at length
In all their own demoniac strength.

"A youthful warrior of the wild,
By words deceived, by smiles beguiled,
Of crime the cheated instrument,
Upon our fatal errands went.
    Through camp and town and wilderness
He tracked his victim ; and, at last,
Just when the tide of hate had passed,
And milder thoughts came warm and fast,
Exulting, at my feet he cast
    The bloody token of success.

"O God ! with what an awful power
    I saw the buried past uprise,
And gather, in a single hour,
    Its ghost-like memories !
And then I felt, alas ! too late,
That underneath the mask of hate,
That shame and guilt and wrong had thrown
O'er feelings which they might not own,
    The heart's wild love had known no change ;
And still that deep and hidden love,
With its first fondness, wept above
    The victim of its own revenge !
There lay the fearful scalp, and there
The blood was on its pale brown hair !
I thought not of the victim's scorn,
    I thought not of his baleful guile,
My deadly wrong, my outcast name,
The characters of sin and shame
On heart and forehead drawn ;
    I only saw that victim's smile,
The still, green places where we met, —
The moonlit branches, dewy wet ;
I only felt, I only heard
The greeting and the parting word, —
The smile, the embrace, the tone, which made
An Eden of the forest shade.

" And oh, with what a loathing eye,
  With what a deadly hate, and deep,
I saw that Indian murderer lie
Before me, in his drunken sleep !
What though for me the deed was done,
And words of mine had sped him on !
Yet when he murmured, as he slept,
  The horrors of that deed of blood,
The tide of utter madness swept
  O'er brain and bosom, like a flood.
And, father, with this hand of mine " —
  " Ha ! what didst thou ? " the Jesuit cries,
Shuddering, as smitten with sudden pain,
  And shading, with one thin hand, his eyes,
With the other he makes the holy sign.
" — I smote him as I would a worm ;
  With heart as steeled, with nerves as firm :
  He never woke again ! " "

" Woman of sin and blood and shame,
  Speak, I would know that victim's name."

" Father," she gasped, " a chieftain, known
  As Saco's Sachem, — Mogg Megone ! ' "

Pale priest ! What proud and lofty dreams,
What keen desires, what cherished schemes,
What hopes, that time may not recall,
Are darkened by that chieftain's fall !
Was he not pledged, by cross and vow,
  To lift the hatchet of his sire,
And, round his own, the Church's foe,
  To light the avenging fire ?
Who now the Tarrantine shall wake,
For thine and for the Church's sake ?
  Who summon to the scene
Of conquest and unsparing strife,
And vengeance dearer than his life,
  The fiery-souled Castine ? [23]
Three backward steps the Jesuit takes,
His long, thin frame as ague shakes ;
  And loathing hate is in his eye,
As from his lips these words of fear
Fall hoarsely on the maiden's ear, —
  " The soul that sinneth shall surely die ! "

She stands, as stands the stricken deer,
  Checked midway in the fearful chase,
When bursts, upon his eye and ear,
The gaunt, gray robber, baying near,
  Between him and his hiding-place ;
While still behind, with yell and blow,

378 APPENDIX

Sweeps, like a storm, the coming foe.
"Save me, O holy man!" her cry
　Fills all the void, as if a tongue,
　Unseen, from rib and rafter hung,
Thrilling with mortal agony ;
Her hands are clasping the Jesuit's knee,
　And her eye looks fearfully into his own ; —
"Off, woman of sin! nay, touch not me
　With those fingers of blood ; begone!"
With a gesture of horror, he spurns the form
That writhes at his feet like a trodden worm.

　　　Ever thus the spirit must,
　　　　Guilty in the sight of Heaven,
　　　　With a keener woe be riven,
　　　For its weak and sinful trust
　　　In the strength of human dust ;
　　　　And its anguish thrill afresh,
　　　For each vain reliance given
　　　　To the failing arm of flesh.

PART III.

Ah, weary Priest ! with pale hands pressed
　On thy throbbing brow of pain,
Baffled in thy life-long quest,
　Overworn with toiling vain,
How ill thy troubled musings fit
　The holy quiet of a breast
　With the Dove of Peace at rest,
Sweetly brooding over it.
Thoughts are thine which have no part
With the meek and pure of heart,
Undisturbed by outward things,
Resting in the heavenly shade,
By the overspreading wings
Of the Blessed Spirit made.
Thoughts of strife and hate and wrong
Sweep thy heated brain along,
Fading hopes for whose success
　It were sin to breathe a prayer ; —
Schemes which Heaven may never bless, —
　Fears which darken to despair.
Hoary priest ! thy dream is done
Of a hundred red tribes won
　To the pale of Holy Church ;
And the heretic o'erthrown,
And his name no longer known,
And thy weary brethren turning,
Joyful from their years of mourning
'Twixt the altar and the porch.
Hark ! what sudden sound is heard

In the wood and in the sky,
Shriller than the scream of bird,
    Than the trumpet's clang more high!
Every wolf-cave of the hills,
    Forest arch and mountain gorge,
    Rock and dell, and river verge,
With an answering echo thrills.
Well does the Jesuit know that cry,
Which summons the Norridgewock to die,
And tells that the foe of his flock is nigh.
He listens, and hears the rangers come,
With loud hurrah, and jar of drum,
And hurrying feet (for the chase is hot),
And the short, sharp sound of rifle shot,
And taunt and menace, — answered well
By the Indians' mocking cry and yell, —
The bark of dogs, — the squaw's mad scream,
The dash of paddles along the stream,
The whistle of shot as it cuts the leaves
Of the maples around the church's eaves,
And the gride of hatchets fiercely thrown,
On wigwam-log and tree and stone.
Black with the grime of paint and dust,
    Spotted and streaked with human gore,
A grim and naked head is thrust
    Within the chapel-door.
" Ha — Bomazeen! In God's name say,
What mean these sounds of bloody fray? "
Silent, the Indian points his hand
    To where across the echoing glen
Sweep Harmon's dreaded ranger-band,
    And Moulton with his men.
" Where are thy warriors, Bomazeen?
Where are De Rouville [24] and Castine,
And where the braves of Sawga's queen? "
" Let my father find the winter snow
Which the sun drank up long moons ago!
Under the falls of Tacconock,
The wolves are eating the Norridgewock;
Castine with his wives lies closely hid
Like a fox in the woods of Pemaquid!
On Sawga's banks the man of war
Sits in his wigwam like a squaw;
Squando has fled, and Mogg Megone,
    Struck by the knife of Sagamore John,
Lies stiff and stark and cold as a stone."

Fearfully over the Jesuit's face,
Of a thousand thoughts, trace after trace,
Like swift cloud-shadows, each other chase.
One instant, his fingers grasp his knife,
For a last vain struggle for cherished life, —

The next, he hurls the blade away,
And kneels at his altar's foot to pray ;
Over his beads his fingers stray,
And he kisses the cross, and calls aloud
On the Virgin and her Son ;
For terrible thoughts his memory crowd
    Of evil seen and done,
Of scalps brought home by his savage flock
From Casco and Sawga and Sagadahock
    In the Church's service won.

No shrift the gloomy savage brooks,
As scowling on the priest he looks :
"Cowesass — cowesass — tawhich wessa seen ?[25]
Let my father look upon Bomazeen, —
My father's heart is the heart of a squaw,
But mine is so hard that it does not thaw ;
Let my father ask his God to make
    A dance and a feast for a great sagamore,
When he paddles across the western lake,
    With his dogs and his squaws to the spirit's shore.
Cowesass — cowesass — tawhich wessa seen ?
Let my father die like Bomazeen ! ''

Through the chapel's narrow doors,
    And through each window in the walls,
Round the priest and warrior pours
    The deadly shower of English balls.
Low on his cross the Jesuit falls ;
While at his side the Norridgewock,
With failing breath, essays to mock
And menace yet the hated foe,
Shakes his scalp-trophies to and fro
    Exultingly before their eyes,
Till, cleft and torn by shot and blow,
    Defiant still, he dies.

"So fare all eaters of the frog !
Death to the Babylonish dog !
    Down with the beast of Rome ! ''
With shouts like these, around the dead,
Unconscious on his bloody bed,
    The rangers crowding come.
Brave men ! the dead priest cannot hear
The unfeeling taunt, — the brutal jeer ;
Spurn — for he sees ye not — in wrath,
The symbol of your Saviour's death ;
    Tear from his death-grasp, in your zeal,
And trample, as a thing accursed,
The cross he cherished in the dust :
    The dead man cannot feel !

Brutal alike in deed and word,
  With callous heart and hand of strife,
How like a fiend may man be made,
Plying the foul and monstrous trade
  Whose harvest-field is human life,
Whose sickle is the reeking sword !
Quenching, with reckless hand in blood,
Sparks kindled by the breath of God ;
Urging the deathless soul, unshriven,
  Of open guilt or secret sin,
Before the bar of that pure Heaven
  The holy only enter in !
Oh, by the widow's sore distress,
The orphan's wailing wretchedness,
By Virtue struggling in the accursed
Embraces of polluting Lust,
By the fell discord of the Pit,
And the pained souls that people it,
And by the blessed peace which fills
  The Paradise of God forever,
Resting on all its holy hills,
  And flowing with its crystal river, —
Let Christian hands no longer bear
  In triumph on his crimson car
  The foul and idol god of war ;
No more the purple wreaths prepare
To bind amid his snaky hair ;
Nor Christian bards his glories tell,
Nor Christian tongues his praises swell.

Through the gun-smoke wreathing white,
Glimpses on the soldiers' sight
A thing of human shape I ween,
For a moment only seen,
With its loose hair backward streaming,
And its eyeballs madly gleaming,
Shrieking, like a soul in pain,
  From the world of light and breath,
Hurrying to its place again,
  Spectre-like it vanisheth !

Wretched girl ! one eye alone
Notes the way which thou hast gone.
That great Eye, which slumbers never,
Watching o'er a lost world ever,
Tracks thee over vale and mountain,
By the gushing forest-fountain,
Plucking from the vine its fruit,
Searching for the ground-nut's root,
Peering in the she-wolf's den,
Wading through the marshy fen,
Where the sluggish water-snake

Basks beside the sunny brake,
Coiling in his slimy bed,
Smooth and cold against thy tread ;
Purposeless, thy mazy way
Threading through the lingering day.
And at night securely sleeping
Where the dogwood's dews are weeping !
Still, though earth and man discard thee,
Doth thy Heavenly Father guard thee :
He who spared the guilty Cain,
    Even when a brother's blood,
    Crying in the ear of God,
Gave the earth its primal stain ;
He whose mercy ever liveth,
Who repenting guilt forgiveth,
And the broken heart receiveth ;
Wanderer of the wilderness,
    Haunted, guilty, crazed, and wild,
He regardeth thy distress,
    And careth for His sinful child !

'T is springtime on the eastern hills !
Like torrents gush the summer rills ;
Through winter's moss and dry dead leaves
The bladed grass revives and lives,
Pushes the mouldering waste away,
For glimpses to the April day.
In kindly shower and sunshine bud
The branches of the dull gray wood ;
Out from its sunned and sheltered nooks
The blue eye of the violet looks ;
    The southwest wind is warmly blowing,
And odors from the springing grass,
The pine-tree and the sassafras,
    Are with it on its errands going.

A band is marching through the wood
Where rolls the Kennebec his flood ;
The warriors of the wilderness,
Painted, and in their battle dress ;
And with them one whose bearded cheek,
And white and wrinkled brow, bespeak
    A wanderer from the shores of France.
A few long locks of scattering snow
Beneath a battered morion flow,
And from the rivets of the vest
Which girds in steel his ample breast,
    The slanted sunbeams glance.
In the harsh outlines of his face
Passion and sin have left their trace ;
Yet, save worn brow and thin gray hair,

No signs of weary age are there.
  His step is firm, his eye is keen,
Nor years in broil and battle spent,
Nor toil, nor wounds, nor pain have bent
  The lordly frame of old Castine.

No purpose now of strife and blood
  Urges the hoary veteran on :
The fire of conquest and the mood
  Of chivalry have gone.
A mournful task is his, — to lay
  Within the earth the bones of those
Who perished in that fearful day,
When Norridgewock became the prey
  Of all unsparing foes.
Sadly and still, dark thoughts between,
Of coming vengeance mused Castine,
Of the fallen chieftain Bomazeen,
Who bade for him the Norridgewocks ·
Dig up their buried tomahawks
  For firm defence or swift attack ;
And him whose friendship formed the tie
  Which held the stern self-exile back
From lapsing into savagery ;
Whose garb and tone and kindly glance
  Recalled a younger, happier day,
  And prompted memory's fond essay,
  To bridge the mighty waste which lay
  Between his wild home and that gray,
Tall chateau of his native France,
Whose chapel bell, with far-heard din,
Ushered his birth-hour gayly in,
And counted with its solemn toll
The masses for his father's soul.

Hark ! from the foremost of the band
  Suddenly bursts the Indian yell ;
For now on the very spot they stand
  Where the Norridgewocks fighting fell.
No wigwam smoke is curling there ;
The very earth is scorched and bare :
And they pause and listen to catch a sound
  Of breathing life, — but there comes not one,
Save the fox's bark and the rabbit's bound ;
But here and there, on the blackened ground,
  White bones are glistening in the sun.
And where the house of prayer arose,
And the holy hymn, at daylight's close,
And the aged priest stood up to bless
The children of the wilderness,
There is naught save ashes sodden and dank ;
  And the birchen boats of the Norridgewock,

Tethered to tree and stump and rock
Rotting along the river bank !

Blessed Mary ! who is she
Leaning against that maple-tree ?
The sun upon her face burns hot,
But the fixed eyelid moveth not ;
The squirrel's chirp is shrill and clear
From the dry bough above her ear ;
Dashing from rock and root its spray,
  Close at her feet the river rushes ;
  The blackbird's wing against her brushes,
  And sweetly through the hazel-bushes
  The robin's mellow music gushes ;
God save her ! will she sleep alway ?

Castine hath bent him over the sleeper :
  "Wake, daughter, — wake ! " but she stirs no limb:
  The eye that looks on him is fixed and dim ;
And the sleep she is sleeping shall be no deeper,
  Until the angel's oath is said,
And the final blast of the trump goes forth
To the graves of the sea and the graves of earth.
  Ruth Boniton is dead !

THE PAST AND COMING YEAR.

Wave of an awful torrent, thronging down,
With all the wealth of centuries, and the cold
Embraces of eternity, o'erstrown
With the great wrecks of empire, and the old
Magnificence of nations, who are gone ;
Thy last, faint murmur — thy departing sigh,
Along the shore of being, like a tone
Thrilling on broken harp-strings, or the swell
Of the chained winds' last whisper, hath gone by,
And thou hast floated from the world of breath
To the still guidance of o'ermastering Death,
Thy pilot to eternity. Farewell !

Go, swell the throngful past. Go, blend with all
The garnered things of Death ; and bear with thee
The treasures of thy pilgrimage, the tall
And beautiful dreams of Hope, the ministry
Of Love and high Ambition. Man remains
To dream again as idly ; and the stains
Of passion will be visible once more.
The winged spirit will not be confined
By the experience of thy journey. Mind
Will struggle in its prison-house, and still,

With Earth's strong fetters binding it to ill,
Unfurl the pinions fitted but to soar
In that pure atmosphere, where spirits range —
The home of high existences — where change
And blighting may not enter. Love again
Will bloom, a fickle flower, upon the grave
Of old affections ; and Ambition wave
His eagle-plume most proudly, for the rein
Of Conscience will be loosened from the soul
To give his purpose freedom. The control
Of reason will be changeful, and the ties
Which gather hearts together, and make up
The romance of existence, will be rent :
Yea, poison will be poured in Friendship's cup ;
And for Earth's low familiar element,
Even Love itself forsake its kindred skies.

But not alone dark visions ! happier things
Will float above existence, like the wings
Of the starred bird of paradise ; and Love
Will not be all a dream, or rather prove
A dream — a sweet forgetfulness — that hath
No wakeful changes, ending but in Death.
Yea, pure hearts shall be pledged beneath the eyes
Of the beholding heaven, and in the light
Of the love-hallowed moon. The quiet Night
Shall hear that language underneath the skies
Which whispereth above them, as the prayer
And the deep vow are spoken. Passing fair
And gifted creatures, with the light of truth
And undebarred affection, as a crown,
Resting upon the beautiful brow of youth,
Shall smile on stately manhood, kneeling down
Before them, as to Idols. Friendship's hand
Shall clasp its brothers ; and Affection's tear
Be sanctified with sympathy. The bier
Of stricken love shall lose the fears, which Death
Giveth his awful work, and earnest Faith
Shall look beyond the shadow of the clay,
The pulseless sepulchre, the cold decay ;
And to the quiet of the spirit-land
Follow the mourned and lovely. Gifted ones
Lighting the Heaven of Intellect, like suns,
Shall wrestle well with circumstance, and bear
The agony of scorn, the preying care,
Wedded to burning bosoms ; and go down
In sorrow to the noteless sepulchre,
With one lone hope embracing like a crown
The cold and death-like forehead of Despair,
That after times shall treasure up their fame
Even as a proud inheritance and high ;
And beautiful beings love to breathe their name
With the recorded things that never die.

And thou, gray voyager to the breezeless sea
Of infinite Oblivion — speed thou on:
Another gift of time succeedeth thee
Fresh from the hand of God; for thou hast done
The errand of thy destiny; and none
May dream of thy returning. Go, and bear
Mortality's frail records to thy cold,
Eternal prison-house; the midnight prayer
Of suffering bosoms, and the fevered care
Of worldly hearts; the miser's dream of gold;
Ambition's grasp at greatness; the quenched light
Of broken spirits; the forgiven wrong
And the abiding curse — ay, bear along
These wrecks of thy own making. Lo, thy knell
Gathers upon the windy breath of night,
Its last and faintest echo. Fare thee well!

1829.

THE MISSIONARY.

"It is an awful, an arduous thing to root out every affection for earthly things, so as to live only for another world. I am now far, very far, from you all; and as often as I look around and see the Indian scenery, I sigh to think of the distance which separates us." — *Letters of Henry Martyn, from India.*

" Say, whose is this fair picture, which the light
From the unshutter'd window rests upon
Even as a lingering halo? Beautiful!
The keen, fine eye of manhood, and a lip
Lovely as that of Hylas, and impressed
With the bright signet of some brilliant thought;
That broad expanse of forehead, clear and high,
Marked visibly with the characters of mind,
And the free locks around it, raven black,
Luxuriant and unsilver'd! — who was he?"

A friend, a more than brother. In the spring
And glory of his being he went forth
From the embraces of devoted friends,
From ease and quiet happiness, from more —
From the warm heart that loved him with a love
Holier than earthly passion, and to whom
The beauty of his spirit shone above
The charms of perishing nature. He went forth
Strengthened to suffer, gifted to subdue
The might of human passion, to pass on
Quietly to the sacrifice of all

The lofty hopes of boyhood, and to turn
The high ambition written on that brow,
From its first dream of power and human fame,
Unto a task of seeming lowliness,
Yet God-like in its purpose.   He went forth
To bind the broken spirit, to pluck back
The heathen from the wheel of Juggernaut;
To place the spiritual image of a God
Holy and just and true, before the eye
Of the dark-minded Brahmin, and unseal
The holy pages of the Book of Life,
Fraught with sublimer mysteries than all
The sacred tomes of Vedas, to unbind
The widow from her sacrifice, and save
The perishing infant from the worshipped river!

"And, lady, where is he?"   He slumbers well
Beneath the shadow of an Indian palm.
There is no stone above his grave.   The wind,
Hot from the desert, as it stirs the leaves
Heavy and long above him, sighs alone
Over his place of slumber.

                          "God forbid
That he should die alone!"   Nay, not alone.
His God was with him in that last dread hour;
His great arm underneath him, and His smile
Melting into a spirit full of peace.
And one kind friend, a human friend, was near—
One whom his teachings and his earnest prayers
Had snatch'd as from the burning.   He alone
Felt the last pressure of his failing hand,
Caught the last glimpse of his closing eye,
And laid the green turf over him with tears,
And left him with his God.

                          "And was it well,
Dear lady, that this noble mind should cast
Its rich gifts on the waters?   That a heart
Full of all gentleness and truth and love
Should wither on the suicidal shrine
Of a mistaken duty?   If I read
Aright the fine intelligence which fills
That amplitude of brow, and gazes out
Like an indwelling spirit from that eye,
He might have borne him loftily among
The proudest of his land, and with a step
Unfaltering ever, steadfast and secure,
Gone up the paths of greatness, — bearing still
A sister spirit with him, as some star,
Preëminent in Heaven, leads steadily up
A kindred watcher, with its fainter beams
Baptized in its great glory.   Was it well

That all this promise of the heart and mind
Should perish from the earth, and leave no trace.
Unfolding like the Cereus of the clime
Which hath its sepulchre, but in the night
Of pagan desolation — was it well ? "

Thy will be done, O Father ! — it *was* well.
What are the honors of a perishing world
Grasp'd by a palsied finger ? the applause
Of the unthoughtful multitude which greets
The dull ear of decay ? the wealth that loads
The bier with costly drapery, and shines
In tinsel on the coffin, and builds up
The cold substantial monument ?   Can these
Bear up the sinking spirit in that hour
When heart and flesh are failing, and the grave
Is opening under us ?   Oh, dearer then
The memory of a kind deed done to him
Who was our enemy, one grateful tear
In the meek eye of virtuous suffering,
One smile call'd up by unseen charity
On the wan lips of hunger, or one prayer
Breathed from the bosom of the penitent —
The stain'd with crime and outcast, unto whom
Our mild rebuke and tenderness of love
A merciful God hath bless'd.

                              " But, lady, say,
Did he not sometimes almost sink beneath
The burden of his toil, and turn aside
To weep above his sacrifice, and cast
A sorrowing glance upon his childhood's home,
Still green in memory ?   Clung not to his heart
Something of earthly hope uncrucified,
Of earthly thought unchastened ?   Did he bring
Life's warm affections to the sacrifice —
Its loves, hopes, sorrows — and become as one
Knowing no kindred but a perishing world,
No love but of the sin-endangered soul,
No hope but of the winning back to life
Of the dead nations, and no passing thought
Save of the errand wherewith he was sent
As to a martyrdom ? "

                              Nay, though the heart
Be consecrated to the holiest work
Vouchsafed to mortal effort, there will be
Ties of the earth around it, and, through all
Its perilous devotion, it must keep
Its own humanity.   And it is well.
Else why wept He, who with our nature veiled
The spirit of a God, o'er lost Jerusalem,

And the cold grave of Lazarus?   And why
In the dim garden rose his earnest prayer,
That from his lips the cup of suffering
Might pass, if it were possible?

                              My friend
Was of a gentle nature, and his heart
Gushed like a river-fountain of the hills,
Ceaseless and lavish, at a kindly smile,
A word of welcome, or a tone of love.
Freely his letters to his friends disclosed
His yearnings for the quiet haunts of home,
For love and its companionship, and all
The blessings left behind him ; yet above
Its sorrows and its clouds his spirit rose,
Tearful and yet triumphant, taking hold
Of the eternal promises of God,
And steadfast in its faith.

                         Here are some lines
Penned in his lonely mission-house and sent
To a dear friend at home who even now
Lingers above them with a mournful joy,
Holding them well-nigh sacred as a leaf
Plucked from the record of a breaking heart.

EVENING IN BURMAH.

A night of wonder ! piled afar
    With ebon feet and crests of snow,
Like Himalaya's peaks, which bar
The sunset and the sunset's star
    From half the shadowed vale below,
Volumed and vast the dense clouds lie,
And over them, and down the sky,
    Paled in the moon, the lightnings go.

And what a strength of light and shade
    Is chequering all the earth below !
And, through the jungle's verdant braid,
Of tangled vine and wild reed made,
    What blossoms in the moonlight glow !
The Indian rose's loveliness,
The ceiba with its crimson dress,
    The twining myrtle dropped with snow.

And flitting in the fragrant air,
    Or nestling in the shadowy trees,
A thousand bright-hued birds are there —
Strange plumage, quivering wild and rare,
    With every faintly breathing breeze ;
And, wet with dew from roses shed,

The bulbul droops her weary head,
  Forgetful of her melodies.

Uprising from the orange-leaves,
  The tall pagoda's turrets glow ;
O'er graceful shaft and fretted eaves,
Its verdant web the myrtle weaves,
  And hangs in flowering wreaths below;
And where the clustered palms eclipse
The moonbeams, from its marble lips
  The fountain's silver waters flow.

Strange beauty fills the earth and air,
  The fragrant grove and flowering tree,
And yet my thoughts are wandering where
My native rocks lie bleak and bare,
  A weary way beyond the sea.
The yearning spirit is not here ;
It lingers on a spot more dear
  Than India's brightest bowers to me.

Methinks I tread the well-known street —
  The tree my childhood loved is there,
Its bare-worn roots are at my feet,
And through its open boughs I meet
  White glimpses of the place of prayer ;
And unforgotten eyes again
Are glancing through the cottage pane,
  Than Asia's lustrous eyes more fair.

Oh, holy haunts ! oh, childhood's home !
  Where, now, my wandering heart, is thine ?
Here, where the dusky heathen come
To bow before the deaf and dumb,
  Dead idols of their own design ;
Where in their worshipped river's tide
The infant sinks, and on its side
  The widow's funeral altars shine !

Here, where, mid light and song and flowers,
  The priceless soul in ruin lies ;
Lost, dead to all those better powers
Which link this fallen world of ours
  To God's clear-shining Paradise ;
And wrong and shame and hideous crime
Are like the foliage of their clime,
  The unshorn growth of centuries !

Turn, then, my heart ; thy home is here ;
  No other now remains for thee :
The smile of love, and friendship's tear,
The tones that melted on thine ear,

The mutual thrill of sympathy,
The welcome of the household band,
The pressure of the lip and hand,
    Thou mayst not hear, nor feel, nor see.

God of my spirit ! Thou, alone,
    Who watchest o'er my pillowed head,
Whose ear is open to the moan
And sorrowing of thy child, hast known
    The grief which at my heart has fed ;
The struggle of my soul to rise
Above its earth-born sympathies ;
    The tears of many a sleepless bed !

Oh, be Thine arm, as it hath been,
    In every test of heart and faith, —
The tempter's doubt, the wiles of men,
The heathen's scoff, the bosom sin, —
    A helper and a stay beneath ;
A strength in weakness, through the strife
And anguish of my wasting life —
    My solace and my hope, in death !

1833.

MASSACHUSETTS.

Written on hearing that the Resolutions of the Legislature of Massachusetts on the subject of Slavery, presented by Hon. C. Cushing to the House of Representatives of the United States, had been laid on the table unread and unreferred, under the infamous rule of " Patton's Resolution."

And have they spurned thy word,
    Thou of the old Thirteen !
Whose soil, where Freedom's blood first poured,
    Hath yet a darker green ?
To outworn patience suffering long
Is insult added to the wrong ?

And have they closed thy mouth,
    And fixed the padlock fast ?
Dumb as the black slave of the South !
    Is this thy fate at last ?
Oh shame ! thy honored seal and sign
Trod under hoofs so asinine !

Call from the Capitol
    Thy chosen ones again,
Unmeet for them the base control
    Of Slavery's curbing rein !

Unmeet for men like them to feel
The spurring of a rider's heel.

When votes are things of trade
    And force is argument,
Call back to Quincy's shade
    Thy old man eloquent.
Why leave him longer striving thus
With the wild beasts of Ephesus !

Back from the Capital —
    It is no place for thee !
Beneath the arch of Heaven's blue wall,
    Thy voice may still be free !
What power shall chain thy utterance there,
In God's free sun and freer air ?

A voice is calling thee,
    From all the martyr graves
Of those stern men, in death made free,
    Who could not live as slaves.
The slumberings of thy honored dead
Are for thy sake disquieted.

So let thy Faneuil Hall
    By freemen's feet be trod,
And give the echoes of its wall
    Once more to Freedom's God !
And in the midst unseen shall stand
The mighty fathers of thy land.

Thy gathered sons shall feel
    The soul of Adams near,
And Otis with his fiery zeal,
    And Warren's onward cheer ;
And heart to heart shall thrill as when
They moved and spake as living men.

Not on Potomac's side,
    With treason in thy rear,
Can Freedom's holy cause be tried :
    Not there, my State, but here.
Here must thy needed work be done,
The battle at thy hearth-stone won.

Proclaim a new crusade
    Against the foes within ;
From bar and pulpit, press and trade,
    Cast out the shame and sin.
Then speak thy now-unheeded word,
Its lightest whisper shall be heard.

II. POEMS PRINTED IN THE "LIFE OF WHITTIER."

THE HOME-COMING OF THE BRIDE.

[The home of Sarah Greenleaf was upon the Newbury shore of the Merrimac, nearly opposite the home of the Whittiers. Among Mr. Whittier's papers was found the following fragment of a ballad about the home-coming, as a bride, of his grandmother, Sarah Greenleaf, now first published.]

Sarah Greenleaf, of eighteen years,
  Stepped lightly her bridegroom's boat within,
Waving mid-river, through smiles and tears,
  A farewell back to her kith and kin.
With her sweet blue eyes and her new gold gown,
  She sat by her stalwart lover's side —
Oh, never was brought to Haverhill town
  By land or water so fair a bride.
Glad as the glad autumnal weather,
  The Indian summer so soft and warm,
They walked through the golden woods together,
  His arm the girdle about her form.

They passed the dam and the gray gristmill,
  Whose walls with the jar of grinding shook,
And crossed, for the moment awed and still,
  The haunted bridge of the Country Brook.
The great oaks seemed on Job's Hill crown
  To wave in welcome their branches strong,
And an upland streamlet came rippling down
  Over root and rock, like a bridal song.
And lo! in the midst of a clearing stood
  The rough-built farmhouse, low and lone,
While all about it the unhewn wood
  Seemed drawing closer to claim its own.

But the red apples dropped from orchard trees,
  The red cock crowed on the low fence rail,
From the garden hives came the sound of bees,
  On the barn floor pealed the smiting flail.

. . . .

394 *APPENDIX*

THE SONG OF THE VERMONTERS, 1779.

[Written during school-days, and published anonymously
in 1833. The secret of authorship was not discovered for
nearly sixty years.]

Ho — all to the borders ! Vermonters, come down,
With your breeches of deerskin and jackets of brown ;
With your red woollen caps, and your moccasins, come,
To the gathering summons of trumpet and drum.

Come down with your rifles ! Let gray wolf and fox
Howl on in the shade of their primitive rocks ;
Let the bear feed securely from pig-pen and stall ;
Here 's two-legged game for your powder and ball.

On our south came the Dutchmen, enveloped in grease ;
And arming for battle while canting of peace ;
On our east, crafty Meshech has gathered his band
To hang up our leaders and eat up our land.

Ho — all to the rescue ! For Satan shall work
No gain for his legions of Hampshire and York !
They claim our possessions — the pitiful knaves —
The tribute we pay shall be prisons and graves !

Let Clinton and Ten Broek, with bribes in their hands,
Still seek to divide and parcel our lands ;
We 've coats for our traitors, whoever they are ;
The warp is of feathers — the filling of tar.

Does the " old Bay State " threaten ? Does Congress complain ?
Swarms Hampshire in arms on our borders again ?
Bark the war-dogs of Britain aloud on the lake —
Let 'em come ; what they can they are welcome to take.

What seek they among us ? The pride of our wealth
Is comfort, contentment, and labor, and health,
And lands which, as Freemen, we only have trod,
Independent of all, save the mercies of God.

Yet we owe no allegiance, we bow to no throne,
Our ruler is law, and the law is our own ;
Our leaders themselves are our own fellow-men,
Who can handle the sword, or the scythe, or the pen.

Our wives are all true, and our daughters are fair,
With their blue eyes of smiles and their light flowing hair,
All brisk at their wheels till the dark even-fall,
Then blithe at the sleigh-ride, the husking, and ball!

We 've sheep on the hillsides, we 've cows on the plain,
And gay-tasselled corn-fields and rank-growing grain;
There are deer on the mountains, and wood-pigeons fly
From the crack of our muskets, like clouds on the sky.

And there 's fish in our streamlets and rivers which take
Their course from the hills to our broad-bosomed lake;
Through rock-arched Winooski the salmon leaps free,
And the portly shad follows all fresh from the sea.

Like a sunbeam the pickerel glides through the pool,
And the spotted trout sleeps where the water is cool,
Or darts from his shelter of rock and of root
At the beaver's quick plunge, or the angler's pursuit.

And ours are the mountains, which awfully rise,
Till they rest their green heads on the blue of the skies;
And ours are the forests unwasted, unshorn,
Save where the wild path of the tempest is torn.

And though savage and wild be this climate of ours,
And brief be our season of fruits and of flowers,
Far dearer the blast round our mountains which raves,
Than the sweet summer zephyr which breathes over slaves!

Hurrah for Vermont! For the land which we till
Must have sons to defend her from valley and hill;
Leave the harvest to rot on the fields where it grows,
And the reaping of wheat for the reaping of foes.

From far Michiscom's wild valley, to where
Poosoonsuck steals down from his wood-circled lair,
From Shocticook River to Lutterlock town —
Ho — all to the rescue! Vermonters, come down!

Come York or come Hampshire, come traitors or knaves,
If ye rule o'er our land, ye shall rule o'er our graves;
Our vow is recorded — our banner unfurled,
In the name of Vermont we defy all the world!

TO A POETICAL TRIO IN THE CITY OF GOTHAM.

[This *jeu d'esprit* was written by Whittier in 1832. The notes are his own. The authorship was not discovered till after his death.]

> Three wise men of Gotham
> Went to sea in a bowl.

Bards of the island city! — where of old
    The Dutchman smoked beneath his favorite tree,
And the wild eyes of Indian hunters rolled
    On Hudson plunging in the Tappaan Zee,
Scene of Stuyvesant's might and chivalry,
    And Knickerbocker's fame, — I have made bold
To come before ye, at the present time,
And *reason* with ye in the way of *rhyme*.

Time was when poets kept the quiet tenor
    Of their green pathway through th' Arcadian vale, —
Chiming their music in the low sweet manner
    Of song-birds warbling to the "Soft South" gale ;
Wooing the Muse where gentle zephyrs fan her,
    Where all is peace and earth may not assail ;
Telling of lutes and flowers, of love and fear,
Of shepherds, sheep and lambs, and "such small deer."

But ye ! lost recreants — straying from the green
    And pleasant vista of your early time,
With broken lutes and crownless skulls — are seen
    Spattering your neighbors with abhorrent slime
Of the low world's pollution ! [1] Ye have been
    So long apostates from the Heaven of rhyme,
That of the Muses, every mother's daughter
Blushes to own such graceless bards e'er sought her.

"*Hurrah for Jackson !*" is the music now
    Which your cracked lutes have learned alone to utter,
As, crouching in Corruption's shadow low,
    Ye daily sweep them for your bread and butter,[2]

---

[1] Editors of the *Mercantile Advertiser* and the *Evening Post* in New York, — the present organs of Jacksonism.

[2] Perhaps, after all, they get something better ; inasmuch as the Heroites have for some time had exclusive possession of the Hall of St. Tammany, and we have the authority of Halleck that

> "There's a barrel of porter in Tammany Hall,
> And the Bucktails are swigging it all the night long."

Cheered by the applauses of the friends who show
  Their heads above the offal of the gutter,
And, like the trees which Orpheus moved at will,
Reel, as in token of your matchless skill!

Thou son of Scotia![1] — nursed beside the grave
  Of the proud peasant-minstrel, and to whom
The wild muse of thy mountain-dwelling gave
  A portion of its spirit, —if the tomb
Could burst its silence, o'er the Atlantic's wave
  To thee his voice of stern rebuke would come,
Who dared to waken with a master's hand
The lyre of freedom in a fettered land.

And thou ! — once treading firmly the proud deck
  O'er which thy country's honored flag was sleeping,
Calmly in peace, or to the hostile beck
  Of coming foes in starry splendor sweeping, —
Thy graphic tales of battle or of wreck,
  Or lone night-watch in middle ocean keeping,
Have made thy "Leisure Hours" more prized by far
Than those now spent in Party's wordy war.[2]

And last, not least, thou ! — now nurtured in the land
  Where thy bold-hearted fathers long ago
Rocked Freedom's cradle, till its infant hand
  Strangled the serpent fierceness of its foe, —
Thou, whose clear brow in early time was fanned
  By the soft airs which from Castalia flow ![3] —
Where art thou now? feeding with hickory ladle
The curs of Faction with thy daily twaddle !

Men have looked up to thee, as one to be
  A portion of our glory ; and the light
And fairy hands of woman beckoned thee
  On to thy laurel guerdon ; and those bright
And gifted spirits, whom the broad blue sea
  Hath shut from thy communion, bid thee, "*Write*,"
Like John of Patmos. Is all this forgotten,
For Yankee brawls and Carolina cotton ?

---

[1] James Lawson, Esq., of the *Mercantile*. A fine, warm-hearted Scotch-man, who, having unfortunately blundered into Jacksonism, is wondering "how i' the Deil's name" he got there. He is the author of a volume enti-tled *Tales and Sketches*, and of the tragedy of *Giordano*.

[2] William Leggett, Esq., of the *Post*, a gentleman of good talents, favor-ably known as the editor of the *New York Critic*, etc.

[3] William C. Bryant, Esq., well known to the public at large as a poet of acknowledged excellence; and as a very dull editor to the people of New York.

Are autumn's rainbow hues no longer seen ?
  Flows the "Green River" through its vale no more ?
Steals not thy "Rivulet" by its banks of green ?
  Wheels upward from its dark and sedgy shore
Thy "Water Fowl" no longer ? — that the mean
  And vulgar strife, the ranting and the *roar*
Extempore, like Bottom's should be thine, —
Thou feeblest truck-horse in the Hero's line !

Lost trio ! — turn ye to the minstrel pride
  Of classic Britain.   Even effeminate Moore
Has cast the wine-cup and the lute aside
  For Erin and O'Connell ; and before
His country's altar, Bulwer breasts the tide
  Of old oppression.   Sadly brooding o'er
The fate of heroes struggling to be free,
Even Campbell speaks for Poland.   *Where are ye ?*

Hirelings of traitors ! — know ye not that men
  Are rousing up around ye to retrieve
Our country's honor, which too long has been
  Debased by those for whom ye daily weave
Your web of fustian ; that from tongue and pen
  Of those who o'er our tarnished honor grieve,
Of the pure-hearted and the gifted, come
Hourly the tokens of your master's doom ?

Turn from their ruin !   Dash your chains aside !
  Stand up like men for Liberty and Law,
And free opinion.   Check Corruption's pride,
  Soothe the loud storm of fratricidal war, —
And the bright honors of your eventide
  Shall share the glory which your morning saw ;
The patriot's heart shall gladden at your name,
Ye shall be blessed with, and not "damned to fame " !

ALBUM VERSES.

[Written in the album of May Pillsbury of West Newbury, in the fall of 1838, when Whittier was at home on a
visit from Philadelphia, where he was engaged in editorial
work.]

Pardon a stranger hand that gives
Its impress to these gilded leaves.

As one who graves in idle mood
An idler's name on rock or wood,
So in a careless hour I claim
A page to leave my humble name.
Accept it; and when o'er my head
A Pennsylvanian sky is spread,
And but in dreams my eye looks back
On broad and lovely Merrimac,
And on my ear no longer breaks
The murmuring music which it makes,
When but in dreams I look again
On Salisbury beach — Grasshopper plain —
Or Powow stream — or Amesbury mills,
Or old Crane neck, or Pipestave hills,
Think of me then as one who keeps,
Where Delaware's broad current sweeps,
And down its rugged limestone-bed
The Schuylkill's arrowy flight is sped,
Deep in his heart the scenes which grace
And glorify his "native place;"
Loves every spot to childhood dear,
And leaves his heart "untravelled" here;
Longs, midst the Dutchman's kraut and greens,
For pumpkin-pie and pork and beans,
And sighs to think when, sweetly near,
The soft piano greets his ear,
That the fair hands which, small and white,
Glance on its ivory polished light,
Have ne'er an Indian pudding made,
Nor fashioned rye and Indian bread.
And oh! where'er his footsteps turn,
Whatever stars above him burn,
Though dwelling where a Yankee's name
Is coupled with reproach or shame,
Still true to his New England birth,
Still faithful to his home and hearth,
Even 'midst the scornful stranger band
His boast shall be of YANKEE LAND.

WHAT STATE STREET SAID TO SOUTH CAROLINA, AND WHAT SOUTH CAROLINA SAID TO STATE STREET.

[Published in *The National Era*, May 22, 1851.]

Muttering "fine upland staple," "prime Sea Island finer,"
With cotton bales pictured on either retina,

"Your pardon!" said State Street to South Carolina;
"We feel and acknowledge your laws are diviner
   Than any promulgated by the thunders of Sinai!
   Sorely pricked in the sensitive conscience of business
   We own and repent of our sins of remissness:
   Our honor we 've yielded, our words we have swallowed;
   And quenching the lights which our forefathers followed,
   And turning from graves by their memories hallowed,
   With teeth on ball-cartridge, and finger on trigger,
   Reversed Boston Notions, and sent back a nigger!"

"Get away!" cried the Chivalry, busy a-drumming,
   And fifing and drilling, and such Quattle-bumming;
"With your April-fool slave hunt! Just wait till December
   Shall see your new Senator stalk through the Chamber,
   And Puritan heresy prove neither dumb nor
   Blind in that pestilent Anakim, Sumner!"

A FRÉMONT CAMPAIGN SONG.

Sound now the trumpet warningly!
   The storm is rolling nearer,
   The hour is striking clearer,
      In the dusky dome of sky.
If dark and wild the morning be,
   A darker morn before us
   Shall fling its shadows o'er us
      If we let the hour go by.
Sound we then the trumpet chorus!
   Sound the onset wild and high!
      Country and Liberty!
      Freedom and Victory!
   These words shall be our cry, —
      Frémont and Victory!

Sound, sound the trumpet fearlessly!
   Each arm its vigor lending,
   Bravely with wrong contending,
      And shouting Freedom's cry!
The Kansas homes stand cheerlessly,
   The sky with flame is ruddy,
   The prairie turf is bloody,
      Where the brave and gentle die.
Sound the trumpet stern and steady!
   Sound the trumpet strong and high!
      Country and Liberty!
      Freedom and Victory!

These words shall be our cry, —
Frémont and Victory!

Sound now the trumpet cheerily!
Nor dream of Heaven's forsaking
The issue of its making,
That Right with Wrong must try.
The cloud that hung so drearily
The Northern winds are breaking;
The Northern Lights are shaking
Their fire-flags in the sky.
Sound the signal of awaking;
Sound the onset wild and high!
Country and Liberty!
Freedom and Victory!
These words shall be our cry, —
Frémont and Victory!

THE QUAKERS ARE OUT.

[A campaign song written to be sung at a Republican mass meeting held in Newburyport, Mass., October 11, 1860.]

Not vainly we waited and counted the hours,
The buds of our hope have all burst into flowers.
No room for misgiving — no loop-hole of doubt, —
We 've heard from the Keystone!   The Quakers are out.

The plot has exploded — we 've found out the trick;
The bribe goes a-begging; the fusion won't stick.
When the Wide-awake lanterns are shining about,
The rogues stay at home, and the true men are out!

The good State has broken the cords for her spun;
Her oil-springs and water won't fuse into one;
The Dutchman has seasoned with Freedom his kraut,
And slow, late, but certain, the Quakers are out!

Give the flags to the winds! set the hills all aflame!
Make way for the man with the Patriarch's name!
Away with misgiving — away with all doubt,
For Lincoln goes in, when the Quakers are out!

A LEGEND OF THE LAKE.

[This poem, originally printed in the *Atlantic Monthly* was
withheld from publication in his volumes by Mr. Whittier,
in deference to living relatives of the hero of the poem.
Death finally removed the restriction.]

Should you go to Centre Harbor,
  As haply you sometime may,
Sailing up the Winnepesaukee
  From the hills of Alton Bay, —

Into the heart of the highlands,
  Into the north wind free,
Through the rising and vanishing islands,
  Over the mountain sea, —

To the little hamlet lying
  White in its mountain fold,
Asleep by the lake and dreaming
  A dream that is never told, —

And in the Red Hill's shadow
  Your pilgrim home you make,
Where the chambers open to sunrise,
  The mountains, and the lake, —

If the pleasant picture wearies,
  As the fairest sometimes will,
And the weight of the hills lies on you
  And the water is all too still, —

If in vain the peaks of Gunstock
  Redden with sunrise fire,
And the sky and the purple mountains
  And the sunset islands tire, —

If you turn from in-door thrumming
  And the clatter of bowls without,
And the folly that goes on its travels
  Bearing the city about, —

And the cares you left behind you
  Come hunting along your track,

As Blue-Cap in German fable
　Rode on the traveller's pack, —

Let me tell you a tender story
　Of one who is now no more,
A tale to haunt like a spirit
　The Winnepesaukee shore, —

Of one who was brave and gentle,
　And strong for manly strife,
Riding with cheering and music
　Into the tourney of life.

Faltering and failing midway
　In the Tempter's subtle snare,
The chains of an evil habit
　He bowed himself to bear.

Over his fresh young manhood
　The bestial veil was flung, —
The curse of the wine of Circe,
　The spell her weavers sung.

Yearly did hill and lakeside
　Their summer idyls frame ;
Alone in his darkened dwelling
　He hid his face for shame.

The music of life's great marches
　Sounded for him in vain ;
The voices of human duty
　Smote on his ear like pain.

In vain over island and water
　The curtains of sunset swung ;
In vain on the beautiful mountains
　The pictures of God were hung.

The wretched years crept onward,
　Each sadder than the last ;
All the bloom of life fell from him,
　All the freshness and greenness past.

But deep in his heart forever
　And unprofaned he kept
The love of his saintly mother,
　Who in the graveyard slept.

His house had no pleasant pictures;
  Its comfortless walls were bare:
But the riches of earth and ocean
  Could not purchase his mother's chair.

The old chair, quaintly carven,
  With oaken arms outspread,
Whereby, in the long gone twilights,
  His childish prayers were said.

For thence in his long night watches,
  By moon or starlight dim,
A face full of love and pity
  And tenderness looked on him.

And oft, as the grieving presence
  Sat in his mother's chair,
The groan of his self-upbraiding
  Grew into wordless prayer.

At last, in the moonless midnight,
  The summoning angel came,
Severe in his pity, touching
  The house with fingers of flame.

The red light flashed from its windows
  And flared from its sinking roof;
And baffled and awed before it
  The villagers stood aloof.

They shrank from the falling rafters,
  They turned from the furnace glare;
But its tenant cried, "God help me!
  I must save my mother's chair."

Under the blazing portal,
  Over the floor of fire,
He seemed, in the terrible splendor,
  A martyr on his pyre.

In his face the mad flames smote him,
  And stung him on either side;
But he clung to the sacred relic, —
  By his mother's chair he died!

O mother, with human yearnings!
  O saint, by the altar stairs!

Shall not the dear God give thee
  The child of thy many prayers?

O Christ! by whom the loving,
  Though erring, are forgiven,
Hast thou for him no refuge,
  No quiet place in heaven?

Give palms to thy strong martyrs,
  And crown thy saints with gold,
But let the mother welcome
  Her lost one to thy fold!

LETTER TO LUCY LARCOM.

25th 3d mo., 1866.

Believe me, Lucy Larcom, it gives me real sorrow
That I cannot take my carpet-bag and go to town to-morrow;
But I 'm "snow-bound," and cold on cold, like layers of an onion,
Have piled my back and weighed me down as with the pack of Bunyan.
The north-east wind is damper and the north-west wind is colder,
Or else the matter simply is that I am growing older.
And then I dare not trust a moon seen over one's left shoulder,
As I saw this with slender horns caught in a west hill pine,
As on a Stamboul minaret curves the arch-impostor's sign, —
So I must stay in Amesbury, and let you go your way,
And guess what colors greet your eyes, what shapes your steps delay;
What pictured forms of heathen lore, of god and goddess please you,
What idol graven images you bend your wicked knees to.
But why should I of evil dream, well knowing at your head goes
That flower of Christian womanhood, our dear good Anna Meadows.
She 'll be discreet, I 'm sure, although once, in a freak romantic,
She flung the Doge's bridal ring, and married "The Atlantic"!
And spite of all appearances, like the woman in a shoe,
She 's got so many "Young Folks" now, she don't know what to do.
But I must say I think it strange that thee and Mrs. Spaulding,
Whose lives with Calvin's five-railed creed have been so tightly walled in,
Should quit your Puritan homes, and take the pains to go
So far, with malice aforethought, to "walk in a vain show"!
Did Emmons hunt for pictures? Was Jonathan Edwards peeping
Into the chambers of imagery, with maids for Tammuz weeping?
Ah well! the times are sadly changed, and I myself am feeling
The wicked world my Quaker coat from off my shoulders peeling.
God grant that in the strange new sea of change wherein we swim,
We still may keep the good old plank, of simple faith in Him!

LINES ON LEAVING APPLEDORE.

[Sent in a letter to Celia Thaxter.]

Under the shadow of a cloud, the light
Died out upon the waters, like a smile
Chased from a face by grief. Following the flight
Of a lone bird that, scudding with the breeze,
Dipped its crank wing in leaden-colored seas,
I saw in sunshine lifted, clear and bright,
On the horizon's rim the Fortunate Isle
That claims thee as its fair inhabitant,
And glad of heart I whispered, "Be to her,
Bird of the summer sea, my messenger;
Tell her, if Heaven a fervent prayer will grant,
This light that falls her island home above,
Making its slopes of rock and greenness gay,
A partial glory midst surrounding gray,
Shall prove an earnest of our Father's love,
More and more shining to the perfect day."

MRS. CHOATE'S HOUSE-WARMING.

["His washerwoman, Mrs. Choate, by industry and thrift
had been enabled to build for her family a comfortable
house. When it was ready for occupancy, there was a
house-warming, attended by all the neighbors, who brought
substantial tokens of their good-will, including all the furni-
ture needed in her new parlor. Mr. Whittier's hand was to
be seen in the whole movement ; he was present at the fes-
tivity, and made a little speech, congratulating Mrs. Choate
upon her well-deserved success in life, and said he would
read a piece of machine poetry which had been intrusted to
him for the occasion. These are the lines, which were, of
course, of his own composition." — S. T. PICKARD, *Life and
Letters of John Greenleaf Whittier.*]

Of rights and of wrongs
Let the feminine tongues
Talk on — none forbid it.

Our hostess best knew
What her hands found to do,
  Asked no questions, but DID IT.

Here the lesson of work,
Which so many folks shirk,
  Is so plain all may learn it ;
Each brick in this dwelling,
Each timber is telling,
  If you want a home, EARN IT.

The question of labor
Is solved by our neighbor,
  The old riddle guessed out :
The wisdom sore needed,
The truth long unheeded,
  Her flat-iron 's pressed out !

Thanks, then, to Kate Choate !
Let the idle take note
  What their fingers were made for ;
She, cheerful and jolly,
Worked on late and early,
  And bought — what she paid for !

Never vainly repining,
Nor begging, nor whining ;
  The morning-star twinkles
On no heart that 's lighter
As she makes the world whiter
  And smoothes out its wrinkles.

So, long life to Kate !
May her heirs have to wait
  Till they 're gray in attendance ;
And her flat-iron press on,
Still teaching its lesson
  Of brave independence !

AN AUTOGRAPH.

[Written for an old friend, Rev. S. H. Emery, of Quincy
Ill., who revisited Whittier in 1868.]

The years that since we met have flown
Leave as they found me, still alone :

No wife, nor child, nor grandchild dear,
Are mine the heart of age to cheer.
More favored thou, with hair less gray
Than mine, canst let thy fancy stray
To where thy little Constance sees
The prairie ripple in the breeze;
For one like her to lisp thy name
Is better than the voice of fame.

TO LUCY LARCOM.

3d mo., 1870.

.   .   .   .   .   .

Pray give the "Atlantic"
A brief unpedantic
Review of Miss Phelps' book,
Which teaches and helps folk
To deal with the offenders
In love which surrenders
All pride unforgiving,
The lost one receiving
With truthful believing
That she like all others,
Our sisters and brothers,
Is only a sinner
Whom God's love within her
Can change to the whiteness
Of heaven's own brightness.
For who shall see tarnish
If He sweep and garnish?
When He is the cleanser
Shall *we* dare to censure?
Say to Fields, if he ask of it,
I can't take the task of it.

.   .   .   .   .   .

P. S. — For myself, if I 'm able,
And half comfortable,
I shall run for the seashore
To some place as before,
Where blunt we at least find
The teeth of the East wind,
And spring does not tarry
As it does at Amesbury;
But where it will be to
I cannot yet see to.

A FAREWELL.

[Written for Mr. and Mrs. Claflin as they were about to sail to Europe.]

What shall I say, dear friends, to whom I owe
The choicest blessings, dropping from the hands
Of trustful love and friendship, as you go
Forth on your journey to those older lands,
By saint and sage and bard and hero trod?
Scarcely the simple farewell of the Friends
Sufficeth; after you my full heart sends
Such benediction as the pilgrim hears
Where the Greek faith its golden dome uprears,
From Crimea's roses to Archangel snows,
The fittest prayer of parting : "Go with God!"

ON A FLY-LEAF OF LONGFELLOW'S POEMS.

[Written at the Asquam House in the summer of 1882.]

Hushed now the sweet consoling tongue
Of him whose lyre the Muses strung;
His last low swan-song has been sung!

His last! And ours, dear friend, is near;
As clouds that rake the mountains here,
We too shall pass and disappear.

Yet howsoever changed or tost,
Not even a wreath of mist is lost,
No atom can itself exhaust.

So shall the soul's superior force
Live on and run its endless course
In God's unlimited universe.

And we, whose brief reflections seem
To fade like clouds from lake and stream,
Shall brighten in a holier beam.

SAMUEL E. SEWALL.

[An inscription for a marble bust, modelled by Anne Whitney, and placed in the Cary Library, Lexington, Mass., May, 1884.]

> Like that ancestral judge who bore his name,
>   Faithful to Freedom and to Truth, he gave,
> When all the air was hot with wrath and blame,
>   His youth and manhood to the fettered slave.
>
> And never Woman in her suffering saw
>   A helper tender, wise, and brave as he;
> Lifting her burden of unrighteous law,
>   He shamed the boast of ancient chivalry.
>
> Noiseless as light that melts the darkness is,
>   He wrought as duty led and honor bid,
> No trumpet heralds victories like his, —
>   The unselfish worker in his work is hid.

LINES WRITTEN IN AN ALBUM.

[The album belonged to the grandson of Whittier's life-long friend, Theodore D. Weld, and the lines were written in April, 1884.]

> What shall I wish him ? Strength and health
> May be abused, and so may wealth.
> Even fame itself may come to be
> But wearying notoriety.
>
> What better can I ask than this ? —
> A life of brave unselfishness,
> Wisdom for council, eloquence
> For Freedom's need, for Truth's defence,
> The championship of all that 's good,
> The manliest faith in womanhood,
> The steadfast friendship, changing not
> With change of time or place or lot,
> Hatred of sin, but not the less
> A heart of pitying tenderness

And charity, that, suffering long,
  Shames the wrong-doer from his wrong :
One wish expresses all — that he
  May even as his grandsire be !

A DAY'S JOURNEY.

[Written in 1886 for the tenth anniversary of the wedding
of his niece.]

After your pleasant morning travel
  You pause as at a wayside inn,
And take with grateful hearts your breakfast
  Though served in dishes all of TIN.

Then go, while years as hours are counted,
  Until the dial's hand at noon
Invites you to a dinner table
  Garnished with SILVER fork and spoon.

And when the vesper bell to supper
  Is calling, and the day is old,
May love transmute the tin of morning
  And noonday's silver into GOLD.

A FRAGMENT.

[Found among Mr. Whittier's papers, in his handwriting,
but undated.]

The dreadful burden of our sins we feel,
The pain of wounds which Thou alone canst heal,
To whom our weakness is our strong appeal.

From the black depths, the ashes, and the dross
Of our waste lives, we reach out to Thy cross,
And by its fullness measure all our loss !

That holy sign reveals Thee : throned above
No Moloch sits, no false, vindictive Jove —
Thou art our Father, and Thy name is Love ! [1]

[1] This is an alternative reading which has been cancelled : —

   "No lawless Terror dwells in light above,
   Cruel as Moloch, deaf and false as Jove —
   Thou art our Father, and Thy name is Love ! "

III. NOTES TO THE POEMS IN THIS VOLUME.

Note 1, page 15. "O vine of Sibmah ! I will weep for thee with the weeping of Jazer ! " — *Jeremiah* xlviii. 32.

Note 2, page 19. August. Soliloq. cap. xxxi. "Interrogavi Terram," etc.

Note 3, page 79. Dr. Withington, author of *The Puritan*, under the name of Jonathan Oldbug.

Note 4, page 79. Thomas à Kempis in *De Imitatione Christi*.

Note 5, page 236. Goody Cole was brought before the Quarter Sessions in 1680 to answer to the charge of being a witch. The court could not find satisfactory evidence of witchcraft, but so strong was the feeling against her that Major Waldron, the presiding magistrate, ordered her to be imprisoned, with "a lock kept on her leg" at the pleasure of the Court. In such judicial action one can read the fear and vindictive spirit of the community at large.

Note 6, page 249. The reference is to Bayard Taylor's poem, *The Song of the Camp*.

Note 7, page 357. Mogg Megone, or Hegone, was a leader among the Saco Indians, in the bloody war of 1677. He attacked and captured the garrison at Black Point, October 12th of that year ; and cut off, at the same time, a party of Englishmen near Saco River. From a deed signed by this Indian in 1664, and from other circumstances, it seems that, previous to the war, he had mingled much with the colonists. On this account, he was probably selected by the principal sachems as their agent in the treaty signed in November, 1676.

Note 8, page 358. Baron de St. Castine came to Canada in 1644. Leaving his civilized companions, he plunged into the great wilderness, and settled among the Penobscot Indians, near the mouth of their noble river. He here took for his wives the daughters of the great Modocawando,—the most powerful sachem of the East. His castle was plundered by Governor Andros, during his reckless administration ; and the enraged Baron is supposed to have excited the Indians into open hostility to the English.

Note 9, page 358. The owner and commander of the garrison at Black Point, which Mogg attacked and plundered. He was an old man at the period to which the tale relates.

Note 10, page 358. Major Phillips, one of the principal men of the Colony. His garrison sustained a long and terrible siege by the savages. As a magistrate and a gentleman, he exacted of his plebeian neighbors a remarkable degree of deference. The Court Records of the settlement inform us that an individual was fined for the heinous offence of saying that " Major Phillips's mare was as lean as an Indian dog."

Note 11, page 358. Captain Harman, of Georgeana, now of York, was for many years the terror of the Eastern Indians. In one of his expeditions up the Kennebec River, at the head of a party of rangers, he discovered twenty of the savages asleep by a large fire. Cautiously creeping towards them until he was certain of his aim, he ordered his men to single out their objects. The first discharge killed or mortally wounded the whole number of the unconscious sleepers.

Note 12, page 358. Wood Island, near the mouth of the Saco. It was visited by the Sieur de Monts and Champlain, in 1603. The following extract, from the journal of the latter, relates to it : " Having left the Kennebec, we ran along the coast to the westward, and cast anchor under a small island, near the mainland, where we saw twenty or more natives. I here visited an island, beautifully clothed with a fine growth of forest trees, particularly of the oak and walnut ; and overspread with vines, that, in their season, produce excellent grapes. We named it the island of Bacchus." — *Les Voyages de Sieur Champlain*, liv. 2, c. 8.

Note 13, page 359. John Boniton was the son of Richard Bonython, Gent., one of the most efficient and able magistrates of the Colony. John proved to be " a degenerate plant." In 1635, we find by the Court Records that, for some offence, he was fined 40s. In 1640, he was fined for abuse toward R. Gibson, the minister, and Mary, his wife. Soon after he was fined for disorderly conduct in the house of his father. In 1645, the " Great and General Court adjudged John Boniton outlawed, and incapable of any of his Majesty's laws, and proclaimed him a rebel." (*Court Records of the Province*, 1645.) In 1651, he bade defiance to the laws of Massachusetts, and was again outlawed. He acted independently of all law and authority ; and hence, doubtless, his burlesque title of "the Sagamore of Saco," which has come down to the present generation in the following epitaph : —

> " Here lies Boniton, the Sagamore of Saco ;
> He lived a rogue, and died a knave, and went to Hobomoko."

By some means or other, he obtained a large estate. In this poem, I have taken some liberties with him, not strictly warranted by historical facts, although the conduct imputed to him is in keeping with his general character. Over the last years of his life lingers a deep obscurity. Even the manner of his death is uncertain. He was supposed to have been killed by the Indians ; but this is doubted by the able and indefatigable author of the *History of Saco and Biddeford*. — Part I. p. 115.

Note 14, page 359. Foxwell's Brook flows from a marsh or bog, called the " Heath," in Saco, containing thirteen hundred acres. On this brook, and surrounded by wild and romantic scenery, is a beautiful waterfall, of more than sixty feet.

Note 15, page 361. Hiacoomes, the first Christian preacher on Martha's Vineyard ; for a biography of whom the reader is referred to Increase Mayhew's account of the Praying Indians, 1726. The following is related of him : "One Lord's day, after meeting, where Hiacoomes had been preaching, there came in a Powwaw very angry, and said, 'I know all the meeting Indians are liars. You say you don't care for the Powwaws ; ' then calling two or three of them by name, he railed at them, and told them they were deceived, for the Powwaws could kill all the meeting Indians, if they set about it. But Hiacoomes told him that he would be in the midst of all the Powwaws in the island, and they should do the utmost they could against him; and when they should do their worst by their witchcraft to kill him, he would without fear set himself against them, by remembering Jehovah.

He told them also he did put all the Powwaws under his heel. Such was the faith of this good man. Nor were these Powwaws ever able to do these Christian Indians any hurt, though others were frequently hurt and killed by them." — *Mayhew*, pp. 6, 7, c. I.

Note 16, page 363. "The tooth-ache," says Roger Williams in his observations upon the language and customs of the New England tribes, "is the only paine which will force their stoute hearts to cry." He afterwards remarks that even the Indian women never cry as he has heard "some of their men in this paine."

Note 17, page 364. *Wuttamuttata*, "Let us drink." *Wee kan*, "It is sweet." *Vide* Roger Williams's *Key to the Indian Language*, "in that parte of America called New England." — London, 1643, p. 35.

Note 18, page 365. *Wetuomanit*, — a house god, or demon. "They — the Indians — have given me the names of thirty-seven gods which I have, all which in their solemne Worships they invocate!" — R. Williams's *Briefe Observations of the Customs, Manners, Worships, etc., of the Natives, in Peace and Warre, in Life and Death:* on all which is added Spiritual Observations, General and Particular, of Chiefe and Special use — upon all occasions — to all the English inhabiting these parts; yet Pleasant and Profitable to the view of all Mene: p. 110, c. 21.

Note 19, page 368. Mt. Desert Island, the Bald Mountain upon which overlooks Frenchman's and Penobscot Bay. It was upon this island that the Jesuits made their earliest settlement.

Note 20, page 369. Father Hennepin, a missionary among the Iroquois, mentions that the Indians believed him to be a conjurer, and that they were particularly afraid of a bright silver chalice which he had in his possession. "The Indians," says Père Jerome Lallamant, "fear us as the greatest sorcerers on earth."

Note 21, page 370. Bomazeen is spoken of by Penhallow as "the famous warrior and chieftain of Norridgewock." He was killed in the attack of the English upon Norridgewock, in 1724.

Note 22, page 371. Père Ralle, or Rasles, was one of the most zealous and indefatigable of that band of Jesuit missionaries who at the beginning of the seventeenth century penetrated the forests of America, with the avowed object of converting the heathen. The first religious mission of the Jesuits to the savages in North America was in 1611. The zeal of the fathers for the conversion of the Indians to the Catholic faith knew no bounds. For this they plunged into the depths of the wilderness ; habituated themselves to all the hardships and privations of the natives ; suffered cold, hunger, and some of them death itself, by the extremest tortures. Père Brebeuf, after laboring in the cause of his mission for twenty years, together with his companion, Père Lallamant, was burned alive. To these might be added the names of those Jesuits who were put to death by the Iroquois, — Daniel, Garnier, Buteaux, La Riborerde, Goupil, Constantin, and Liegeouis. "For bed," says Father Lallamant, in his *Relation de ce qui s'est dans le pays des Hurons*, 1640, c. 3, "we have nothing but a miserable piece of bark of a tree ; for nourishment, a handful or two of corn. either roasted or soaked in water, which seldom satisfies our hunger ; and after all, not venturing to perform even the ceremonies of our religion without being considered as sorcerers." Their success among the natives, however, by no means equalled their exertions. Père Lallamant says : "With respect to adult persons, in good health, there is little apparent success ; on the contrary, there have been nothing but storms and whirlwinds from that quarter."

Sebastian Ralle established himself, some time about the year 1670, at Norridgewock, where he continued more than forty years. He was accused, and perhaps not without justice, of exciting his Praying Indians against the English, whom he looked upon as the enemies not only of his king, but also of the Catholic religion. He was killed by the English, in 1724, at the foot of the cross which his own hands had planted. His Indian church was broken up, and its members either killed outright or dispersed.

In a letter written by Ralle to his nephew he gives the following account of his church and his own labors : "All my converts repair to the church regularly twice every day : first, very early in the morning, to attend mass, and again in the evening, to assist in the prayers at sunset. As it is necessary to fix the imagination of savages, whose attention is easily distracted, I have composed prayers, calculated to inspire them with just sentiments of the august sacrifice of our altars : they chant, or at least recite them aloud, during mass. Besides preaching to them on Sundays and saints' days, I seldom let a working-day pass without making a concise exhortation, for the purpose of inspiring them with horror at those vices to which they are most addicted, or to confirm them in the practice of some particular virtue." — Vide *Lettres Edifiantes et Cur.*, vol. vi. p. 127.

Note 23, page 377. The character of Ralle has probably never been correctly delineated. By his brethren of the Romish Church, he has been nearly apotheosized. On the other hand, our Puritan historians have represented him as a demon in human form. He was undoubtedly sincere in his devotion to the interests of his church, and not over-scrupulous as to the means of advancing those interests. "The French," says the author of the *History of Saco and Biddeford*, "after the peace of 1713, secretly promised to supply the Indians with arms and ammunition, if they would renew hostilities. Their principal agent was the celebrated Ralle, the French Jesuit." — p. 215.

Note 24, page 379. Hertel de Rouville was an active and unsparing enemy of the English. He was the leader of the combined French and Indian forces which destroyed Deerfield and massacred its inhabitants, in 1703. He was afterwards killed in the attack upon Haverhill. Tradition says that, on examining his dead body, his head and face were found to be perfectly smooth, without the slightest appearance of hair or beard.

Note 25, page 380. *Cowesass ? — tawhich wessaseen ?* Are you afraid ? — why fear you ?

IV. A LIST OF MR. WHITTIER'S POEMS,

ARRANGED CHRONOLOGICALLY.

This list follows the dates given with the poems. In the few cases where the dates have not been determined exactly, the poems are placed in the group with which they were published, when collected in volumes. The order is by years, and no attempt has here been made to preserve the exact order of composition under the year.

1825. The Exile's Departure.
        The Deity.
        The Vale of the Merrimac.
        Benevolence.
1827. Ocean.
1828. The Sicilian Vespers.
        The Earthquake.
1829. The Spirit of the North.
        Judith at the Tent of Holofernes.
        Metacom.
        The Drunkard to his Bottle.
        The Past and Coming Year.
1830. The Fair Quakeress.
        Bolivar.
        The Vaudois Teacher.
        The Star of Bethlehem.
        The Frost Spirit.
1831. Isabella of Austria.
        The Fratricide.
        The Cities of the Plain.
1832. Isabel.
        Stanzas : " Bind up thy tresses."
        To William Lloyd Garrison.
1833. The Female Martyr.
        The Missionary.
        The Call of the Christian.
        Extract from " A New England Legend."
        Toussaint L'Ouverture.

1834. Mogg Megone.
The Crucifixion.
Hymn : " O Thou whose presence went before."
The Slave-Ships.
To the Memory of Charles B. Storrs.
Follen.
A Lament.
1835. The Demon of the Study.
The Yankee Girl.
The Hunters of Men.
Stanzas for the Times.
1836. A Day.
Clerical Oppressors.
A Summons.
To the Memory of Thomas Shipley.
The Moral Warfare.
1837. Massachusetts.
The Fountain.
Palestine.
Hymns from the French of Lamartine.
Hymn : "O Holy Father, just and true."
Ritner.
The Pastoral Letter.
Lines on the Death of S. Oliver Torrey.
1838. Pentucket.
The Familist's Hymn.
Pennsylvania Hall.
The Farewell of a Virginia Slave Mother.
The Quaker of the Olden Time.
1839. The New Year.
The Relic.
The World's Convention.
1840. To ——, with a copy of Woolman's Journal.
1841. The Cypress Tree of Ceylon.
St. John.
The Exiles.
Funeral Tree of the Sokokis.
The Norsemen.
Memories.

The Merrimac.
Lucy Hooper.
To a Friend.
Leggett's Monument.
Democracy.

1842.   Follen.
The Gallows.
Raphael.

1843.   The Knight of St. John.
Cassandra Southwick.
The New Wife and the Old.
Hampton Beach.
Ego.
To J. P.
Chalkley Hall.
Massachusetts to Virginia.
The Christian Slave.
Seed-Time and Harvest.
To the Reformers of England.
The Human Sacrifice.

1844.   The Pumpkin.
The Bridal of Pennacook.
Ezekiel.
Channing.
To Massachusetts.
The Sentence of John L. Brown.
To Faneuil Hall.
Texas.

1845.   New Hampshire.
At Washington.
To my Friend on the Death of his Sister.
Gone.
The Shoemakers.
The Fishermen.
The Lumbermen.

1846.   The Ship-Builders.
The Pine-Tree.
Lines from a Letter to a Young Clerical Friend.
To Ronge.

Kathleen.
The Prisoner for Debt.
Our State.
To Fredrika Bremer.
The Men of Old.
The Christian Tourists.
The Lakeside.
Autumn Thoughts.
The Legend of St. Mark.
1850.   The Well of Loch Maree.
Ichabod.
In the Evil Day.
Elliott.
The Hill-Top.
To Avis Keene.
A Sabbath Scene.
Derne.
Lines on the Portrait of a Celebrated Publisher.
All 's Well.
1851.   Remembrance.
The Chapel of the Hermits.
The Prisoners of Naples.
To my Old Schoolmaster.
Invocation.
Wordsworth.
In Peace.
Kossuth.
To——. Lines written after a Summer Day's Excursion.
1852.   Pictures.
The Cross.
First-Day Thoughts.
Questions of Life.
April.
The Disenthralled.
The Peace of Europe.
Eva.
Astræa.
1853.   Tauler.

Summer by the Lakeside.
Trust.
My Namesake.
The Dream of Pio Nono.
The Hero.
Rantoul.
Official Piety.
1854. The Voices.
Burns.
William Forster.
Charles Sumner.
The Rendition.
The Haschish.
The Fruit Gift.
Maud Muller.
The Hermit of the Thebaid.
Letter from a Missionary of the Methodist Episcopal
    Church, South.
The Kansas Emigrants.
A Memory.
1855. The Barefoot Boy.
My Dream.
Flowers in Winter.
Arisen at Last.
For Righteousness' Sake.
1856. The Ranger.
The Mayflower.
The Conquest of Finland.
The New Exodus.
A Lay of Old Time.
A Song, inscribed to the Frémont Clubs.
What of the Day.
A Song for the Time.
The Pass of the Sierra.
The Panorama.
Burial of Barber.
To Pennsylvania.
Mary Garvin.
1857. Moloch in State Street.

Naples.

The Summons.

The Quaker Alumni.

1861. To William H. Seward.

Thy Will be done.

To John C. Frémont.

A Word for the Hour.

"Ein feste Burg ist unser Gott."

Cobbler Keezar's Vision.

Our River.

1862. Amy Wentworth.

At Port Royal.

The Cry of a Lost Soul.

Mountain Pictures.

To Englishmen.

The Watchers.

The Waiting.

The Battle Autumn of 1862.

Astræa at the Capitol.

1863. The Proclamation.

The Answer.

To Samuel E. Sewall and Harriet W. Sewall.

A Memorial.

Andrew Rykman's Prayer.

The Countess.

Barbara Frietchie.

Anniversary Poem.

Hymn sung at Christmas by the Scholars of St. Helena's Island, S. C.

Mithridates at Chios.

1864. The Vanishers.

What the Birds said.

The Brother of Mercy.

The Wreck of Rivermouth.

Bryant on his Birthday.

Thomas Starr King.

Hymn for the Opening of Thomas Starr King's House of Worship.

1865. Revisited.

To the Thirty-ninth Congress.
The Changeling.
The Grave by the Lake.
Kallundborg Church.
Hymn for the Celebration of Emancipation at New-
    buryport.
Laus Deo.
The Mantle of St. John de Matha.
The Peace Autumn.
The Eternal Goodness.

1866. Snow-Bound.
The Common Question.
Our Master.
Abraham Davenport.
Lines on a Fly Leaf.
The Maids of Attitash.
The Dead Ship of Harpswell.

1867. George L. Stearns.
The Worship of Nature.
Freedom in Brazil.
The Palatine.
The Tent on the Beach.

1868. The Hive at Gettysburg.
Divine Compassion.
The Clear Vision.
The Meeting.
The Two Rabbins.
Among the Hills.
The Dole of Jarl Thorkell.
Hymn for the House of Worship at Georgetown.

1869. Howard at Atlanta.
Garibaldi.
Norumbega.
The Pageant.

1870. Miriam.
In School-Days.
To Lydia Maria Child.
My Triumph.
Nauhaught, the Deacon.

The Prayer-Seeker.
The Laurels.
A Spiritual Manifestation.

1871. The Sisters.
Marguerite.
The Robin.
The Singer.
Disarmament.
How Mary Grew.
Chicago.
My Birthday.

1872. The Pressed Gentian.
A Woman.
The Pennsylvania Pilgrim.
The Three Bells.
King Volmer and Elsie.
The Brewing of Soma.
Hymn for the Opening of Plymouth Church.

1873. Conductor Bradley.
John Underhill.
A Mystery.
In Quest.
The Friend's Burial.
The Prayer of Agassiz.
A Christmas Carmen.

1874. Kinsman.
The Golden Wedding of Longwood.
Vesta.
A Sea Dream.
Hazel Blossoms.
Summer.

1875. "I was a Stranger and ye took me in."
The Two Angels.
The Healer.
Child Songs.
Lexington.
The Library.

1876. June on the Merrimac.
Sunset on the Bearcamp.
Centennial Hymn.

Greeting.
The Rock Tomb of Bradore.
Help.
Requirement.
Utterance.
By their Works.
The Word.
The Memory.

1882. The Bay of Seven Islands.
Garden.
An Autograph.
An Easter Flower Gift.
Godspeed.
The Wishing Bridge.
Storm on Lake Asquam.
At Last.
A Greeting.
The Poet and the Children.
Wilson.
The Mystic's Christmas.

1883. Our Country
St. Gregory's Guest.
How the Women went from Dover.
What the Traveller said at Sunset.
A Summer Pilgrimage.
Winter Roses.

1884. The Light that is felt.
The Two Loves.
The "Story of Ida."
Sweet Fern.
Abram Morrison.
Birchbrook Mill.

1885. Hymns of the Brahmo Somaj.
The Two Elizabeths.
Requital.
The Wood Giant.
The Reunion.
Adjustment.
An Artist of the Beautiful.
A Welcome to Lowell.

INDEXES OF FIRST LINES
AND TITLES.

INDEX OF FIRST LINES

INDEX OF TITLES

Date D